Global Economic Prospects

*A World Bank Group
Flagship Report*

JUNE 2023

Global
Economic
Prospects

 **WORLD BANK GROUP**

Summary of Contents

Contents

Acknowledgments

This World Bank Group Flagship Report is a product of the Prospects Group in the Development Economics (DEC) and Equitable Growth, Finance, and Institutions (EFI) Vice Presidencies. The project was managed by M. Ayhan Kose and Franziska Ohnsorge, under the general guidance of Indermit Gill.

Global and regional surveillance work was led by Carlos Arteta. The report was prepared by a team that included Marie Albert, Francisco Arroyo Marioli, John Baffes, Samuel Hill, Osamu Inami, Steven Kamin, Sergiy Kasyanenko, Philip Kenworthy, Jeetendra Khadan, Patrick Kirby, Joseph Mawejje, Nikita Perevalov, Dominik Peschel, Franz Ulrich Ruch, Naotaka Sugawara, Garima Vasishtha, and Shu Yu.

Research assistance was provided by Lule Bahtiri, Mattia Coppo, Franco Derossi Diaz Laura, Jiayue Fan, Yi Ji, Maria Hazel Macadangdang, Rafaela Martinho Henriques, Muneeb Ahmad Naseem, Vasiliki Papagianni, Lorëz Qehaja, Juan Felipe Serrano Ariza, Shijie Shi, Kaltrina Temaj, and Juncheng Zhou. Modeling and data work was provided by Shijie Shi.

Online products were produced by Graeme Littler. Joe Rebello managed communications and media outreach with a team that included Nandita Roy, Paul Blake, Kristen Milhollin, and Mariana Lozzi Teixeira, and with extensive support from the World Bank's media and digital communications teams. Graeme Littler provided editorial support, with contributions from Adriana Maximiliano and Michael Harrup.

The print publication was produced by Adriana Maximiliano, in collaboration with Andrew Berghauser, Cindy Fisher, Michael Harrup, Maria Hazel Macadangdang, and Jewel McFadden.

Regional projections and write-ups were produced in coordination with country teams, country directors, and the offices of the regional chief economists.

Many reviewers provided extensive advice and comments. The analysis also benefited from comments and suggestions by staff members from World Bank Group country teams and other World Bank Group Vice Presidencies as well as Executive Directors in their discussion of the report on May 30, 2023. However, both forecasts and analysis are those of the World Bank Group staff and should not be attributed to Executive Directors or their national authorities.

Foreword

More than three years after the coronavirus touched off the deepest global recession since World War II, the world economy remains hobbled—far short of the strength that will be necessary to make substantial progress on global ambitions to eliminate extreme poverty, counter climate change, and replenish human capital.

Emerging market and developing economies (EMDEs) today are struggling just to cope—deprived of the wherewithal to create jobs and deliver essential services to their most vulnerable citizens. The optimism that arose with the end of China's COVID-19 shutdown earlier this year proved to be fleeting. In EMDEs other than China, a pronounced slump is underway: growth is set to slow to 2.9 percent in 2023 from 4.1 percent in 2022. Besieged by high inflation, tight global financial markets, and record debt levels, many countries are simply growing poorer. By the end of 2024, per-capita income growth in about a third of EMDEs will be lower than it was on the eve of the pandemic. In low-income countries—especially the poorest—the damage is even larger: in about one-third of these countries, per capita incomes in 2024 will remain below 2019 levels by an average of 6 percent.

Yet, as the World Bank Group's latest *Global Economic Prospects* report makes clear, new hazards are threatening to make matters worse. Despite the steepest global interest-rate hiking cycle in four decades, inflation remains high; even by end-2024, it will remain above the target range of most inflation-targeting central banks. Policymakers in most economies will need to be exceptionally agile to cope with the risks that come with such rate hikes. Today, high interest rates aren't merely crimping growth in EMDEs; they are also dampening investment and intensifying the risk of financial crises. These challenges would intensify in the event of more widespread banking-sector strains in advanced economies.

Low-income countries are especially vulnerable. Relative to the average EMDE, these countries spend only the tiniest fraction of government revenues on their most vulnerable citizens—barely 3 percent of GDP. Today, interest payments are taking an ever-bigger bite out of these resources—more than one-fifth of revenues in many countries—leaving them with little fiscal space to cope with the next shock or make the investments necessary to revive growth.

In addition, all the major drivers of global growth—including productivity, trade, labor force and investment growth—are expected to weaken over the remainder of this decade. Potential growth—the maximum growth the global economy can sustain over the longer term without igniting inflation—is expected to fall to a three-decade low over the remainder of the 2020s.

These problems must be tackled promptly if the world is to establish the economic footing necessary for even a semblance of success on global development goals. To curb climate change, stave off pandemics, and rebuild after conflict, developing countries need substantial resources. The necessary financing ramp-up to generate these resources depends both on faster growth and a more dynamic private sector.

The World Bank's latest projections indicate that the world economy will remain frail—and at risk of a deeper downturn—this year and in 2024. Our baseline scenario calls for global growth to slow from 3.1 percent in 2022 to 2.1 percent in 2023, before inching up to 2.4 percent in 2024. Even this tepid growth assumes that stress in the banking sector of advanced economies does not spill over to EMDEs.

The lessons of economic history are forbidding. Rapid interest-rate increases of the kind that have been underway in the United States over the past year are correlated with a higher likelihood of financial crises in EMDEs. And if the current banking stress in advanced economies metastasizes into widespread financial turmoil affecting EMDEs, the worst-case scenario would have arrived: the global economy would experience a deep downturn next year.

This report offers a roadmap for policymakers—not only for avoiding the worst outcomes but also on how to put the global economy back on track. Five steps can make the difference:

1. *Mitigating financial contagion*: Central banks—especially those in advanced economies—can curb the risk of disruptive spillovers to global financial markets by communicating their intentions as early and clearly as possible and calibrating their strategies so as to avoid abrupt changes in the policy outlook.

2. *Reducing domestic vulnerabilities*: EMDE monetary authorities may need to tighten their own policies in order to moderate capital outflows, currency depreciation, and resultant increases in inflation. Prudential standards and capital and liquidity buffers at EMDE banks and other financial institutions can be shored up to reduce the risk of financial contagion from banks in advanced economies. In addition, EMDEs need to rebuild currency reserve buffers to mitigate the impact of volatile capital flows.

3. *Restoring fiscal sustainability.* Among EMDEs, tax collection and administration must be improved to shore up revenues. Revenues in low-income countries have long been well below EMDE averages—and heavily dependent on grants from donors. But since 2015, grant financing has been declining as a share of their GDP. These countries will need to prioritize domestic resource mobilization, spending efficiency, and better debt management.

4. *Reinvigorating long-term growth.* The slowdown in potential growth can be reversed with steps to accelerate productivity-enhancing investment, strengthen health systems, improve student learning, and increase the participation of women and older workers in the labor force. Policies that promote trade and private capital mobilization—particularly for investments in digital technology and climate-related projects—will help a great deal.

5. *Alleviating debt distress and strengthening the global financial safety net.* This means ensuring that international financial institutions are adequately funded and focused on rapid support for EMDEs in distress. It also requires new mechanisms to speedily and sensibly restructure the public debt of countries in debt distress. In the wake of bank failures in advanced economies, a renewed focus on global financial regulatory reform is also necessary.

The global economy is in rough shape—and the extraordinary series of severe economic shocks and serious policy misjudgments are both to blame. Yet years before COVID-19 arrived, governments had already been turning their backs on free and fair trade. And long before the outbreak of the pandemic, governments across the world had developed an appetite for huge budget deficits. They turned a blind eye to the dangers of rising debt-to-GDP ratios. If a lost decade is to be avoided, these failures must be corrected—*now, not later.*

Indermit Gill
Senior Vice President and Chief Economist
World Bank Group

Executive Summary

The global economy remains in a precarious state amid the protracted effects of the overlapping negative shocks of the pandemic, the Russian Federation's invasion of Ukraine, and the sharp tightening of monetary policy to contain high inflation. Global growth is projected to slow significantly in the second half of this year, with weakness continuing in 2024. Inflation pressures persist, and tight monetary policy is expected to weigh substantially on activity. Recent banking sector stress in advanced economies will also likely dampen activity through more restrictive credit conditions. The possibility of more widespread bank turmoil and tighter monetary policy could result in even weaker global growth. Rising borrowing costs in advanced economies could lead to financial dislocations in the more vulnerable emerging market and developing economies (EMDEs). In low-income countries, in particular, fiscal positions are increasingly precarious. Comprehensive policy action is needed at the global and national levels to foster macroeconomic and financial stability. Among many EMDEs, and especially in low-income countries, bolstering fiscal sustainability will require generating higher revenues, making spending more efficient, and improving debt management practices. Continued international cooperation is also necessary to tackle climate change, support populations affected by crises and hunger, and provide debt relief where needed. In the longer term, reversing a projected decline in EMDE potential growth will require reforms to bolster physical and human capital and labor-supply growth.

Global Outlook. After growing 3.1 percent last year, the global economy is set to slow substantially in 2023, to 2.1 percent, amid continued monetary policy tightening to rein in high inflation, before a tepid recovery in 2024, to 2.4 percent. Tight global financial conditions and subdued external demand are expected to weigh on growth across emerging market and developing economies (EMDEs). Projections for many countries have been revised down over the forecast horizon, with upgrades primarily due to stronger-than-expected data at the beginning of 2023 more than offset by downgrades thereafter. Inflation has been persistent but is projected to decline gradually as demand weakens and commodity prices moderate, provided longer-term inflation expectations remain anchored.

Global growth could be weaker than anticipated in the event of more widespread banking sector stress, or if more persistent inflation pressures prompt tighter-than-expected monetary policy. Weak growth prospects and heightened risks in the near term compound a long-term slowdown in potential growth, which has been exacerbated by the overlapping shocks of the pandemic, the Russian Federation's invasion of Ukraine, and the sharp tightening of global financial conditions. This difficult context highlights a multitude of

policy challenges. Recent bank failures call for a renewed focus on global financial regulatory reform. Global cooperation is also necessary to accelerate the clean energy transition, mitigate climate change, and provide debt relief for the rising number of countries experiencing debt distress. At the national level, it is imperative to implement credible policies to contain inflation and ensure macroeconomic and financial stability, as well as undertake reforms to set the foundations for a robust, sustainable, and inclusive development path.

Regional Prospects. Growth is projected to diverge across EMDE regions this year and next. It is expected to pick up in 2023 in East Asia and Pacific (EAP) and Europe and Central Asia (ECA), as China's reopening spurs a recovery and as growth prospects in several large economies improve. In contrast, growth is forecast to moderate in all other regions, particularly in Latin America and the Caribbean (LAC) and the Middle East and North Africa (MNA). Headwinds from weak external demand, tight global financial conditions, and high inflation will drag on activity this year, especially in LAC, South Asia (SAR), and Sub-Saharan Africa (SSA). The lingering impact of Russia's invasion of Ukraine will continue to weigh on growth across regions, particularly in ECA. Next year, growth is projected to moderate in EAP and SAR but to pick up elsewhere as domestic headwinds ease and external demand strengthens. Downside risks to the outlook for all regions include possible further global financial stress and more persistent domestic inflation than projected in the baseline. Geopolitical tensions, conflict and social unrest, and natural disasters stemming from climate change also present downside risks, to varying degrees. The materialization of such risks could further weaken potential growth, leading to a prolonged period of slower growth in all EMDE regions.

Financial Spillovers of Rising U.S. Interest Rates. The rapid rise in interest rates in the United States poses a significant challenge to EMDEs. As the Federal Reserve has pivoted toward a more hawkish stance to rein in inflation, a substantial part of the sharp increases in U.S. interest rates since early 2022 has been driven by shocks that capture changes in perceptions of the Fed's reaction function. These reaction shocks are associated with especially adverse financial market effects in EMDEs, including a higher likelihood of experiencing a financial crisis. Their effects also appear to be more pronounced in EMDEs with greater economic vulnerabilities. These findings suggest that major central banks can alleviate adverse spillovers through proper communication that clarifies their reaction functions. They also highlight that EMDEs need to adjust macroeconomic and financial policies to mitigate the negative impact of rising global and U.S. interest rates.

Fiscal Policy Challenges in Low-Income Countries. The room for fiscal policy to maneuver has narrowed in low-income countries (LICs) over the past decade: LIC debt has grown rapidly as sizable and widening deficits offset the debt-reducing effects of growth. Fiscal deficits have reflected growing spending pressures, including on debt service, amid persistent revenue weakness, especially for grants and income tax revenues. As a result, 14 out of the 28 LICs were assessed as being in debt distress or at a high risk of debt distress as of end-February 2023. Creating room for fiscal policy requires generating higher revenues, making spending more efficient, and improving debt management practices. These measures need to be embedded in improvements to domestic institutional frameworks and supported by well-coordinated global policies both to improve fiscal policy management and to address debt challenges.

Abbreviations

AE	advanced economy
CA	Central Asia
CE	Central Europe and Baltic Countries
CPI	consumer price index
EAP	East Asia and Pacific
ECA	Europe and Central Asia
ECB	European Central Bank
EE	Eastern Europe
EMBI	emerging market bond index
EMDE	emerging market and developing economy
EU	European Union
FDI	foreign direct investment
FY	fiscal year
G20	Group of Twenty: Argentina, Australia, Brazil, Canada, China, France, Germany, India, Indonesia, Italy, Japan, Republic of Korea, Mexico, Russia, Saudi Arabia, South Africa, Türkiye, the United Kingdom, the United States, and the European Union
GCC	Gulf Cooperation Council
GDP	gross domestic product
GEP	Global Economic Prospects
GFC	Global Financial Crisis
GNFS	goods and nonfactor services
IMF	International Monetary Fund
LAC	Latin America and the Caribbean
LIC	low-income country
MNA	Middle East and North Africa
NBFIs	non-bank financial institutions
OECD	Organization for Economic Co-operation and Development
OPEC	Organization of the Petroleum Exporting Countries
OPEC+	OPEC and Azerbaijan, Bahrain, Brunei Darussalam, Kazakhstan, Malaysia, Mexico, Oman, the Russian Federation, South Sudan, and Sudan
PMI	Purchasing Managers' Index
PPP	purchasing power parity
RHS	right-hand scale
RRF	Recovery and Resilience Facility
SAR	South Asia
SCC	South Caucasus
SOE	state-owned enterprise
SSA	Sub-Saharan Africa
TFP	total factor productivity
VAR	vector autoregression
WAEMU	West African Economic and Monetary Union
WDI	World Development Indicators

CHAPTER 1

GLOBAL OUTLOOK

After growing 3.1 percent last year, the global economy is set to slow substantially in 2023, to 2.1 percent, amid continued monetary policy tightening to rein in high inflation, before a tepid recovery in 2024, to 2.4 percent. Tight global financial conditions and subdued external demand are expected to weigh on growth across emerging market and developing economies (EMDEs). Projections for many countries have been revised down over the forecast horizon, with upgrades primarily due to stronger-than-expected data at the beginning of 2023 more than offset by downgrades thereafter. Inflation has been persistent but is projected to decline gradually as demand weakens and commodity prices moderate, provided longer-term inflation expectations remain anchored. Global growth could be weaker than anticipated in the event of more widespread banking sector stress or if more persistent inflation pressures prompt tighter-than-expected monetary policy. Weak growth prospects and heightened risks in the near term compound a long-term slowdown in potential growth, which has been exacerbated by the overlapping shocks of the pandemic, the Russian Federation's invasion of Ukraine, and the sharp tightening of global financial conditions. This difficult context highlights a multitude of policy challenges. Recent bank failures call for a renewed focus on global financial regulatory reform. Global cooperation is also necessary to accelerate the clean energy transition, mitigate climate change, and provide debt relief for the rising number of countries experiencing debt distress. At the national level, it is imperative to implement credible policies to contain inflation and ensure macroeconomic and financial stability, as well as undertake reforms to set the foundations for a robust, sustainable, and inclusive development path.

Summary

The global economy remains in a precarious state amid the protracted effects of the overlapping negative shocks of the pandemic, the Russian Federation's invasion of Ukraine, and the sharp tightening of monetary policy to contain high inflation. The resilience that global economic activity exhibited earlier this year is expected to fade. Growth in several major economies was stronger than envisaged at the beginning of the year, with faster-than-expected economic reopening in China and resilient consumption in the United States. Nonetheless, for 2023 as a whole, global activity is projected to slow, with a pronounced deceleration in advanced economies and a sizable pickup in China (figure 1.1.A). Inflation pressures persist, and the drag on growth from the ongoing monetary tightening to restore price stability is expected to peak in 2023 in many major economies. Recent banking sector stress will further tighten credit conditions. This will result in a substantial growth deceleration in the second half of this year. This slowdown will compound a period of already-subdued growth—over the first half of the 2020s (2020-2024), growth in EMDEs

is expected to average just 3.4 percent, one of the weakest half-decades of the past 30 years (figure 1.1.B). This slowdown reflects both cyclical dynamics and the current trend of declining global potential output growth (figure 1.1.C).

Global financial conditions have tightened as a result of policy rate hikes and, to a lesser extent, recent bouts of financial instability. Many banks experienced substantial unrealized losses due to the sharp rise in policy interest rates. Concerns about the viability of balance sheets of some banks led to depositor flight and market volatility in the United States and Europe earlier in the year, which were stemmed by a swift and extensive policy response. Financial markets remain highly sensitive to evolving expectations about the future path of interest rates of major central banks. Spillovers from banking turmoil in advanced economies to EMDEs have so far been limited. However, countries with more pronounced macroeconomic policy vulnerabilities, as reflected by lower credit ratings, have experienced slower growth and greater financial stress, including large currency depreciations and a sharp widening of sovereign spreads. Projections for 2023 growth in these economies have fallen by more than half over the past year (figure 1.1.D).

Inflation pressures persist. Although global headline inflation has been decelerating as a result of base effects, abating supply chain pressures, and

Note: This chapter was prepared by Carlos Arteta, Phil Kenworthy, Patrick Kirby, Nikita Perevalov, Dominik Peschel, and Garima Vasishtha, with contributions from John Baffes, Samuel Hill, Osamu Inami, Sergiy Kasyanenko, Jeetendra Khadan, and Naotaka Sugawara.

TABLE 1.1 Real GDP[1]

(Percent change from previous year unless indicated otherwise)

Percentage point differences from January 2023 projections

	2020	2021	2022e	2023f	2024f	2025f	2023f	2024f
World	**-3.1**	**6.0**	**3.1**	**2.1**	**2.4**	**3.0**	**0.4**	**-0.3**
Advanced economies	**-4.3**	**5.4**	**2.6**	**0.7**	**1.2**	**2.2**	**0.2**	**-0.4**
United States	-2.8	5.9	2.1	1.1	0.8	2.3	0.6	-0.8
Euro area	-6.1	5.4	3.5	0.4	1.3	2.3	0.4	-0.3
Japan	-4.3	2.2	1.0	0.8	0.7	0.6	-0.2	0.0
Emerging market and developing economies	**-1.5**	**6.9**	**3.7**	**4.0**	**3.9**	**4.0**	**0.6**	**-0.2**
East Asia and Pacific	1.2	7.5	3.5	5.5	4.6	4.5	1.2	-0.3
China	2.2	8.4	3.0	5.6	4.6	4.4	1.3	-0.4
Indonesia	-2.1	3.7	5.3	4.9	4.9	5.0	0.1	0.0
Thailand	-6.1	1.5	2.6	3.9	3.6	3.4	0.3	-0.1
Europe and Central Asia	-1.7	7.1	1.2	1.4	2.7	2.7	1.3	-0.1
Russian Federation	-2.7	5.6	-2.1	-0.2	1.2	0.8	3.1	-0.4
Türkiye	1.9	11.4	5.6	3.2	4.3	4.1	0.5	0.3
Poland	-2.0	6.9	5.1	0.7	2.6	3.2	0.0	0.4
Latin America and the Caribbean	-6.2	6.9	3.7	1.5	2.0	2.6	0.2	-0.4
Brazil	-3.3	5.0	2.9	1.2	1.4	2.4	0.4	-0.6
Mexico	-8.0	4.7	3.0	2.5	1.9	2.0	1.6	-0.4
Argentina	-9.9	10.4	5.2	-2.0	2.3	2.0	-4.0	0.3
Middle East and North Africa	-3.8	3.8	5.9	2.2	3.3	3.0	-1.3	0.6
Saudi Arabia	-4.3	3.9	8.7	2.2	3.3	2.5	-1.5	1.0
Iran, Islamic Rep. [2]	1.9	4.7	2.9	2.2	2.0	1.9	0.0	0.1
Egypt, Arab Rep. [2]	3.6	3.3	6.6	4.0	4.0	4.7	-0.5	-0.8
South Asia	-4.1	8.3	6.0	5.9	5.1	6.4	0.4	-0.7
India [2]	-5.8	9.1	7.2	6.3	6.4	6.5	-0.3	0.3
Pakistan [2]	-0.9	5.8	6.1	0.4	2.0	3.0	-1.6	-1.2
Bangladesh [2]	3.4	6.9	7.1	5.2	6.2	6.4	0.0	0.0
Sub-Saharan Africa	-2.0	4.4	3.7	3.2	3.9	4.0	-0.4	0.0
Nigeria	-1.8	3.6	3.3	2.8	3.0	3.1	-0.1	0.1
South Africa	-6.3	4.9	2.0	0.3	1.5	1.6	-1.1	-0.3
Angola	-5.6	1.1	3.5	2.6	3.3	3.1	-0.2	0.4
Memorandum items:								
Real GDP[1]								
High-income countries	-4.3	5.4	2.8	0.8	1.3	2.3	0.2	-0.3
Middle-income countries	-1.2	7.1	3.4	4.2	4.0	4.1	0.8	-0.3
Low-income countries	1.4	4.2	4.8	5.1	5.9	5.9	0.1	0.3
EMDEs excluding China	-3.8	5.9	4.1	2.9	3.4	3.8	0.2	-0.2
Commodity-exporting EMDEs	-3.7	5.1	3.2	1.9	2.8	2.9	0.0	0.0
Commodity-importing EMDEs	-0.3	7.9	3.9	5.0	4.4	4.5	0.9	-0.4
Commodity-importing EMDEs excluding China	-4.0	7.0	5.3	4.2	4.2	4.8	0.4	-0.3
EM7	-0.4	7.7	3.3	4.7	4.1	4.2	1.2	-0.4
World (PPP weights) [3]	-2.8	6.3	3.3	2.7	2.9	3.4	0.5	-0.3
World trade volume [4]	**-7.8**	**11.0**	**6.0**	**1.7**	**2.8**	**3.0**	**0.1**	**-0.6**
Commodity prices [5]							Level differences from January 2023 projections	
WBG commodity price index	63.1	101.0	143.3	110.1	109.2	110.5	-14.9	-7.3
Energy index	52.7	95.4	152.6	108.9	109.1	111.0	-21.6	-9.2
Oil (US$ per barrel)	42.3	70.4	99.8	80.0	82.0	84.4	-8.0	2.0
Non-energy index	84.1	112.5	124.4	112.5	109.5	109.5	-1.2	-3.5

Source: World Bank.

Note: e = estimate (actual data for commodity prices); f = forecast. WBG = World Bank Group. World Bank forecasts are frequently updated based on new information. Consequently, projections presented here may differ from those contained in other World Bank documents, even if basic assessments of countries' prospects do not differ at any given date. For the definition of EMDEs, developing countries, commodity exporters, and commodity importers, please refer to table 1.2. EM7 includes Brazil, China, India, Indonesia, Mexico, the Russian Federation, and Türkiye. The World Bank is currently not publishing economic output, income, or growth data for Turkmenistan and República Bolivariana de Venezuela owing to lack of reliable data of adequate quality. Turkmenistan and República Bolivariana de Venezuela are excluded from cross-country macroeconomic aggregates.

1. Headline aggregate growth rates are calculated using GDP weights at average 2010-19 prices and market exchange rates.

2. GDP growth rates are on a fiscal year basis. Aggregates that include these countries are calculated using data compiled on a calendar year basis. For India and the Islamic Republic of Iran, the column labeled 2022 refers to FY2022/23. For Bangladesh, the Arab Republic of Egypt, and Pakistan, the column labeled 2022 refers to FY2021/22. Pakistan's growth rates are based on GDP at factor cost.

3. World growth rates are calculated using average 2010-19 purchasing power parity (PPP) weights, which attribute a greater share of global GDP to emerging market and developing economies (EMDEs) than market exchange rates.

4. World trade volume of goods and nonfactor services.

5. Indexes are expressed in nominal U.S. dollars (2010 = 100). Oil refers to the Brent crude oil benchmark. For weights and composition of indexes, see https://worldbank.org/commodities.

falling commodity prices, core inflation in many countries remains elevated, and inflation is above target in almost all inflation-targeting economies. Inflation is expected to continue to be above its pre-pandemic level beyond 2024 (figure 1.1.E). That said, inflation expectations in most inflation-targeting countries have so far not undergone a major shift and appear to remain anchored.

Energy prices have eased considerably since their peak in 2022 on account of weaker global growth prospects and a warmer-than-expected Northern winter, which reduced natural gas and electricity consumption. Metal prices increased in early 2023, reflecting signs of a stronger-than-anticipated recovery in China, but subsequently retraced those gains. Agricultural prices have been easing on the back of good production prospects for most crops.

In all, global growth is forecast to slow from 3.1 percent in 2022 to 2.1 percent in 2023, before edging up to 2.4 percent in 2024. Relative to the January projections, this is 0.4 percentage point stronger in 2023 and 0.3 percentage point weaker in 2024. Greater-than-expected resilience of major economies at the end of 2022 and early in 2023 led to the overall upgrade to growth in 2023.

However, the drag on activity from tighter monetary policy is increasingly apparent, particularly in more interest-rate-sensitive activities such as business and residential investment, including construction. Growth over the rest of 2023 is set to slow substantially as it is weighed down by the lagged and ongoing effects of monetary tightening, and more restrictive credit conditions. These factors are envisaged to continue to affect activity heading into next year, leaving global growth below previous projections. Notwithstanding a continued recovery in tourism, global trade growth is likewise expected to slow in view of the ongoing rotation of consumption toward services, which tend to be less trade-intensive. Fiscal policy is expected to have little net impact on global growth over the forecast horizon, with modest tightening in EMDEs generally offsetting support in advanced economies.

Growth in advanced economies is set to decelerate substantially for 2023 as a whole, to 0.7 percent, and to remain feeble in 2024, due to monetary

FIGURE 1.1 Global prospects

The global economy is projected to slow substantially this year, with a pronounced deceleration in advanced economies. The first half of the 2020s is expected to be one of the weakest half-decades of the past 30 years for emerging market and developing economies (EMDEs), as a result of both cyclical dynamics and slowing potential growth. EMDEs with lower credit ratings are set to experience a particularly sharp slowdown this year. Inflation remains elevated in many countries and is envisaged to remain above pre-pandemic levels beyond 2024. Excluding China, EMDEs are expected to make next to no progress at closing the gap in per capita incomes with advanced economies over the forecast horizon.

A. Contributions to global growth

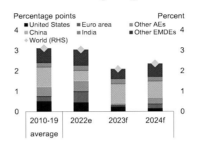

B. Growth in EMDEs

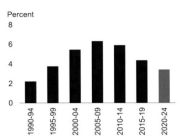

C. Contributions to potential growth

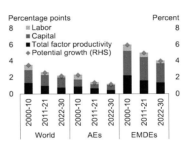

D. EMDE growth in 2023, by credit rating

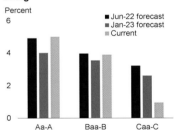

E. Model-based global CPI inflation projections

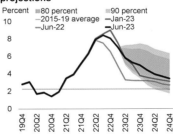

F. EMDE GDP per capita

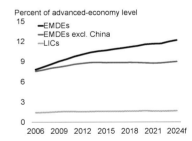

Sources: Consensus Economics; Haver Analytics; Kose and Ohnsorge (2023a); Moody's Analytics; Oxford Economics; Penn World Tables; World Bank.
Note: AEs = advanced economies; CPI = consumer price index; EMDEs = emerging market and developing economies; LICs = low-income countries.
A.B.F. Aggregate growth rates and GDP per capita calculated using real U.S. dollar GDP weights at average 2010-19 prices and market exchange rates. Data for 2023-24 are forecasts.
B. Figure shows the non-overlapping 5-year average growth in EMDEs.
C. Figure shows GDP-weighted averages of production function-based potential growth estimates for 29 advanced economies and 53 EMDEs, as in Kose and Ohnsorge (2023a). Data for 2022-30 are forecasts.
D. Comparison of GDP-weighted growth across editions of the Global Economic Prospects report, by credit ratings. Sample includes 9 Aa-A, 62 Baa-B, and 25 Caa-C EMDEs.
E. Model-based GDP-weighted projections of year-on-year country-level CPI inflation using Oxford Economics' Global Economic Model, using global oil price forecasts presented in table 1.1. Uncertainty bands constructed from the distribution of forecast errors for total CPI from Consensus Economics for an unbalanced panel of 18 economies.
F. GDP per capita aggregates calculated as aggregated GDP divided by the aggregate population.

tightening, less favorable credit conditions, softening labor markets, and still-high energy prices. In EMDEs, aggregate growth is projected to edge up to 4 percent in 2023, almost entirely due to a rebound in China following the removal of strict pandemic-related mobility restrictions. Excluding China, growth in EMDEs is set to slow substantially to 2.9 percent this year. This projection is predicated on the assumption of a protracted period of tight global monetary policy, fiscal consolidation in most EMDEs, and weak external demand. The slowdown is expected to be even more severe for EMDEs with elevated fiscal vulnerabilities and external financing needs. Persistent weak growth means that, excluding China, EMDEs are expected to continue making next to no progress at closing the differential in per capita incomes relative to advanced economies (figure 1.1.F). By 2024, economic activity in EMDEs will still be about 5 percent below levels projected on the eve of the pandemic.

Global inflation is projected to gradually edge down as growth decelerates, labor demand in many economies softens, and commodity prices remain stable. The slow pace of improvement means that core inflation is expected to remain above central bank targets in many countries throughout 2024.

Risks to the outlook remain tilted to the downside. Recent advanced-economy bank turmoil highlights the possibility of more disorderly failures, which could lead to systemic banking crises and protracted economic downturns, with spillovers to sovereigns and across borders. These failures could be triggered by mounting concerns about balance sheet quality, continued losses in the heavily leveraged commercial real estate sector, or by the ongoing decline in house prices in many countries.

In a scenario where banking stress results in a severe credit crunch and broader financial stress in advanced economies, global growth in 2024 would only be 1.3 percent, about half the pace in the baseline forecast (figure 1.2.A). In another scenario where financial stress propagates globally to a far greater degree, the world economy would fall into recession in 2024, as global growth of only 0.3 percent would imply a contraction in global per capita GDP.

Another risk to the forecast pertains to the possibility of higher-than-expected global inflation. This would result in additional monetary policy tightening, which could trigger financial stress. This would be particularly important in the case of the United States, given the scale of international spillovers from hawkish policy reaction by the Federal Reserve to rein in inflation—such spillovers could include a substantial further rise in borrowing costs in EMDEs, especially in those with underlying vulnerabilities (figure 1.2.B). In the longer term, the decades-long slowdown of the fundamental drivers of potential growth—labor supply, capital accumulation, and total factor productivity—may be exacerbated by trade fragmentation and climate-related natural disasters.

Debt distress in various EMDEs, including low-income countries (LICs), highlights the need for globally coordinated debt relief that overcomes the challenges posed by the increasing diversity of lenders (figure 1.2.C). Sustained international cooperation is needed to accelerate the clean energy transition, help countries improve both energy security and affordability, and incentivize the investments needed to pursue a path toward resilient, low-carbon growth (figure 1.2.D). The global community also has a vital role to play in mitigating humanitarian crises stemming from food shortages and conflict.

At the national level, central banks in some EMDEs face persistent inflation and heightened risks due to the impact of their policies on fiscal positions and the financial sector. The increase in central bank credibility in many EMDEs in recent decades is an important policy accomplishment. Any erosion of credibility at this critical juncture would make the job of inflation control much more difficult and could trigger destabilizing capital outflows. Policy makers can also reduce financial market volatility by maintaining adequate foreign reserve buffers, promoting rigorous financial supervision, and strengthening bank resolution frameworks. Proper monitoring of financial system exposure to an increase in defaults and other dislocations can ensure that prompt corrective action can be taken, as needed.

Tighter financing conditions, slowing growth, and elevated debt levels create significant fiscal challenges for EMDEs. The rising cost of servicing debt is increasing the risk of debt distress among EMDEs, particularly LICs (figure 1.2.E). Countries need to pursue a carefully calibrated policy mix that avoids inflationary fiscal stimulus and ensures that government support is appropriately targeted to vulnerable groups. Measures to improve fiscal space without unduly damaging activity need to be prioritized. Across many EMDEs, especially LICs, strengthened institutions and improvements to domestic governance are needed to boost the efficiency of spending and taxation.

Many of the current challenges reflect underlying longer-run trends. Potential growth in EMDEs has been on a decades-long declining path because of slowing growth rates of labor force, investment, and productivity. The slowdown in these fundamental factors has been exacerbated by the overlapping shocks of the pandemic, Russia's invasion of Ukraine, and the sharp tightening of global monetary policy in response to high inflation. Reversing the decline in potential growth will require decisive structural reforms (figure 1.2.F). These include measures to improve investment conditions, develop human capital and infrastructure, increase participation in the formal labor force, foster productivity growth in services, and promote international trade. In particular, fostering investment in green energy and climate resilience can ensure that growth is both robust and sustainable.

Global context

Global trade is being dampened by subdued global demand and the continued rotation of consumption toward services. Energy prices have eased considerably since their peak in 2022 as a result of weaker global growth prospects and a warmer-than-usual winter, which reduced demand for energy for heating. Core inflation around the world has been persistent, resulting in continued monetary tightening. EMDE financial conditions continue to be restrictive, with less creditworthy borrowers facing greater financial strains.

Global trade

Global goods trade growth slowed in the first half of 2023 in tandem with weakening global indus-

FIGURE 1.2 Global risks and policy challenges

An intensification of advanced-economy banking stress could result in a sharp slowdown in global growth in 2024, or even a global recession if it had major spillovers to emerging market and developing economies (EMDEs). A more hawkish U.S. monetary policy reaction to inflation could also further raise borrowing costs in EMDEs, especially in those with underlying vulnerabilities. There is an increasing need for debt relief for low-income countries amid a greater diversity of lenders. Substantial investments are needed to achieve resilient and low-carbon growth. Rising debt servicing costs are increasing the risk of debt distress. Reversing the decline in potential growth requires decisive structural reforms.

A. Global growth under different scenarios

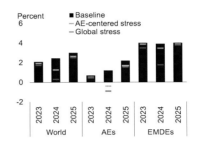

B. Impact of 25-basis-point reaction shock on EMDE financial variables after one quarter

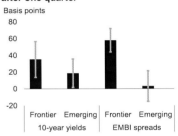

C. Composition of external debt, by creditor

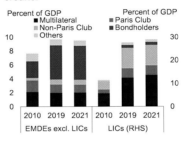

D. Additional investment for a resilient and low-carbon pathway, 2022-30

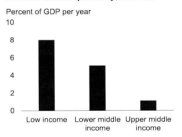

E. Government net interest payments in EMDEs and LICs

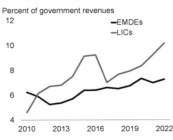

F. Global potential growth under reform scenarios

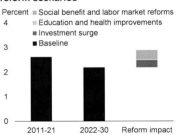

Sources: IDS (database); JP Morgan; Kose and Ohnsorge (2023a); Kose et al. (2022); MSCI; Oxford Economics; WDI (database); World Bank (2022a); World Bank.
Note: AEs = advanced economies; EMBI = emerging market bond index; EMDEs = emerging market and developing economies; LICs = low-income countries.
A. Global growth is computed by aggregating GDP at 2015 market exchange rates and prices from the Oxford Economics Model.
B. Estimated with panel non-linear local projection model with fixed effects and robust standard errors. Sample includes up to 9 frontier markets and up to 19 emerging markets, using 2022 MSCI classification. Whiskers are 90 percent confidence intervals. "EMBI spreads" based on EMBI global.
C. Figure shows U.S. dollar GDP-weighted average of public and publicly guaranteed external debt. "Others" includes multiple lenders. Sample includes 119 EMDEs, including 24 LICs.
D. Bars show annual investment needs to build resilience to climate change and reduce emissions by 70 percent by 2050. Estimates include investment needs for transport, energy, water, urban adaptations, industry, and landscape. In some Country Climate and Development Reports estimates cannot be considered entirely "additional" to pre-existing financing needs.
E. Net interest payments are the difference between primary balances and overall fiscal balances. Aggregates computed with government revenues in U.S. dollars as weights, based on 150 EMDEs, including 27 LICs.
F. Figure shows annual GDP-weighted averages. Scenarios assume a repeat of each country's best 10-year improvement as described in Kose and Ohnsorge (2023a). Data for 2022-30 are forecasts.

FIGURE 1.3 Global trade

Supply chain pressures and supplier delivery times have dropped back to pre-pandemic levels as goods demand has weakened and global shipping conditions have improved. A rising number of new trade measures have been protectionist. The ongoing shift in global consumption toward less trade-intensive goods will likely continue to lower the growth rate of trade relative to output. This shift and subdued demand are expected to dampen global trade growth substantially this year.

A. Global supply chain pressures

B. New trade measures

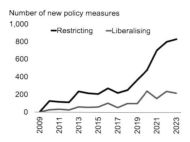

C. Global trade and output growth

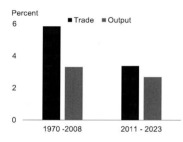

D. Global trade forecast

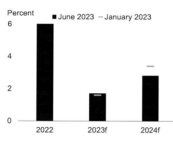

Sources: Federal Reserve Bank of New York; GTA (database); Haver Analytics; World Bank.

A. Figure shows manufacturing Purchasing Managers' Index (PMI) suppliers' delivery times and the Global Supply Chain Pressure Index (GSCPI). Data for delivery times are inverted by subtracting data from 100; therefore, increasing (decreasing) PMI data indicate slower (faster) delivery times. GSCPI is normalized such that zero indicates the average value for January 1998-April 2023, while positive (negative) values represent how many standard deviations the index is above (below) the average. Last observation is April 2023.

B. Figure shows the number of implemented trade policy interventions since November 2008. Restrictive (liberalizing) measures are interventions that discriminate against (benefit) foreign commercial interests. Last observation is May 24, 2023.

C. Bars indicate annual average growth. Global output growth is real GDP growth computed as a weighted average at 2010-19 average prices and exchange rates. Trade growth is the average growth of import and export volumes.

D. Trade is measured as the average of export and import volumes. "June 2023" and "January 2023" refer to the forecasts presented in the respective editions of the *Global Economic Prospects* report.

trial production. Services trade, by contrast, continued to strengthen following the easing of pandemic-induced mobility restrictions. International tourist arrivals are expected to approach 95 percent of 2019 levels in 2023, an increase from 63 percent in 2022 (UNWTO 2023).

Pressures on global supply chains have abated as goods demand has weakened and global shipping conditions have improved (figure 1.3.A). The global supply chain pressures index and suppliers'

delivery times reached their lowest levels in almost four years in the first half of 2023 and are expected to remain low.

During the pandemic, trade growth was supported by a shift in the composition of demand toward tradable goods and away from services, which are less trade-intensive. The gradual rotation of demand back to its pre-pandemic composition is now slowing trade growth—as is the fact that the recovery in China is expected to be predominantly driven by services, which will limit positive spillovers to its trading partners through demand for goods and commodities. The growing number of restrictive trade measures reflects a rising degree of geopolitical tensions and attempts by some major economies to follow more inward-looking policies (figure 1.3.B). In the longer term, this will likely reshape global supply chains and increase trade costs (EBRD 2023; Góes and Bekkers 2022).

Together, these factors are expected to further reduce the responsiveness of global trade to changes in output—responsiveness that had already declined in the 2010s relative to previous decades (figure 1.3.C; Kose and Ohnsorge 2023a). Against this backdrop, global trade growth is forecast to slow from 6 percent in 2022 to 1.7 percent in 2023 (figure 1.3.D). As global consumption returns to its pre-pandemic mix between goods and services, trade is expected to recover to 2.8 percent in 2024, only slightly stronger than GDP growth. The trade outlook is subject to various downside risks, including weaker-than-expected global demand, tighter global financial conditions, worsening trade tensions between major economies, mounting geopolitical uncertainty, and a further rise in protectionist measures (Aiyar et al. 2023; Metivier et al. 2023).

Commodity markets

Energy prices have eased considerably since their peak in the third quarter of 2022. A warmer-than-expected northern hemisphere winter reduced natural gas and electricity consumption, especially in Europe (figure 1.4.A). Oil prices have averaged $80/bbl in 2023 to date, but they have been volatile. This volatility reflected uncertainty about global growth prospects in the first quarter of 2023, followed by the announcement in early April by Saudi Arabia and other OPEC+ members of a cut to oil production of 1.16 mb/d. This pledge brings the total OPEC+ expected cuts over the course of 2023 to 3.6 percent of global demand. Russia has changed the destination of its oil exports without a material change in volumes (figure 1.4.B). The internationally coordinated price cap on its exports (currently set at $60/bbl) also does not appear to be a binding constraint to exports. Metal prices increased in early 2023 on expectations of a strong recovery in China, but have subsequently retraced those gains. Most agricultural commodity prices have eased this year, reflecting good production prospects for most crops, including grains and oilseeds.

Crude oil prices are projected to average $80/bbl in 2023, a $8/bbl downward revision from the January forecast, and to edge up to $82/bbl in 2024, reflecting a modest pickup in demand. Prices for natural gas and coal are expected to moderate in 2023 and decline further in 2024, as Europe has made substantial progress in improving efficiency and reducing energy demand. Natural gas prices in Europe are expected to remain well above their pre-pandemic five-year average, despite elevated inventories (figure 1.4.C). Energy prices could be lower if global demand is weaker than expected. In this respect, prospects in China play a particularly important role, as it is expected to account for more than half of the increase in global oil demand in 2023. On the upside, risks to the price forecast relate to a lack of expansion in U.S. oil production, low levels of spare capacity among OPEC members, and to the possibility that the cartel may decide to cut output further.

Metal prices are expected to decline in 2023 and 2024, albeit to levels higher than their 2015-19 average. Price declines reflect a recovery of supply following production disruptions last year, as well as subdued global demand. Metal prices may be higher if China's real estate sector recovers faster than expected or if supply disruptions persist—the importance of developments in China is illustrated by the fact that the country has accounted for a substantial proportion of global demand growth in recent months (figure 1.4.D).

FIGURE 1.4 Commodity markets

Commodity prices have returned to their pre-invasion levels but remain historically high. Energy prices have eased considerably this year, as a warmer-than-expected winter and lower European demand reduced natural gas, coal, and electricity consumption. Russian oil export volumes have not changed materially, but their destination has shifted sharply away from Europe, which has built up substantial natural gas inventories. Metals prices have remained subdued amid a weaker-than-expected industrial recovery in China.

A. Commodity price indexes

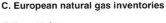
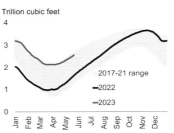

B. Destination of Russian Federation's oil exports

C. European natural gas inventories

D. Metals demand growth

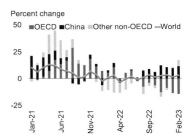

Sources: GSE (database); IEA (2023a); World Bank; World Bureau of Metal Statistics.
Note: OECD = Organisation for Economic Co-operation and Development.
A. Monthly data, last observation is April 2023.
B. Figure shows the share of the Russian Federation's oil exports by destination.
C. Sample includes 20 EU countries and the United Kingdom. Last observation is May 22, 2023.
D. Figure shows year-on-year, percent change. Last observation is February 2023.

Agricultural prices are projected to fall 7.2 percent in 2023 and ease further in 2024, as production of grains and oilseeds is expected to increase. Nonetheless, food prices have risen significantly faster than overall inflation since the pandemic, with substantially larger increases in some countries as a result of weaker currencies and transport disruptions. Overall, the agricultural price index is expected to remain well above pre-pandemic nominal levels in 2024. The key risks to agricultural production are adverse weather patterns (including the emerging El Niño), trade policy restrictions, and higher energy costs. Food insecurity remains a critical challenge in some EMDEs, reflecting severe weather events, geopolitical conflict, and distortive trade measures.

FIGURE 1.5 Global inflation

Global core inflation remains elevated. Projections suggest inflation will continue to be above its pre-pandemic level beyond 2024. Market-based measures of long-term inflation compensation in advanced economies remain above 2 percent, despite a decline in oil prices. In many emerging market and developing economies (EMDEs), inflation is either accelerating or has stabilized at high levels. One-year-ahead EMDE inflation expectations have declined only slightly. Longer-term projections point to a faster decline in inflation in countries with inflation targets.

A. Core inflation

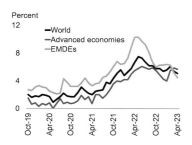

B. Model-based global CPI inflation projections

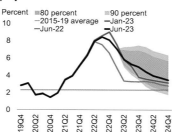

C. Deviation of long-term market inflation compensation from 2 percent

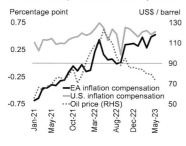

D. Inflation momentum in EMDEs

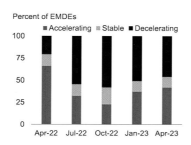

E. One-year-ahead expectations for EMDE inflation

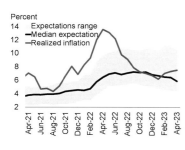

F. Share of EMDEs with five-year-ahead inflation projections substantially above pre-pandemic inflation

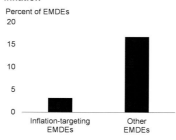

Sources: Bloomberg; Consensus Economics; Haver Analytics; International Monetary Fund; Oxford Economics; World Bank.

Note: CPI = consumer price index; EA = euro area; EMDEs = emerging market and developing economies.

A. Figure shows median 3-month core inflation at an annualized rate. Sample includes 31 advanced economies and 40 EMDEs. Last observation is April 2023.

B. Model-based GDP-weighted projections of year-on-year country-level CPI inflation using Oxford Economics' Global Economic Model, using global oil price forecasts presented in table 1.1. Uncertainty bands constructed from the distribution of forecast errors for total CPI from Consensus Economics for an unbalanced panel of 18 economies.

C. Figure shows the deviation of month-end coupon on 5-year inflation swaps 5-years forward. Oil price refers to Brent crude spot price. Last observation is May 2023.

D. Accelerating (decelerating) is defined as annualized 3-month inflation 1 percentage point or more above (below) its level in the preceding quarter. Sample includes 83 EMDEs.

E. Inflation expectations calculated as a time-weighted average of consensus inflation expectations for the current and following calendar year. Expectations range is the interquartile range. Realized inflation is median 3-month inflation for a sample of up to 101 EMDEs.

F. Figure shows the proportion of EMDEs for which the 2028 inflation projection is more than 1 percentage point above average inflation in 2010-19. Sample includes 146 EMDEs.

Global inflation

Inflation remains above target in almost all inflation-targeting economies. Median headline global inflation stood at 7.2 percent year-on-year in April, down from a peak of 9.4 percent in July 2022. This deceleration largely reflects favorable base effects from commodity prices falling below their 2022 peaks, along with abating supply chain pressures. Moderating energy prices help explain global inflation being somewhat softer in the first quarter of 2023 than previously anticipated. However, recent core inflation measures suggest the disinflation that started last year has made only halting progress. Across EMDEs, three-month median core inflation has decelerated somewhat in recent months, while it has picked up in advanced economies (figure 1.5.A). Amid these developments, global inflation is envisaged to remain further above its 2015-19 average than was expected in January, and for a longer period (figure 1.5.B).

With supply chain pressures easing and energy prices declining, excess demand appears to be a key driver of continuing high inflation in advanced economies, though lingering impairments to supply capacity may also still play a role (Bernanke and Blanchard 2023). In Europe, the role of energy prices is particularly important—the pass-through of energy costs into broader prices may be adding to inflation persistence, which could be further exacerbated by the sunsetting of fiscal programs that have attenuated price spikes for end-users (Pill 2023). The absence of economic slack may also be increasing the ability of firms and workers to exercise pricing power, such that inflation has become more responsive to economic activity (Borio et al. 2023; Gagnon and Sarsenbayev 2022).

In some advanced economies, particularly the euro area, market-derived measures of long-term inflation compensation have moved up since last year, despite a decline in oil prices, with which they have been correlated in the past (figure 1.5.C; Elliot et al. 2015). This could signal greater risks of inflation remaining above target, but may also reflect increased inflation risk aversion among market participants (Böninghausen, Kidd, and de Vincent Humphreys 2018; Lane 2023). Consumer surveys indicate that medium-term inflation expectations in the United States and the euro area have been fairly stable in 2023.

In many EMDEs, inflation is either accelerating once again or has stabilized at high levels (figure 1.5.D). Some common responses to recent shocks, including (tacit or explicit) indexation of wages to inflation and increases in untargeted fossil fuel subsidies, may have added to generalized inflation pressures (IEA 2023b). A protracted period of high inflation could be especially challenging for EMDEs, where inflation expectations are generally less stable than in advanced economies and more influenced by current inflation rates (Kamber, Mohanty, and Morley 2020). Consensus-derived expectations for EMDE inflation one-year-ahead moved up substantially as inflation initially picked up, but declined more slowly as inflation decelerated last year.

The distribution of short-term inflation forecasts across EMDEs has also widened markedly, with double-digit inflation expected in more than a quarter of EMDEs (figure 1.5.E). Long-term forecasts suggest that EMDEs with inflation-targeting central banks may have an advantage in durably bringing inflation down. Five years ahead, only one-in-twenty inflation-targeting EMDEs is projected to have inflation more than 1 percentage point above 2010-19 average levels, compared with about one-in-six non-inflation-targeting EMDEs (figure 1.5.F).

The reopening of China's economy is not expected to have a material impact on global inflation. While strengthening activity will put upward pressure on domestic inflation, this will likely be limited by slack in China's economy, including in the labor market. In addition, the recovery in China is projected to be less commodity-intensive than in past episodes of growth accelerations, and therefore less likely to boost global prices.

Global financial developments

Global financial conditions have become restrictive as a result of the fastest global monetary policy tightening cycle since the 1980s, along with bouts of financial instability. For nearly a year, markets have interpreted U.S. policy rates as being well

above their long-term level. This pushed the U.S. yield curve into its steepest inversion (that is, two-year yields exceeding ten-year yields) since 1981 (figure 1.6.A). Such yield curve inversions have often preceded U.S. recessions.

Advanced-economy banks started the year with unrealized losses on bond portfolios, which increased as interest rates rose. This, combined with shortcomings in risk management, contributed to the failure of several regional banks in the United States. In Europe, Credit Suisse came under intense market pressure in March and was subject to an emergency takeover. The initial emergence of banking stress drove a surge in market volatility, including the sharpest five-day drop in two-year U.S. yields in more than two decades and a large decline in bank equity prices (figure 1.6.B). To bolster market confidence and limit contagion to the broader financial system, authorities have responded with emergency liquidity facilities. The U.S. authorities also introduced an expanded deposit guarantee for the banks that failed in March. Central banks have nonetheless reaffirmed intentions to maintain, or increase, the tightness of monetary policy until inflation shows a clear trend toward target. Even with continued signs of banking stress, broader risk appetite in advanced-economy financial markets has been notably resilient. High-yield corporate risk spreads have mostly stayed below their post-2010 average, despite bank lending standards reaching their most restrictive levels since the global financial crisis (figure 1.6.C).

For EMDEs, higher interest rates in advanced economies often entail an extended period of costly external financing. Nonresident investors have remained cautious, which has persistently weighed on portfolio capital flows to EMDEs excluding China. Under the pressure of tight financial conditions, EMDEs have diverged into two broad subsets.[1] The first subset includes those

---

[1] According to recent Moody's credit ratings, 73 percent of EMDEs have sovereign ratings of B or above, while 27 percent have ratings below B. This classification is similar to, but does not perfectly align with, the common practice in capital markets of dividing countries into "emerging" and "frontier" markets, which is done on the basis of a variety of characteristics such as financial market depth and liquidity.

FIGURE 1.6 Global financial developments

Prior to the advanced-economy bank failures in March, the U.S. yield curve registered its deepest inversion in four decades. During the banking stress, short-term government bond yields and bank stocks fell sharply. Despite these events, and much tightened bank lending standards, advanced-economy credit spreads remain contained. As borrowing costs have risen globally, currency depreciation and credit spread widening in emerging market and developing economies have been disproportionately concentrated in the countries with the weakest credit ratings.

A. Yield curve inversions in the United States

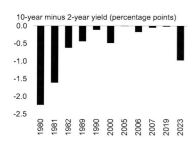

B. Advanced-economy yields and bank stocks during March 2023 banking stress

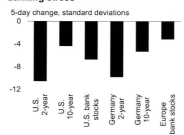

C. Bank lending standards and high-yield spreads in advanced economies

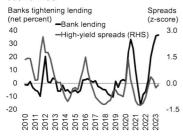

D. Change in EMDE borrowing costs since February 2022, by credit rating

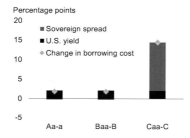

E. EMDE U.S. dollar exchange rate, by credit rating

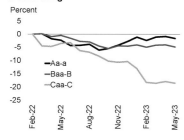

F. EMDE CDS premia around advanced-economy bank failures

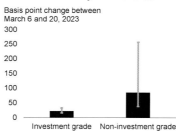

Sources: Bloomberg; European Central Bank; Federal Reserve Economic Data; Haver Analytics; J.P.Morgan; Moody's Analytics; World Bank.
Note: EMDEs = emerging market and developing economies.
A. Figure shows the largest negative value for the 5-day moving average of the 10-year minus the 2-year U.S. Treasury yield during each inversion. An inversion begins when this average turns negative and ends when it turns positive.
B. Figure shows the largest 5-day changes in March 2023 as multiples of the standard deviation of 5-day changes. "2-year" and "10-year" refer to 2- and 10-year government bond yields; "bank stocks" refers to price of an index of U.S. regional bank stocks and the banks subindex of the European STOXX 600 index. Sample is January 4, 2000 to March 21, 2023 for yields and January 3, 2012 to March 21, 2023 for spreads.
C. Bank lending is a simple average of the net percentage of banks tightening lending standards to non-financial enterprises in the United States and the euro area. "High-yield spreads" is an average of z-scores of high-yield bonds spread indices for the United States and the euro area.
D. U.S. yield is the 5-year Treasury yield. Sovereign spread is the spread over U.S. yields for EMDE dollar-denominated sovereign debt. Changes are since February 2022 for 45 EMDEs.
E. Indexes constructed by compounding daily average changes in exchange rates for each group. Sample includes 76 EMDEs. Last observation is May 25, 2023.
F. Median change in 5-year U.S. dollar-denominated credit default swaps for 48 EMDEs, including 19 investment-grade and 29 non-investment-grade countries. Whiskers indicate interquartile range.

with credit ratings of B or above (the majority of EMDEs), which have so far proved able to withstand global monetary tightening without incurring substantial increases in risk premia on external debt (figure 1.6.D). In some such EMDEs where inflation has been high, central banks have helped assuage market concerns by raising policy rates earlier, and by more than, advanced-economy counterparts. Nonetheless, since the Federal Reserve started to raise its policy rate, marginal dollar-denominated borrowing costs have increased by close to 200 basis points even among the most resilient EMDEs.

The second subset includes EMDEs with the lowest credit ratings (below B), which have proved far more vulnerable. Their risk premia have increased substantially, in part because they have also experienced much greater currency depreciation than most other EMDEs (figure 1.6.E). Many of these countries have limited fiscal capacity, large unhedged foreign currency liabilities, and other economic vulnerabilities. With little or no access to commercial debt markets, they have become reliant on official creditors, or their own diminishing reserves, to meet external financing needs. Some have slipped into crises.

Spillovers from advanced-economy banking stress have so far been limited in most EMDEs, but have exhibited a similar divergence. Market perceptions of the creditworthiness of investment grade EMDEs (as measured by credit-default swap premia) were little affected in March, after the first bank failures in advanced economies; in contrast, credit default swap spreads for non-investment-grade sovereign borrowers widened notably (figure 1.6.F).

Major economies: Recent developments and outlook

Activity in advanced economies slowed less than expected in early 2023 but is set to weaken substantially later this year. Past and ongoing monetary policy rate hikes, tighter credit conditions amid banking sector stress, softening labor markets, and the lingering effects of the energy price spike of 2022 are expected to weigh on activity. In China, growth is projected to rebound more quickly than previously expected, reflecting the economic reopening and supportive policy, before moderating toward the end of 2023.

Advanced economies

Growth in advanced economies in late 2022 and early 2023 slowed less than expected, as tight labor markets supported robust wage growth and prevented a sharper slowdown in consumption (figure 1.7.A). The tightness in labor markets is in part related to a slowdown in labor supply, with labor force participation rates falling (partly because of a rise in early retirements) and, in the United States, a decline in hours worked by those employed (Lee, Park, and Shin 2023). In the first quarter of 2023, GDP expanded by 1.1 percent in the United States on a quarterly basis, supported by broadly robust consumption. Euro area GDP grew by 0.3 percent at an annualized rate, reflecting lower energy prices, easing supply bottlenecks, and fiscal policy support for firms and households.

Advanced-economy growth is projected to slow to an annual average of 0.7 percent in 2023. This largely reflects the continued effect of considerable central bank policy rate hikes since early 2022. More restrictive credit conditions due to banking sector stress in advanced economies should slow domestic demand further in 2023. Past increases in energy prices and the expected softening in labor markets are also projected to weigh on activity. Growth is expected to accelerate modestly to 1.2 percent in 2024 due to a pickup in the euro area.

Stronger-than-expected activity in early 2023 is projected to push average annual growth 0.2 percentage point above the January forecast, despite an expected weakening in the second half. In contrast, the pickup in growth in 2024 is weaker than previously forecast, owing to the more delayed impact of monetary policy rate increases, as well as additional headwinds from tighter credit conditions.

In the **United States**, growth is expected to weaken significantly through 2023 and early 2024, mainly as a result of the lagged effects of the sharp rise in policy rates over the past year and a half aimed at bringing down the highest inflation

FIGURE 1.7 Major economies: Recent developments and outlook

Tight labor markets and high wage growth prevented a sharper slowdown in advanced economies in early 2023. Policy rate hikes and recent bank failures have contributed to a tightening of financial conditions and a slowdown in bank lending. Historically high job vacancy rates should decline as labor markets slow in advanced economies. The recovery in China is expected to be led by services activity, which tends to be less trade intensive.

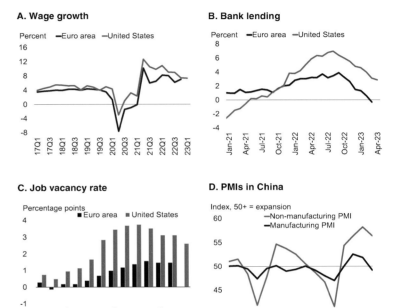

Sources: European Central Bank; Eurostat; Federal Reserve Economic Data; Haver Analytics; National Bureau of Statistics of China; U.S. Bureau of Economic Analysis; U.S. Bureau of Labor Statistics; World Bank.
A. Figure shows the year-on-year percentage change in wages and salaries. Last observation is 2023Q1 for the United States and 2022Q4 for the euro area.
B. Figure shows six-month percentage change in the stock of credit, which is bank lending to nonfinancial private sector, monthly end of period, for the euro area and bank loans and leases from the H8 release by the Federal Reserve, monthly end of period, for the United States. Last observation is April 2023 for the United States and March 2023 for the euro area.
C. Figure shows job openings rate in the United States and the job vacancy rate in the euro area, as percentage points deviation from the average value for the period 2010-2019. Last observation is 2023Q1 for the United States and 2022Q4 for the euro area.
D. Figure shows official manufacturing and non-manufacturing Purchasing Managers' Index (PMI). PMI readings above (below) 50 indicate expansion (contraction) in economic activity. Last observation is April 2023.

rates since the early 1980s. Model-based estimates show that the peak impact on growth from this tightening is likely to take place in 2023. In addition, recent bank failures have contributed to a slowdown in credit creation (figure 1.7.B). Tighter credit will also weigh on near-term activity.

Consumption has been resilient but is expected to slow substantially. Higher borrowing costs and tighter financial conditions will weigh on household spending as the large stock of savings accumulated during the pandemic is depleted, and unusually tight labor markets begin to rebalance, gradually reducing the historically high job vacancy rates (figure 1.7.C). Decelerating consumption and residential investment will likely contribute to very feeble activity in the second half of 2023. After growing 1.1 percent in 2023, the U.S. economy is likely to remain weak in 2024, decelerating to 0.8 percent. Activity is expected to pick up toward the end of next year, as inflation eases and the effects of monetary policy tightening fade.

In the **euro area**, growth proved more resilient than expected at the turn of the year, supported by warmer weather and lower natural gas prices. Energy price pressures have been fading, but core inflation has remained elevated, reflecting the strength of the labor market, robust wage growth, lagged effects from high gas and electricity prices, and broadening price pressures. The persistence of underlying inflation pressures, as seen in the core services component which excludes shelter, suggests that monetary policy may need to be tighter than previously expected.

Growth is forecast to slow to 0.4 percent in 2023, from 3.5 percent in 2022, owing mainly to the lagged effects of monetary policy tightening. The upward revision of 0.4 percentage point to growth this year relative to January mainly reflects the better-than-expected data at the beginning of the year and the downgrade to energy price projections. After bottoming out in 2023, growth is expected to firm to 1.3 percent in 2024, supported by reforms and investments funded by the Recovery and Resilience Facility. The 0.3 percentage point downward revision to the forecast for 2024 partly reflects the effects of tight monetary policy over a longer period than previously expected.

In **Japan**, growth is expected to slow to 0.8 percent in 2023, as the lagged effects of synchronized monetary policy tightening in major advanced economies weigh on external demand. Although price pressures are expected to subside in the second half of 2023 as the pass-through from a surge in import prices runs its course, persistent weakness in real wage growth will hold back consumer demand. Growth is anticipated to edge

down further to 0.7 percent in 2024, partly as a result of the gradual unwinding of macroeconomic policy support.

China

Economic activity in China bounced back in early 2023, spurred by the earlier-than-expected economic reopening, which bolstered consumer spending, including on services-related activity (figure 1.7.D). The property sector began to emerge from a protracted slump, supported by wide-ranging policies. These included liquidity provisions to developers and measures to ensure the completion of unfinished projects. Meanwhile, goods trade remained subdued.

Growth is projected to rebound to 5.6 percent in 2023, as the economic reopening drives consumer spending, particularly on domestic services. Investment is expected to pick up only modestly as infrastructure-related stimulus fades, and high debt levels weigh on the property sector recovery. Weak external demand will also dampen growth. While the reopening will support services trade, subdued infrastructure and manufacturing sector activity will weigh on overall trade, as services activity tends to be less trade intensive. Inflation is expected to remain below target, allowing monetary policy to remain mildly accommodative. The fiscal policy stance is expected to be broadly neutral.

With the reopening boost fading in the second half of the year, growth will slow to 4.6 percent in 2024, as moderating consumption offsets a small pickup in exports. Key downside risks include continuing stress in the real estate sector, a sharper-than-anticipated slowdown in global growth and trade, and the lingering possibility of disruptive COVID-19 waves. On the upside, a more vigorous consumption recovery could support growth for longer than expected.

Emerging market and developing economies

EMDE growth is expected to pick up in 2023 almost entirely due to China's economic reopening. Excluding China, growth in EMDEs is set to slow markedly. A protracted period of tight domestic monetary policy, fiscal consolidation, and weak external demand will curb growth in many EMDEs. Although advanced-economy banking stress has so far not translated to EMDE financial sectors, the effects of more restrictive global financial conditions will remain a headwind to growth, particularly for EMDEs with weaker credit ratings. In LICs, domestic vulnerabilities, increased fragility, and persistently high poverty rates, will continue to weigh on economic recoveries.

Recent developments

EMDE growth firmed somewhat in early 2023. External demand for many countries was supported by the pickup in growth in China and the unexpected resilience in advanced economies. Indicators of EMDE domestic demand have improved, but from a low level. Consumer confidence, for example, has improved slightly from its trough in the last quarter of 2022, but remains well below recent averages (figure 1.8.A). Services activity also picked up to start the year, with services PMIs indicating solid expansion in several large EMDEs.

Although measures of EMDE financial stress have generally declined since last year, financing costs remain elevated, reflecting both domestic and advanced-economy monetary policy tightening. This has weighed on EMDE investment and output in sectors that are more sensitive to interest rate movements, such as industrial production and construction (figure 1.8.B). Industrial production in EMDEs excluding China declined sharply in the second half of last year but rebounded somewhat in the first quarter of 2023 (figure 1.8.C). New orders in EMDE manufacturing PMIs have shown modestly increasing output, after signaling contraction for much of 2022. International tourism flows have been slow to respond to China's reopening but have normalized substantially compared with last year (figure 1.8.D).

Activity in EMDE energy exporters remains firm, despite a decline in energy prices (especially for coal and gas), reflecting momentum from a prolonged period of elevated export earnings. In the context of decelerating advanced-economy demand, subdued metal prices will provide little support for growth in EMDE metal exporters,

FIGURE 1.8 Recent developments in emerging market and developing economies

Indicators of domestic demand in emerging market and developing economies (EMDEs), such as consumer confidence, have started to recover but remain weak. Tighter financial conditions have weighed on activity in sectors more sensitive to interest rates, such as construction and industrial production, both of which have been subdued. Tourism has recovered substantially since 2022.

A. EMDE consumer confidence

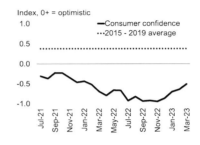

B. EMDE construction activity and financial conditions

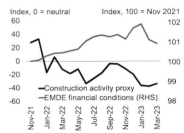

C. Growth of EMDE industrial production

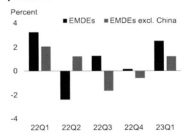

D. International tourist arrivals

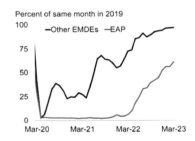

Sources: Bloomberg; Goldman Sachs; Haver Analytics; World Bank.
Note: EAP = East Asia and Pacific; EMDEs = emerging market and developing economies.
A. Figure shows the simple average of consumer confidence indices standardized against their historical values for 12 EMDEs (Albania, Argentina, Brazil, China, Colombia, Hungary, India, Indonesia, Mexico, Pakistan, Thailand, and Türkiye). Standard deviations for constituent scores are based on the period from 2015 to the last observation, which is March 2023.
B. Increases in the financial conditions index imply more restrictive conditions. Increases in the EMDE construction activity proxy indicate greater confidence and increasing year-on-year activity in EMDE construction sectors. The construction activity proxy is a simple average of z-scores, multiplied by 100, for variables capturing confidence and activity in construction sectors for 9 EMDEs (Argentina, Brazil, Mexico, Chile, China, Hungary, Romania, South Africa, and Thailand). EMDE financial conditions is a GDP-weighted average of the Goldman Sachs financial conditions indices for 12 EMDEs, lagged by 3 months (that is, the July 2022 value signifies conditions in April 2022).
C. Figure shows the quarterly growth of industrial production in 31 EMDEs.
D. Figure shows total arrivals for country groups, expressed as a percentage of the same month in 2019. Sample includes 26 EMDEs, of which 5 are EAP.

many of which are also facing headwinds from tight financing conditions. In large agricultural exporters, stable high prices have supported investment in machinery and equipment, softening the contractionary impact of increased borrowing costs. Among poorer agricultural exporters, however, prohibitive fertilizer costs are crimping output. Among EMDE commodity importers, the decline in energy import costs has partially reversed the squeeze on consumers and industrial activity from last year's worsening terms of trade.

Across LICs, high prices for food and energy continue to weigh on consumption—especially in fragile countries and in small agricultural commodity producers, where violence, adverse weather shocks, and elevated production costs have dampened activity. Sizable financing needs, together with rising debt service costs, present a growing fiscal burden.

Outlook

EMDE outlook

Growth in EMDEs is projected to edge up to 4 percent in 2023, which almost entirely reflects the rebound in China. Excluding China, EMDE growth is set to decline to 2.9 percent this year, from 4.1 percent last year, due to the drag from high inflation and the associated monetary tightening—both domestically and via monetary policy spillovers from advanced economies—as well as from slowing external demand. From a regional perspective, growth is set to slow in all regions except EAP and ECA (box 1.1). Growth in EMDEs excluding China is expected to pick up modestly to 3.4 percent in 2024, as the effects of monetary tightening diminish and several larger EMDEs emerge from domestic strains, including natural disasters, power shortages, and political turbulence.

Substantial upgrades to projections for China and, to a lesser extent, Russia are the main drivers of the 0.6 percentage point upward revision to EMDE growth this year (figure 1.9.A). The improved near-term outlook for China reflects a greater-than-expected boost from economic reopening. In Russia, the contraction this year is envisaged to be milder than initially forecast, partially due to the continued flow of energy exports.

EMDE growth is expected to receive little support from external demand. China's recovery is envisaged to be services oriented, rather than trade-intensive. Aside from a pickup in tourism flows to Southeast Asian countries, the projections therefore entail only a muted growth impulse from

China to other EMDEs. Similarly, near-term EMDE growth will benefit only marginally from stronger-than-expected advanced-economy growth in 2023, which largely reflects positive surprises at the beginning of the year giving way to weak subsequent growth in the second half of 2023 and in 2024.

Gradual fiscal consolidation is expected in the majority of EMDEs in 2023; however, in aggregate, this is offset by a few larger EMDEs with increasing deficits. Where consolidation takes place, adjustment is foreseen to occur primarily via reduced spending, as weak growth weighs on government revenue. Spending-led retrenchment is expected to intensify in 2024. This will help rebuild fiscal buffers, but also dampen demand. Accordingly, the aggregate EMDE fiscal impulse is about neutral for growth this year and negative in 2024 (figure 1.9.B).

Many EMDE central banks have also continued to tighten monetary policies, or retained high rates for longer than previously expected. Given lags in the transmission of monetary tightening, investment growth is expected to be weak throughout the year, with labor markets and consumption also softening. Moreover, market pricing suggests that inflation-adjusted policy rates will rise further in many EMDEs, as inflation declines only gradually, taking aggregate EMDE real rates further into positive territory (figure 1.9.C). This should help to combat inflation in many countries but will entail a continued drag on EMDE activity throughout 2024.

The global tightening cycle has weighed especially on growth prospects in EMDEs with weaker sovereign credit profiles, which are expected to grow just 0.9 percent in 2023. Projections for these economies have been repeatedly downgraded as global financial conditions have tightened (figure 1.9.D). In many such countries, debt service is consuming a large proportion of limited government revenues, and non-concessional external finance has largely dried up. In the absence of fiscal capacity to buffer commodity price shocks and support populations, living standards and macroeconomic stability have deteriorated.

BOX 1.1 Regional perspectives: Outlook and risks

Growth is projected to diverge across EMDE regions this year and next. It is expected to pick up in 2023 in East Asia and Pacific (EAP) and Europe and Central Asia (ECA), as China's reopening spurs a recovery and as growth prospects in several large economies improve. In contrast, growth is forecast to moderate in all other regions, particularly in Latin America and the Caribbean (LAC) and the Middle East and North Africa (MNA). Headwinds from weak external demand, tight global financial conditions, and high inflation will drag on activity this year, especially in LAC, South Asia (SAR), and Sub-Saharan Africa (SSA). The lingering impact of the Russian Federation's invasion of Ukraine will continue to weigh on growth across regions, particularly in ECA. Next year, growth is projected to moderate in EAP and SAR but to pick up elsewhere as domestic headwinds ease and external demand strengthens. Downside risks to the outlook for all regions include possible further global financial stress and more persistent domestic inflation than projected in the baseline. Geopolitical tensions, conflict and social unrest, and natural disasters stemming from climate change also present downside risks, to varying degrees. The materialization of such risks could further weaken potential growth, leading to a prolonged period of slower growth in all EMDE regions.

Introduction

EMDE regions are contending with a mix of predominately negative global headwinds, resulting in diverging growth prospects. Amid weak growth of global demand and output, trade growth is expected to remain subdued and weigh on activity in all regions. Inflation is moderating but remains elevated, prolonging monetary policy tightening cycles in many countries. Growth is projected to strengthen in EAP and ECA in 2023 but to decline in other regions. Commodity prices, particularly for energy and food, are expected to moderate this year. This will help lower inflation and support activity in commodity-importing regions, including EAP and SAR, as well as some countries in LAC, but weigh on commodity exporters, particularly in ECA and MNA.

Against the backdrop of subdued growth, all regions face a suite of downside risks. These include financial sector stress and weaker growth stemming from tighter global financial conditions, with highly indebted regions, particularly ECA, LAC and SSA, and many oil-importing countries in MNA, especially vulnerable. In all regions persistently high inflation could lead to further domestic monetary policy tightening. Heightened geopolitical tensions could disrupt trade and damage globally integrated sectors, especially in EAP and ECA. Further risks are posed by conflicts and social instability, already severe in ECA, LAC and MNA, and natural disasters, including extreme weather events related to climate change, with SSA and small states in EAP and LAC heavily exposed.

In this context, this box considers two questions:

- What are the cross-regional differences in the growth outlook?

- What are the key risks to the outlook for each region?

Outlook

Growth is projected to diverge across EMDE regions in 2023 in the face of persistently high inflation and global headwinds—notably slower growth in the major advanced economies and tight global financial conditions (figure B1.1.1.A). In EAP and ECA, growth is forecast to strengthen in 2023, to rates higher than projected in January, mainly reflecting developments in the two regions' largest economies—China and the Russian Federation. In China, an earlier-than-expected reopening of the economy is driving a rebound in growth this year, supported by consumer spending, particularly on services. Output in Russia is projected to contract less than anticipated in January mainly due to more resilient-than-expected oil production and higher-than-expected growth momentum from 2022. Persistent contraction in export volumes, weak domestic demand, policy uncertainty, and sanctions in response to Russia's invasion of Ukraine will continue to weigh on activity.

In other EMDE regions, growth is forecast to weaken this year, and, except in LAC and SAR, more steeply than projected in January (figure B1.1.1.B). Growth in LAC and MNA is forecast to slow the most in 2023, following strong expansions in 2022 supported by economic reopening and high commodity prices. In MNA's oil exporters, cuts to oil production—with

---

Note: This box was prepared by Samuel Hill.

BOX 1.1 Regional perspectives: Outlook and risks (*continued*)

FIGURE B1.1.1 Regional outlooks

Growth in EAP and ECA is projected to pick up, and to be faster than previously forecast, in 2023 owing to improved prospects for China and a few large economies. Growth in other EMDE regions is forecast to weaken this year, broadly in line with January projections, except in MNA, owing to lower-than-expected oil production. While headline inflation appears to have peaked in all regions, in most regions it remains elevated by recent historical standards—and a key drag on growth.

A. Output growth

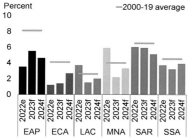

B. Growth forecast revisions

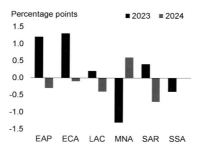

C. Consumer price inflation

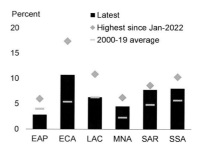

Sources: Haver Analytics; World Bank.
Note: EAP = East Asia and Pacific, ECA = Europe and Central Asia, LAC = Latin America and the Caribbean, MNA = Middle East and North Africa, SAR = South Asia, SSA = Sub-Saharan Africa.
A. Aggregate growth rates are calculated using GDP weights at average 2000-19 prices and market exchange rates. 2000-2019 refers to the simple average of growth rates for each region. Data for 2023 and 2024 are World Bank forecasts.
B. Revisions reflect differences in forecasts presented in the January 2023 edition of the Global Economic Prospects report. Data for 2023 and 2024 are forecasts.
C. Bars show regional median year-on-year consumer price inflation in April 2023 where available and otherwise March 2023. Lines shows the regional median of the simple country average of year-on-year consumer price inflation between January 2000 and December 2019. Diamonds show the regional median of the highest year-on-year consumer price inflation since January 2022. Sample includes 106 EMDEs (9 in EAP, 21 in ECA, 20 in LAC, 12 in MNA, 6 in SAR, and 23 in SSA).

spillovers to broader economic activity—are expected to weigh on growth. In MNA's oil importers, high inflation, external financing pressures, and limited access to foreign currency are expected to constrain activity. Growth is also projected to moderate in SAR— albeit only marginally—and SSA, as combinations of weak external demand, high inflation, and instability, including from debt distress and natural disasters, weigh on activity.

While headline inflation has declined from recent peaks in all EMDE regions, it remains elevated by historical standards, except in EAP and LAC, and above central bank targets in most inflation-targeting countries in most regions (figure B1.1.1.C). Inflation remains especially high in ECA and SSA, reflecting ongoing energy and food supply disruptions. While headline inflation is expected to continue moderating in the coming months, core inflation is likely to remain elevated, as higher production costs, including for labor, feed through to consumer prices. In crisis-afflicted economies, particularly in MNA and SAR, significant currency depreciations have added to inflationary

pressures. Persistently high inflation will continue to be a drag on growth this year, eroding real wages and weighing on consumption, increasing uncertainty, and holding back investment. The drag on consumption is expected to be particularly pronounced in low-income countries, predominantly in SAR and SSA, where food accounts for above-average shares of household spending.

With global trade growth projected to slow sharply this year, external demand is set to remain weak for all EMDE regions. Consumption- and services-led growth in China is expected to provide limited support to global goods trade but boost the global tourism recovery. Tepid external demand for goods, including commodities, will weigh on growth in all regions, especially EAP, ECA, and LAC. However, this will be partly offset by a pickup in international tourism, particularly in EAP and to a lesser extent in LAC. Commodity prices are projected to continue easing in 2023 from the very high levels reached last year, helping to cool inflation in all regions and supporting activity in commodity-importing regions, including EAP and SAR.

BOX 1.1 Regional perspectives: Outlook and risks (*continued*)

FIGURE B1.1.2 **Regional risks**

EMDE regions are subject to various downside risks, including from tighter global financial conditions—particularly ECA, LAC, and SSA—amid high external debt levels. Rising public-debt-servicing costs in all regions add to the risk of debt distress. Inflation has exceeded expectations in all regions and could remain stubbornly high in most regions. Intensifying geopolitical tensions could disrupt international trade and global value chains, damaging globally integrated manufacturing sectors in EAP and ECA, while further intensification of conflicts—already severe in ECA, LAC, and MNA—could cause broad economic and social damage. The materialization of downside risks, especially those harming investment, could weaken potential growth.

A. External debt

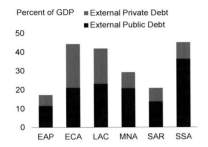

B. Public-debt-servicing costs

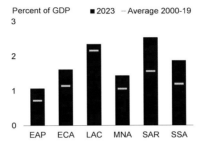

C. Expected inflation in 2023

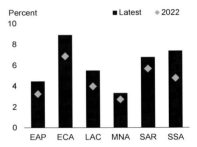

D. Manufacturing exports

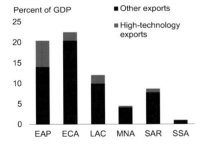

E. Conflict in EMDEs

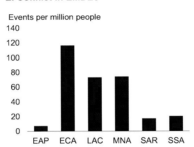

F. Potential growth and its sources

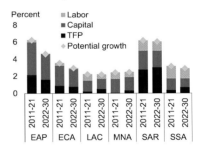

Sources: ACLED (Database); International Monetary Fund; Kilic Celik et al. (2023a); WDI (database); World Bank.
Note: EAP = East Asia and Pacific, ECA = Europe and Central Asia, LAC = Latin America and the Caribbean, MNA = Middle East and North Africa, SAR = South Asia, SSA = Sub-Saharan Africa.
A. GDP-weighted average of gross external debt as a share of GDP. Annual data as of 2022. Sample includes 60 EMDEs (8 in EAP, 14 in ECA, 18 in LAC, 6 in MNA, 5 in SAR, and 9 in SSA).
B. Bars show the regional median of the difference between general government net lending/borrowing and general government primary net lending/borrowing. Lines show the regional median of the simple country average between 2000 and 2019. Sample includes 135 EMDEs (20 in EAP, 21 in ECA, 26 in LAC, 15 in MNA, 6 in SAR and, 47 in SSA).
C. Bars show median inflation projections for 2023 from April 2023 World Bank projections. Diamonds show median inflation projections for 2023 from April 2022 World Bank projections. Sample includes 134 EMDEs (16 in EAP, 20 in ECA, 27 in LAC, 16 in MNA, 7 in SAR, and 48 in SSA).
D. Bars show the GDP-weighted averages of manufacturing exports as a share of GDP in 2021. Sample includes 74 EMDEs (9 in EAP, 12 in ECA, 18 in LAC, 8 in MNA, 4 in SAR, and 23 in SSA).
E. Bars show the number of reported conflict events in since June 2022; conflict events include battles, explosions, violence against civilians, riots and protests. Last observation is May 19, 2023. Sample includes 134 EMDEs (14 in EAP, 23 in ECA, 26 in LAC, 18 in MNA, 7 in SAR, and 46 in SSA).
F. Figure shows GDP-weighted averages of production function-based annual average potential growth estimates. TFP growth stands for total factor productivity growth. Sample includes 53 EMDEs (6 in EAP, 9 in ECA, 16 in LAC, 5 in MNA, 3 in SAR, and 14 in SSA).

However, for commodity-exporting regions, including ECA, LAC, MNA, and SSA, this will be a drag on growth and government revenues, and will weaken their terms of trade.

Macroeconomic policies are expected to be a drag on growth in all EMDE regions in 2023. Persistently high core inflation has prompted many EMDE central banks to delay monetary policy easing, particularly in LAC. The effects of tighter monetary policy will continue to be felt this year, with real interest rates rising as inflation moderates. Except in MNA's oil exporters, where high oil prices have boosted government revenues, fiscal consolidation is expected to continue in 2023 in most

BOX 1.1 Regional perspectives: Outlook and risks (*continued*)

regions as governments seek to rebuild fiscal buffers, although mostly at a gradual pace. Policy uncertainty, social instability, and conflicts are also expected to weigh on activity, particularly in ECA where Russia's invasion of Ukraine continues to have a negative impact on regional output. In LAC, MNA, and SSA, political instability and protests continue to weigh on sentiment and activity in some countries.

In 2024, economic growth is expected to diverge further among the regions. In EAP, growth is projected to slow as the rebound in China fades. In SAR, growth is also forecast to slow next year, owing in part to the repercussions of economic and humanitarian crises and natural disasters, and the lagged effects of monetary and fiscal policy tightening. In the other regions, growth is projected to increase toward potential rates, as domestic headwinds from high inflation and monetary policy tightening ease. Further moderation in global food prices, together with broadly stable energy prices, is expected to help lower inflation and support consumption, particularly in commodity-importing EMDEs. In LAC and SSA, the projected pickup in growth still implies only limited reductions in poverty. In all regions, growth will be supported by stronger external demand as activity picks up in advanced economies and global trade growth firms.

Risks

The baseline projections for EMDE regions are subject to a number of downside risks. Tighter-than-expected global financial conditions could be sparked by renewed stress in the global banking sector, heightened investor risk aversion, or additional monetary policy tightening in major advanced economies in response to persistent inflation. Slower-than-expected growth in advanced economies would further weaken external demand for EMDEs. An intensification in geopolitical tensions, persistently high domestic inflation, and disruptions from domestic conflict and climate change pose further downside risks. The materialization of these risks could further weaken both actual and potential growth.

Tighter-than-expected global financial conditions would have adverse consequences for all EMDE regions, particularly where creditworthiness is lower and where some countries are already grappling with financial crises. This risk was underscored by the jump in sovereign risk premia in March across EMDE

regions—most notably in SSA—in response to bank failures in Europe and the United States. ECA, LAC, and SSA, as well as some countries in SAR, are particularly at risk, given high levels of external debt and the associated exposure to higher borrowing costs (figure B1.1.2.A). The need to finance sizable current account deficits in many countries in LAC, SAR and SSA also increases vulnerabilities to sudden increases in borrowing costs.

High levels of public debt heighten the risk of government debt crises. While fiscal deficits have generally fallen from the very high levels reached in the early phases of the pandemic, they remain above pre-pandemic levels in EAP, ECA, LAC and SAR, adding to debt and increasing the risk of a forced sharp pivot toward budgetary consolidation, which would dampen activity. As indebtedness and borrowing costs have risen, so too have public-debt-servicing costs in all regions (figure B1.1.2.B). Absent well-calibrated fiscal consolidation, further increases in borrowing costs could threaten fiscal sustainability in economies where fiscal space is limited, particularly in LAC and SSA. In MNA, and to a lesser extent LAC, government revenues—and therefore fiscal positions—are also vulnerable to sharper-than-expected declines in commodity prices.

High inflation may be more persistent than expected; indeed, expected inflation has increased in most countries in several regions, most prominently in ECA, LAC and SSA (figure B1.1.2.C). Further unexpectedly persistent high inflation would imply further erosion of household purchasing power, higher interest rates, and heightened uncertainty, leading to weaker consumption and investment. Continued high inflation also increases the risk of inflation becoming entrenched by feeding into expectations and leading to increases in wages and production costs, particularly where the outlook for demand remains robust, as in SAR. Signs that inflation expectations were becoming de-anchored could spur central banks to further tighten monetary policy.

An intensification of geopolitical tensions could further erode growth prospects in all EMDE regions by stoking uncertainty and disrupting global trade and supply chains. This applies to trade in commodities, as underscored by changes in global energy trade flows following the imposition of sanctions on Russia's energy exports in response to its invasion of Ukraine. Repercussions of

BOX 1.1 Regional perspectives: Outlook and risks (*continued*)

increased tensions could put renewed upward pressure on commodity prices and further stoke inflation. Geopolitical tensions could also drive a further reorientation of production lines through friend-shoring, near-shoring, or on-shoring, particularly of high-technology manufactured goods. While potentially creating opportunities for some countries, trade diversion could force a disruptive realignment or shortening of global value chains, stoking uncertainty and dampening investment, with the regions most highly integrated into global manufacturing trade, particularly EAP and ECA, at greatest risk (figure B1.1.2.D). Conflict and civil unrest—already high in many EMDEs, including in ECA, LAC, MNA, and SSA—could also escalate, increasing uncertainty and causing greater economic and social harm (figure B1.1.2.E).

As underscored by the earthquakes in the Syrian Arab Republic and Türkiye in February, natural disasters could cause severe damage and economic disruption. Extreme weather events, which are becoming more frequent and intense with climate change, could also substantially weaken growth, as highlighted by severe

droughts in LAC, MNA, and SSA, and storms in EAP. Risks are particularly large for small island states concentrated in EAP and LAC. While agricultural prices are expected to moderate this year, worsening conflicts or adverse weather-related events could reduce agricultural output, push up food prices anew, and exacerbate enduring food security challenges, especially in MNA, SAR, and SSA. This could feed further social unrest and conflict.

Growth could be weaker than projected for longer if the materialization of downside risks undermines the drivers of potential growth. Absent substantial reforms, over the remainder of this decade potential growth is already set to decline in EAP and, to a lesser extent, in ECA and to remain lackluster elsewhere (figure B1.1.2.F). In particular, investment, an important potential growth driver in all regions, could weaken if financial conditions tighten more than expected. Protracted slow global growth—or worse, recession—and trade disruptions could also depress investment. Longer-term investment growth would also suffer in the event of financial crisis.

Excluding China and Russia, growth is forecast to decline slightly more in commodity exporters than in commodity importers, and from a lower starting point (figure 1.9.E). Growth in commodity importers excluding China is set to fall to 4.2 percent in 2023, from 5.3 percent in 2022. Continued high local prices for energy and food will take a toll on private demand in most countries, while heightened macroeconomic vulnerabilities in some large commodity-importing economies are likely to weigh on business confidence. In commodity exporters excluding Russia, growth is expected to slow to 2.2 percent, from 4.2 percent last year. This largely reflects slowing growth in oil exporters, as the boom in industrial activity associated with high energy prices fades.

Over the first half of the 2020s (2020-2024), growth in EMDEs is expected to be unusually weak, averaging just 3.4 percent. This can be largely attributed to the overlapping adverse shocks of recent years—the COVID-19 pandemic, the repercussions from Russia's invasion of

Ukraine, and the ongoing global monetary policy tightening cycle. However, a longer-term perspective suggests that a fundamental structural slowdown is also at work, which is likely to persist throughout the remainder of the decade. This involves a reduction in the prospects for potential output, resulting from a slowing in all the major underlying drivers of growth: labor force growth (associated with aging populations); capital accumulation; and improvement in total factor productivity.

Labor force growth in EMDEs is set to decelerate as populations age in all regions except Sub-Saharan Africa. Weak investment growth, which weighed on EMDE growth for much of the past decade, is expected to continue as economies grapple with elevated debt and a long-term slowdown in trade growth. This implies a diminished contribution to growth from capital accumulation. Subdued investment is also a major driver of projections of declining total factor productivity growth, since new investment can

FIGURE 1.9 Outlook for emerging market and developing economies

Growth in emerging market and developing economies (EMDEs) excluding China is forecast to slow markedly in 2023. Upgrades to China and the Russian Federation account for most of the upward revision to growth this year. Both fiscal and monetary policy are expected to weigh on activity in 2023 and 2024. Amid high borrowing costs, growth projections for countries with weak credit profiles have on average more than halved from a year ago. Excluding China and Russia, growth is expected to slow more in commodity exporters than commodity importers, from a lower starting point. In the longer term, EMDE potential growth is weakening.

A. Growth forecast revisions

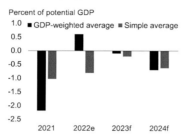

B. Fiscal impulse

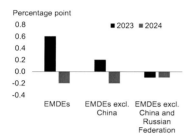

C. Real policy rates and one-year ahead market expectations

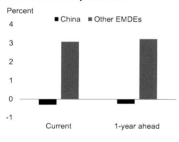

D. Growth in 2023, by credit rating

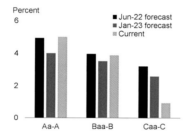

E. Growth, by commodity exporter status

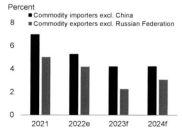

F. Potential growth

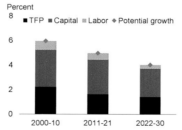

Sources: Bloomberg; Kose and Ohnsorge (2023a); WEO (database); World Bank.
Note: EMDEs = emerging market and developing economies.
A. Figure shows the difference between the latest projections and forecasts from the January 2023 *Global Economic Prospects* report.
B. Fiscal impulse is the negative annual change in the structural primary balance for up to 43 EMDEs, using data from the April 2023 WEO (database). A positive value indicates fiscal expansion, while a negative value indicates consolidation. Structural primary balance is the general government structural balance excluding net interest costs.
C. "Current" real rate is the policy rate minus a one-year ahead inflation expectation derived as a time-weighted average of 2023 and 2024 Bloomberg consensus inflation forecasts. "1-year ahead" is the market expectation derived from interest rate futures for the 1-year-ahead policy rate, minus a one-year inflation expectation for mid-2024 to mid-2025. 'Other EMDEs' is the GDP-weighted average for Brazil, Chile, Colombia, Hungary, India, Malaysia, Mexico, Philippines, Poland, Romania, South Africa, and Thailand. Last observation is May 30, 2023.
D. Comparison of GDP-weighted growth between different editions of the *Global Economic Prospects* report. Sample size includes 9 Aa-A, 62 Baa-B, and 25 Caa-C economies.
E. Aggregates calculated using GDP weights at average 2010-19 prices and market exchange rates.
F. Based on the production function approach as described in Kose and Ohnsorge (2023a). Sample includes 53 EMDEs. Data for 2022-30 are forecasts.

embody efficiency improvements and technology transfer. Model-based estimates suggest that EMDE potential growth may weaken from a rate of 5 percent per year in 2011-21, to 4 percent in 2022-2030 (figure 1.9.F; Kose and Ohnsorge 2023a). This would likely further delay the attainment of poverty reduction goals.

LICs outlook

LICs are forecast to grow by 5.1 percent this year, little changed from previous projections but below the pre-pandemic average. Forecast upgrades for several large countries are offset by the sizable downgrades in many other LICs, where worsening domestic vulnerabilities and fragility are dampening growth (box 1.2). Progress with poverty alleviation is expected to remain feeble, as past increases in the cost of living continue to weigh on activity. In some countries, fiscal consolidations amid elevated debt and high borrowing costs are projected to temper growth further by dampening public spending and investment.

In a number of fragile LICs, the effects of recent cost-of-living increases were exacerbated by sharp increases in violence and insecurity and climate-change-induced adverse weather events. Humanitarian needs across some fragile LICs (Afghanistan, Somalia, South Sudan, Sudan) are severe, with substantial risks of further deterioration in extreme poverty and food security. Some smaller agricultural-commodity exporters are struggling with complex challenges, including elevated input costs for seed, fertilizer, and energy, shortages of imported raw materials, floods, pest infestations (Burkina Faso, Mali), and disruptions caused by tropical cyclones (Madagascar, Malawi, Mozambique). In some other LICs, forecasts have been revised up on the basis of supportive mining-related activity, moderating inflation, and a peace agreement in Ethiopia—the largest LIC.

Per capita income growth

In per capita terms, the baseline forecasts represent a weak recovery from the overlapping shocks of the past three years. Over the first half of the 2020s (2020-2024), about one-third of EMDEs are expected to experience negative per capita growth (figure 1.10.A).

BOX 1.2 Recent developments and outlook for low-income countries

The challenges facing low-income countries (LICs) have become more formidable. The number of people struggling with extreme poverty and food insecurity in LICs has risen significantly as sharp increases in the cost of living have, in many cases, come on top of severe droughts or floods, or intensified violence. Although the overall growth forecast for 2023 has been revised upward marginally—to 5.1 percent, mostly owing to stronger recoveries in the largest economies—forecasts have been downgraded for over 40 percent of LICs. The deterioration in the outlook for many LICs reflects persistent inflation, rising indebtedness, depleted policy space, heightened insecurity, and weather-induced disruptions to activity. Risks to the outlook are tilted to the downside, including increased debt distress, higher-than-projected inflation, more frequent or intense weather events, increased insecurity, and weaker global growth.

Introduction

Growth in low-income countries (LICs) is expected to firm this year, as several metal and energy exporters expand production, and peacebuilding in Ethiopia gradually yields dividends. Nonetheless, many LICs struggle with increased vulnerabilities and fragility stemming partly from sharp increases in the cost of living since early 2022. Despite recent declines, consumer prices remain elevated, restricting food affordability for vulnerable populations. Almost 100 million people in LICs are still experiencing severe food insecurity (WFP and FAO 2022). Policy space to support the poor has been depleted, while substantial financing needs endanger debt sustainability in many countries. High levels of violence and extreme weather events continue to displace people, disrupt food supplies, and exacerbate poverty.

The outlook for LICs is subject to substantial uncertainty and various downside risks. Volatility of global commodity prices could intensify as markets remain vulnerable to renewed supply shocks. If global inflation pressures persist, further policy tightening could not only weigh on external demand but also heighten the risk of debt crises in some LICs. A stronger-than-expected rebound in China could support activity in some commodity exporters, but it could also lead to a surge in energy and food prices. Lastly, worsening insecurity would further retard economic development and poverty reduction, especially in LICs confronting the devastating impacts of climate change.

Against this backdrop, this box addresses the following questions.

- What have been the main recent economic developments in LICs?

- What is the outlook for LICs?

- What are the risks to the outlook?

Recent developments

Growth in LICs strengthened last year to 4.8 percent, reflecting continued post-pandemic rebounds in non-resource sectors and agriculture (Ethiopia, Mozambique, Niger, Uganda), and stronger mining activity in several metal and oil producers (Chad, the Democratic Republic of Congo, Equatorial Guinea, Guinea). Nevertheless, recoveries slowed in over 60 percent of LICs as domestic vulnerabilities—including extreme poverty and food insecurity, lack of fiscal space, and large external financing needs—worsened considerably across many countries alongside sharp cost-of-living increases stemming partly from the repercussions of Russia's invasion of Ukraine (figure B1.2.1.A).

Pervasive violence, especially in the Sahel region (Burkina Faso, Mali, Somalia, South Sudan, Sudan), and adverse weather patterns overlapped with macroeconomic instability and worsened humanitarian situations across LICs last year. Although the incidence of violence has fallen from its peak in mid-2022—with improved security in several large countries—peacebuilding remains fragile in the Democratic Republic of Congo and Ethiopia, while conflict has escalated in other LICs (Burkina Faso, Sudan; figure B1.2.1.B).

Several agricultural commodity exporters, already coping with increased inter-communal violence, have been facing other challenges, including elevated costs of fertilizer and fuel, shortages of foreign exchange (Burundi, Eritrea) and imported raw materials, infestations of cotton leafhoppers (Burkina Faso, Mali), and disruptions caused by floods (Chad, Sudan) and tropical cyclones (Madagascar, Malawi, Mozambique; Engel et al. 2023). On the upside, better rainfall has

Note: This box was prepared by Sergiy Kasyanenko.

BOX 1.2 Recent developments and outlook for low-income countries (*continued*)

FIGURE B1.2.1 LICs: Recent developments

Although growth in low-income countries (LICs) continued to improve in 2022, recoveries slowed in many countries because of heightened domestic vulnerabilities and increased external economic headwinds. Many LICs are still coping with worsening domestic vulnerabilities following last year's cost-of-living shocks and increased insecurity.

A. Interrupted recoveries

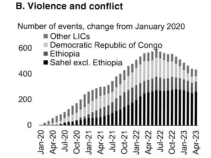

B. Violence and conflict

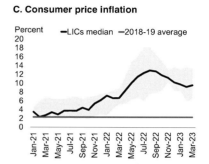

C. Consumer price inflation

Sources: ACLED (database); Haver Analytics; World Bank.
Note: f = forecast; LICs = low-income countries.
B. Twelve-months moving average; violent events include battles, explosions, violence against civilians, riots, and protests. Last observation is April 2023.
C. Annual consumer price inflation. Sample of 9 LICs. Shaded area shows the 25-75 percentile range of inflation rates among the countries. Last observation is March 2023.

been supporting agricultural activity in a number of countries (Niger, Uganda), while improved security has put growth prospects in Ethiopia on a firmer footing.

Annual consumer price inflation in the median LIC has cooled, to below 10 percent in March 2023; however, this remains more than four times higher than before the COVID-19 pandemic and double-digit annual inflation persists in 40 percent of countries (figure B1.2.1.C; World Bank 2023a). Continued price pressures include weak currencies, elevated costs of energy and farming inputs, depleted stocks of staple foods, and adverse weather events. Furthermore, armed conflicts have been causing significant food price spikes in many local markets across LICs by disrupting major transportation and distribution routes (Alfano and Cornelissen 2022).

LICs' current account and budget deficits widened to post-pandemic highs last year because of soaring import bills and increased government spending to mitigate cost-of-living increases and improve security. Public debt in LICs remains about 70 percent of GDP on average, and in over 80 percent of LICs both the current account and the budget are in deficit. In over a quarter of LICs, these deficits both exceed 5 percent of GDP (Malawi, Rwanda, Uganda). Such considerable

financing needs, together with limited access to external borrowing, have heightened the risk of debt distress in many countries.

Outlook

Growth in LICs is projected to firm to 5.1 percent in 2023—a 0.1 percentage point upgrade from the previous forecast, but with revisions differing widely among countries. Solid activity in several commodity producers is expected to be supported by firming exports boosted by the reopening of China's economy, as well as by the continued expansion of large extractive projects (Democratic Republic of Congo, Mozambique, Zambia). Nonetheless, forecasts have been downgraded for over 40 percent of LICs by 0.7 percentage point on average. Recoveries in many of those LICs are expected to remain constrained by the legacy of past shocks, including the pandemic and the invasion of Ukraine, which worsened poverty, triggered cost-of-living surges, and undermined debt sustainability.

Growth in LICs is forecast to strengthen further to 5.9 percent in 2024 (table B1.2.1). The growth pickup assumes that cost-of-living pressures ease, supply disruptions caused by recent weather events gradually dissipate, and security situations improve in some

BOX 1.2 Recent developments and outlook for low-income countries (*continued*)

FIGURE B1.2.2 LICs: Outlook and risks

Output growth in LICs is projected to strengthen further in 2023-24 as inflation moderates and disruptions caused by recent adverse weather and insecurity gradually ease. In many fragile LICs, however, recoveries are expected to remain weak, tempered by debt distress and unfavorable terms of trade, with slowing per capita income growth. Risks to the baseline forecast are tilted firmly to the downside, especially for those LICs most vulnerable to climate change.

A. GDP growth

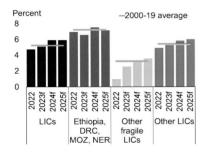

B. Real income per capita in fragile LICs

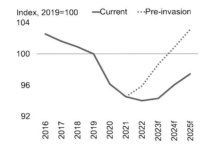

C. LIC population affected by extreme weather events

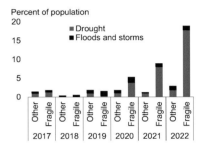

Sources: Guha Sapir, Below, and Hoyois (EM-DAT); World Bank.
Note: f = forecast; Fragile LICs = fragile and conflict-affected LICs; LICs = low-income countries.
A. DRC = Democratic Republic of Congo, MOZ = Mozambique, and NER = Niger; Ethiopia, Democratic Republic of Congo, Mozambique, and Niger age fragile LICs. Average GDP growth rates calculated using constant GDP weights at average 2010-19 prices and market exchange rates. Fragile LICs sample comprises 22 LICs, which include 13 Fragile LICs.
B. Fragile LICs exclude the Democratic Republic of Congo and Ethiopia. Pre-invasion projections are forecasts from the January 2023 *Global Economic Prospects* report.
C. Bars indicate percent of population in the affected group countries.

countries. Elevated metal prices and investment in mining and infrastructure are expected to support growth and exports of metal producers, although fiscal consolidations and political uncertainty will temper recoveries in some cases (Liberia, Sierra Leone). However, for a number of LICs, especially those in fragile and conflict-affected situations, the outlook is less favorable, with worsening humanitarian situations, high inflation, and substantial external financing needs (Burkina Faso, Malawi, South Sudan, Sudan).

In fragile LICs, growth is expected to firm to 5.6 percent a year on average in 2023-24—representing a return to past average long-term growth rates as the recovery from recent shocks accelerates. However, much of this improvement is accounted for by a few large economies where better security (Ethiopia) or expanding extractive sectors (Democratic Republic of Congo) are expected to boost growth. In Ethiopia, economic activity is projected to normalize in the Tigray region following last year's peace agreement. In the Democratic Republic of Congo, increasing production and exports of copper and a strong pick up of growth in

nonmining sectors are expected to sustain a 7.7 average growth in 2023-24, implying continued poverty reduction. In a number of other fragile LICs, the completion of large energy projects is expected to underpin robust growth and exports (Mozambique, Niger).

The remaining fragile LICs, most of which are agricultural commodity exporters, are expected to grow more slowly—by only 2.7 percent a year on average in 2023-24, a 0.7 percentage point downgrade from the January forecast and barely faster than population growth (figure B1.2.2.A). This downgrade reflects an intensification of domestic challenges—such as resurgent violence (Sudan)—amplified by the unfavorable external environment and increased vulnerability to extreme climate events.

Recoveries in nonfragile LICs are forecast to regain momentum as the drag from last year's shocks lessens. Growth is projected to improve in 2023-24 in several economies because of recovering tourism (Rwanda), recent funding from multilateral organizations

BOX 1.2 Recent developments and outlook for low-income countries (*continued*)

TABLE B1.2.1 Low-income country forecasts[a]
(Real GDP growth at market prices in percent, unless indicated otherwise)

	2020	2021	2022e	2023f	2024f	2025f	Percentage point differences from January 2023 projections 2023f	2024f
Low-Income Country, GDP [b]	**1.4**	**4.2**	**4.8**	**5.1**	**5.9**	**5.9**	**0.1**	**0.3**
GDP per capita (US dollars)	-1.4	1.3	1.9	2.3	3.1	3.1	0.1	0.4
Afghanistan[c]	-2.4	-20.7	..	..	..	..	..	..
Burkina Faso	1.9	6.9	2.5	4.3	4.8	5.1	-0.7	-0.5
Burundi	0.3	3.1	1.8	3.0	4.0	4.2	0.0	0.0
Central African Republic	1.0	1.0	0.0	3.0	3.8	3.8	0.0	0.0
Chad	-1.6	-1.2	2.2	3.2	3.4	3.1	-0.1	0.1
Congo, Dem. Rep.	1.7	6.2	8.6	7.7	7.6	7.5	1.3	1.0
Eritrea	-0.5	2.9	2.5	2.7	2.9	2.8	0.0	0.0
Ethiopia[d]	6.1	6.3	6.4	6.0	6.6	7.0	0.7	0.5
Gambia, The	0.6	4.3	4.3	5.0	5.5	5.8	1.0	0.0
Guinea	4.9	4.3	4.7	5.6	5.8	5.6	0.3	0.2
Guinea-Bissau	1.5	6.4	3.5	4.5	4.5	4.5	0.0	0.0
Liberia	-3.0	5.0	4.8	4.3	5.5	5.6	-0.4	-0.2
Madagascar	-7.1	5.7	3.8	4.2	4.8	5.1	0.0	0.2
Malawi	0.8	2.8	0.9	1.4	2.4	3.0	-1.6	-1.0
Mali	-1.2	3.1	1.8	4.0	4.0	5.0	0.0	0.0
Mozambique	-1.2	2.3	4.1	5.0	8.3	5.3	0.0	0.3
Niger	3.6	1.4	11.5	6.9	12.5	9.1	-0.2	2.4
Rwanda	-3.4	10.9	8.1	6.2	7.5	7.5	-0.5	0.5
Sierra Leone	-2.0	4.1	3.0	3.4	3.7	4.4	-0.3	-0.7
South Sudan[d]	9.5	-5.1	-2.3	-0.4	2.3	2.4	0.4	0.2
Sudan	-3.6	-1.9	-1.0	0.4	1.5	2.0	-1.6	-1.0
Syrian Arab Republic [c]	-0.2	1.3	-3.5	-5.5	..	..	-2.3	..
Togo	1.8	5.3	4.9	4.9	5.3	5.5	-0.7	-1.1
Uganda[d]	3.0	3.4	4.7	5.7	6.2	6.7	0.2	0.1
Yemen, Rep. [c]	-8.5	-1.0	1.5	-0.5	2.0	..	-1.5	..
Zambia	-2.8	4.6	3.9	4.2	4.7	4.8	0.3	0.6

Source: World Bank.
Note: e = estimate; f = forecast. World Bank forecasts are frequently updated based on new information and changing (global) circumstances. Consequently, projections presented here may differ from those contained in other Bank documents, even if basic assessments of countries' prospects do not significantly differ at any given moment in time.
a. The Democratic People's Republic of Korea and Somalia are not forecast on account of data limitations.
b. Aggregate growth rates are calculated using GDP weights at average 2010-19 prices and market exchange rates.
c. Forecasts for Afghanistan (beyond 2021), the Syrian Arab Republic (beyond 2023), and the Republic of Yemen (beyond 2024) are excluded because of a high degree of uncertainty.
d. GDP growth rates are on a fiscal year basis. For example, the column labeled 2022 refers to FY2021/22.

(Rwanda, Uganda), increasing output in agriculture (The Gambia), and moderating inflation.

Progress with poverty reduction in LICs—set back by the cost-of-living shock following Russia's invasion of Ukraine—is expected to remain slow, given the subdued per capita income growth projected for many countries, especially those affected by fragility (figure B1.2.2.B). Although per capita incomes in LICs are projected to grow by 2.7 percent a year on average in 2023-24, they are expected to increase at only half this pace in the fragile LICs, excluding the Democratic Republic of Congo and Ethiopia—the two most populous LICs. At the end of 2024, per capita incomes are expected to remain below 2019 levels in about 40 percent of LICs. Moreover, in 40 percent of LICs—

BOX 1.2 Recent developments and outlook for low-income countries (*continued*)

accounting for half of the total LIC population—average per capita income growth rates in 2023-24 are expected to still fall short of their pre-pandemic averages.

Risks

Risks to the outlook remain tilted to the downside, especially for countries affected by fragility or those vulnerable to sharp cost-of-living increases and adverse weather events. Pressures in global commodity markets could lead to increased price volatility, especially if the war in Ukraine were to escalate. The economic recovery in China could further amplify commodity market volatility if its pace were to falter.

Debt sustainability risks are considerable in a number of LICs, as increased current account and budget deficits, combined with weak growth and high debt-service costs, have lifted LICs' financing needs. If inflation persists above targets and causes global monetary policy to tighten more than expected or if stress in the global banking system re-emerges, financing conditions and access to external borrowing could become even more challenging for LICs. With over half of all LICs at high risk of, or already in, debt distress, unfavorable debt dynamics could trigger severe financial stress or even debt crises in some countries.

Domestic vulnerabilities and fragility have worsened across many LICs, while depleted policy space has eroded buffers to absorb additional shocks (Burkina Faso, Malawi). Meanwhile, climate change is exacerbat-

ing overlapping exposures to macroeconomic and weather-related shocks, as LICs are generally more reliant on natural resources to support the growth of output, exports, and jobs than other EMDEs (UNCTAD 2022). Countries that are most vulnerable to climate change often also have large vulnerable populations, elevated levels of civil insecurity, and are at high risk of debt distress (Chad, Sudan; World Bank 2022b; figure B1.2.2.C). An escalation in violence or adverse weather events could substantially worsen ongoing humanitarian crises and dampen growth.

Progress with economic development in LICs—already upended by the COVID-19 pandemic and the repercussions of the invasion of Ukraine—may face further reversals as the adverse impacts of climate change become more severe. Several LICs are already experiencing catastrophic consequences of extreme weather. In the Sahel region, which is warming faster than the global average (IPCC 2023), nearly 40 million people need emergency food assistance. The number of people facing extreme hunger is rising rapidly across Eastern Africa, which is confronting the worst drought in recorded history. Last year, over 40 thousand people—half of them children younger than 5 years—are estimated to have died in Somalia because of the drought (UNICEF 2023). These risks could intensify sharply if global greenhouse gas emissions continue to rise and LICs with substantial adaptation gaps are unable to secure adequate financing to improve their climate resilience.

In LICs, especially the very poorest economies, the damage is stark. In close to half of LICs, per capita incomes will remain below their 2019 levels this year, by about 5 percent on average. Income per capita in the poorest LICs is expected to recover at a much slower pace compared with other LICs (figure 1.10.B). More broadly, fragility continues to aggravate humanitarian crises and remains a substantial deterrent to development across EMDEs—income per capita growth in fragile EMDEs is expected to average only 1.1 percent a year in 2023-24, further entrenching extreme poverty.

The unequal distribution of growth is weighing on median living standards in many EMDEs. In the upper quartile of EMDEs, food prices have risen more than 40 percent since end-2020, with disproportionate impacts on the consumption of the least well-off, who spend more of their income on food. Moreover, informal workers, who tend to have lower incomes, are likely to have seen steeper real income cuts in the context of high inflation (Ohnsorge and Yu 2021). In contrast, workers in formal employment have greater capacity to wage-bargain to retain purchasing power.

FIGURE 1.10 Per capita GDP growth

In the first half of this decade, per capita GDP is expected to decline in about one-third of emerging market and developing economies (EMDEs). For many low-income countries (LICs), especially the very poorest economies, income per capita remains below its pre-pandemic level. Catch-up of EMDEs excluding China—especially of LICs—with advanced-economy income per capita levels has been feeble for an extended period. For nearly two-thirds of EMDEs in fragile and conflict-affected situations, per capita incomes are expected to be lower in 2024 than they were in 2019.

A. EMDEs with declining GDP per capita

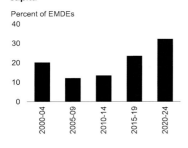

B. Income per capita in LICs

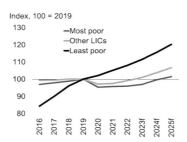

C. EMDE GDP per capita

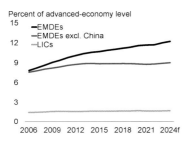

D. Countries with lower GDP per capita in 2024 than in 2019

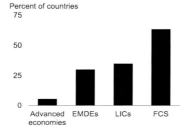

Sources: World Bank (2023b); World Bank.
Note: EMDEs = emerging market and developing economies; FCS= fragile and conflict-affected situations; LICs = low-income countries. Data for 2023-25 are forecasts.
A.C.D. GDP per capita for aggregates are calculated as aggregated GDP divided by the aggregate population. GDP aggregates are calculated using real U.S. dollar GDP weights at average 2010-19 prices and market exchange rates.
A. Figure shows the proportion of EMDEs for which per capita growth was negative, on average, in each 5-year period. Sample includes 149 EMDEs.
B. Most poor LICs refer to countries with the poverty headcount ratio at $2.15 a day above the 75th percentile (63.5 percent); least poor are the ones where the poverty headcount is below the 25th percentile (25.3 percent). Poverty headcount estimates for 2023 are from the World Bank (2023b). Per capita income is calculated as each group's GDP divided by its population.
D. Figure shows the share of countries in respective groups with real per capita GDP in 2024 lower than in 2019.

Subdued per capita income growth is a long-term trend in many EMDEs. On present projections, EMDEs excluding China will register only modest catch-up toward advanced economy income levels in 2022-2024, following several years of backsliding (figure 1.10.C). In fact, nearly a third of EMDEs, including two-thirds of countries in fragile and conflict-affected situations, are expected to have lower per capita incomes in 2024 than they did in 2019 (figure 1.10.D). Even in the medium term, EMDEs as a whole are likely to

make only incremental progress in this regard. Under current assumptions about the expected evolution of its fundamental drivers, potential per capita growth in EMDEs is projected to be 3.5 percent per year in 2022-30, 0.6 percentage point lower than in 2011-21.

Global outlook and risks

Global growth is expected to slow this year as credit conditions tighten due to ongoing monetary tightening and banking sector stress in advanced economies. The drag from tighter financial conditions is becoming increasingly apparent and is expected to peak this year. Inflation has proved persistent but should decline as demand slows and commodity prices moderate, provided longer-term inflation expectations remain stable. Stress in systemically important banks could lead to financial crisis and protracted economic losses. Unexpected persistence in core inflation or further commodity price shocks could result in greater-than-expected monetary tightening and hence increase the risk of a resurgence of financial stress. In the longer term, the slowdown in the fundamental drivers of growth may be exacerbated by trade fragmentation and intensified climate change.

Global outlook

Global growth is expected to slow to 2.1 percent in 2023 before rebounding to 2.4 percent in 2024. The weakness in activity projected for this year is widespread across countries—especially in advanced economies (figure 1.11.A). The primary driver of the short-term dynamics continues to be the combination of elevated inflation, alongside the global monetary policy tightening it has provoked. The drag from these factors is expected to peak this year before gradually dissipating. In the longer term, global output is expected to decelerate because of a broad-based slowdown in all the fundamental drivers of growth.

Nonetheless, developments since the beginning of the year have resulted in the forecast for global growth being revised up by 0.4 percentage point for 2023. Activity in major advanced economies and some EMDEs did not slow as much as expected at the turn of the year. Notably, the rapid reopening of China's economy contributed materially to an upward revision to this year's growth forecast. While the aggregate global forecast has been revised up, projections for most economies have been revised down, with larger downgrades among countries that have had a greater degree of monetary tightening (figure 1.11.B).

The surprising economic strength at the turn of the year is not expected to last. According to model-based estimates, the impact of monetary tightening on growth in the United States—which has substantial global spillovers—is envisaged to peak this year (figure 1.11.C). Although household consumption has been quite resilient in the first half of 2023, the impact of rising borrowing costs has been apparent in interest-rate-sensitive activities such as business and residential investment (figure 1.11.D). Banking sector stress has encouraged lenders to strengthen balance sheets and tighten credit standards, which may further slow credit issuance (Gropp et al. 2019).

The pace of monetary transmission may be somewhat slower than usual in the current cycle for a variety of reasons. In some major economies, the share of variable-rate mortgages has fallen in recent years, delaying the pass-through from policy rates to mortgage payments by households (Berger et al. 2021). The substantial buffers built up through excess household savings and elevated corporate profits may also be muting or delaying the response to higher interest rates. Similarly, increasing market concentration and high profit margins may insulate some firms from the impacts of rising borrowing costs and slow the pace of monetary policy pass-through (Duval et al. 2021). The lagged effects of monetary tightening and the slowdown in credit growth have been factored into the 0.3 percentage point downward revision to the baseline 2024 forecast for global growth.

Headline inflation remains high despite a recent deceleration due to falling energy prices. Elevated core inflation has proven more persistent than expected. As a result, the global inflation forecast for this year has been revised up by 0.3 percentage point since January. Headline inflation is now projected to fall from 7.3 percent in 2022 to 5.5 percent in 2023. The combination of weaker

FIGURE 1.11 Global outlook

Global growth is expected to slow substantially this year, with a pronounced deceleration in advanced economies and a sizable pickup in China. Most country forecasts have been revised down, particularly for those countries that have had greater monetary policy tightening. The impact of central bank tightening on growth is expected to peak this year in many countries, including the United States, and is already apparent in rate-sensitive activities such as manufacturing.

A. Contributions to global growth

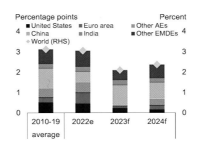

B. Average revision to 2023 forecast, by degree of monetary tightening

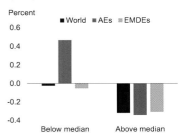

C. Estimated impact of latest Federal Reserve tightening cycle on annual U.S. growth

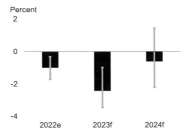

D. Global industrial production and manufacturing PMI

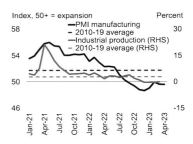

Sources: Anderson et al. (2013); Blagrave et al. (2020); Brayton, Laubach, and Reifschneider (2014); CPB Netherlands Bureau for Economic Policy Analysis; Haver Analytics; Oxford Economics; World Bank.

Note: AEs = advanced economies; EMDEs = emerging market and developing economies.

A. Aggregate growth rates are calculated using real U.S. dollar GDP weights at average 2010-19 prices and market exchange rates. Data for 2023-24 are forecasts.

B. Figure shows average 2023 forecast change between the January and June 2023 editions of the *Global Economic Prospects* report according to whether the central bank's policy rate has increased by more or less than the global median. This is expressed in country-specific standard deviations. Sample includes 19 advanced economies and 77 EMDEs.

C. Estimated impact on U.S. GDP growth of the rise in the U.S. policy rate from 0.25 to 5.25 percent, between 2022Q1 and 2023Q4, according to several major published global projection models. This includes the Oxford Economic Model, the Federal Reserve's FRB/US model (using both adaptive and forward-looking expectations), the Bank of Canada's IMPACT model, and the IMF's GIMF model. Bars indicate simple averages; orange whiskers indicate minimum-maximum values.

D. Figure shows global manufacturing Purchasing Managers' Index (PMI) and annual percentage change of global industrial production. PMI readings above (below) 50 indicate expansion (contraction) in economic activity. Last observation is April 2023 for the PMI and March 2023 for industrial production.

growth, lower commodity prices, and still-anchored inflation expectations is expected, by 2024, to dampen core inflation, with headline inflation falling to 3.7 percent. Despite this expected decline, inflation is set to remain above central bank targets in many countries throughout next year.

FIGURE 1.12 Risk of financial stress

Bank balance sheets have sustained losses from recent economic weakness and the unusually rapid rise in interest rates. This could be exacerbated by declines in house prices, which are already taking place in countries accounting for half of global activity. The nature of banking sector vulnerabilities varies, with greater risks in some regions associated with potential loss of liquidity, and others suffering from low bank profitability or limited capital buffers.

A. Magnitude of monetary policy tightening since 2020

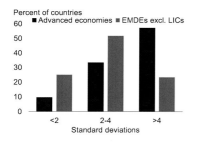

B. Share of the global economy in countries with falling housing prices

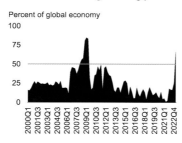

C. Banking exposure to liquidity risks

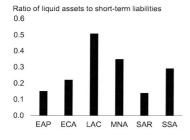

D. Banking exposure to solvency risks

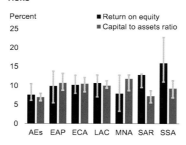

Sources: BIS (database); FinStats 2023 (database); Haver Analytics; J.P. Morgan; World Bank.
Note: AEs = advanced economies; EMDEs = emerging market and developing economies; EAP = East Asia and Pacific, ECA = Europe and Central Asia, LAC = Latin America and the Caribbean, MNA = Middle East and North Africa, SAR = South Asia, SSA = Sub-Saharan Africa; LICs = low-income countries.
A. Figure shows the number of standard deviations from the lowest point since January 2021 to its peak. The standard deviation is calculated on the sample period between 2011-2023. Sample includes 21 advanced economies and 71 EMDEs; the countries in the euro area are counted as 1 unit.
B. Figure shows the GDP-weighted share of the global residential real estate market where nominal prices declined over the preceding 2 quarters. Sample includes up to 36 advanced economies and 21 EMDEs. Orange line indicates 50 percent.
C. Bars show GDP-weighted data. Short-term liabilities include deposits and short-term funding. Data are as of 2021.
D. Capital to assets ratio shows banks' capital to assets. Bars indicate medians. Whiskers indicate interquartile range. Data are as of 2021.

Risks to the outlook

Risks to the outlook remain tilted to the downside. The collapse of multiple banks this year highlights the possibility of more disorderly failures, which could lead to systemic banking crises and protracted economic losses. These failures could be triggered by rising non-performing loans, lower asset values impairing balance sheets, a deeper correction in house prices, or losses from the heavily leveraged commercial real estate sector. In addition, higher or more persistent inflation—especially, more persistent core inflation—could trigger further monetary tightening. In the longer term, the slowdown in the fundamental drivers of growth may be exacerbated by trade fragmentation and climate change. On the upside, the resilience of economic activity in the face of substantial headwinds, thus far, points to the risk that the prospects for major economies may be stronger than currently estimated.

Financial stress

Balance sheets in many banks and non-bank financial institutions (NBFIs) have been weakened by the rise in interest rates, which has reduced the value of long-term assets acquired when interest rates were low and were expected to remain so for an extended period. The scale of the increase in interest rates has been outside of recent historical norms, particularly in advanced economies, and outside of the range of many regulators' stress tests (figure 1.12.A; Federal Reserve 2023). High interest rates, along with slowing activity, may lead to an increase in non-performing loans, further reducing asset quality.

Banks with a large share of loans backed by commercial real estate are especially vulnerable, as the sector's high leverage makes it exposed to rising borrowing costs in the context of protracted weakness in demand for office space since the emergence of COVID-19. Another important source of potential bank losses could be falling real estate prices. House prices are already falling in many countries that constitute more than half of global activity (figure 1.12.B). A combination of falling house prices and softening job markets could raise mortgage defaults. This would further weaken bank balance sheets, while also weighing on household wealth and consumption (Berger et al. 2017).

As borrowing costs rise, the decline in the market value of banks' assets can trigger concerns that they may lack the resources to repay their depositors, especially when the funds are withdrawn from low-yielding deposits in search of higher rates elsewhere. When deposits are not fully insured, this can result in a self-reinforcing bank run. These dynamics have been apparent in the failures of several banks this year, with contagion throughout the financial system so far avoided by aggressive policy responses. New revelations of financial weakness in some systemically important banks or NBFIs could raise investor risk aversion, result in disorderly flight to safety, tighten financial conditions, and further weaken bank and firm balance sheets (Agénor and da Silva 2018). Increasing cross-border linkages between banks and NBFIs can be an important channel of transmission of financial stress between advanced economies and EMDEs (Feyen et al. 2022).

Banking system vulnerabilities differ across various parts of the world. Some regions have greater risks associated with potential loss of liquidity (LAC, MNA, SSA), while others suffer from low bank profitability (advanced economies) or limited capital buffers (SAR, SSA; figures 1.12.C and D). Depending on the nature of adverse shocks, governments may be unable to respond rapidly enough to stem contagion or may lack the resources to engineer a rescue. In some cases, the health of the financial system and that of the sovereign may be interlinked as a result of large bank holdings of government debt and government support for failing banks—the so-called "sovereign-bank nexus"—resulting in financial stress being transmitted to governments, which could lead to sovereign defaults (Feyen and Zuccardi 2019). This nexus has become more important since the pandemic, as many EMDEs have increased their reliance on local banks and NBFIs for local-currency debt issuance (Hardy and Zhu 2023; IMF 2023a).

A severe banking crisis would likely cause substantial and persistent economic damage. The median magnitude of cumulative losses around banking crises is estimated at a third of output in high-income economies and 14 percent in low- and middle-income countries (Laeven and Valencia 2018). High levels of debt function as a shock amplifier, making financial crises more likely and more severe (Kose et al. 2021). Financial crises also weigh on long-term productivity through multiple channels, the clearest of which is through investment as corporate earnings, confidence, and access to finance are reduced while uncertainty is

heightened (Dieppe, Celik, and Okou 2021). Furthermore, a cascading banking crisis in a major economy would have global spillovers through cross-border financial linkages and confidence.

Quantifying scenarios of financial stress

In the baseline, credit conditions in advanced economies are expected to continue worsening for the rest of the year amid a higher cost of deposit retention and funding and remain tight over the remainder of the projection horizon. Nonetheless, as discussed above, financial conditions could worsen more drastically, with significant repercussions on global activity.

To quantify these repercussions, two scenarios of financial stress are considered, centered on the banking system in advanced economies. In these scenarios, the revelation of financial weakness in more banks or NBFIs causes a tightening in financial conditions. The two scenarios mainly differ in the extent of global spillovers from the bank failures. The impacts of these shocks on activity, inflation, and interest rates are quantified using a global macroeconomic model.[2]

First scenario: Financial stress in advanced economies. In this scenario, banking stress would result in a severe credit crunch but would remain largely contained within advanced economies. Financial conditions—as modeled by investor risk aversion, widening corporate and sovereign spreads, and lower confidence—would tighten considerably more than the moderate amount assumed in the baseline, worsening approximately 30 percent as much as seen in advanced economies during the 2007-09 global financial crisis (figure 1.13.A). This shock is assumed to occur in the third quarter of 2023 and persist for four quarters before gradually fading. Policy makers would take meaningful steps that limit contagion, such as bailing out failing banks and providing liquidity to markets. As a result, spillovers to EMDEs would

---

[2] These scenarios are produced using the Oxford Economics' Global Economic Model, a global semi-structural macroeconomic projection model which includes 81 individual country blocks, most of which are available at a quarterly frequency, with behavioral equations governing domestic economic activity, monetary and fiscal policy, global trade, and commodity prices (Oxford Economics 2019).

FIGURE 1.13 Quantifying scenarios of financial stress

Financial stress scenarios center on a sharp tightening of financial conditions in advanced economies equivalent to 30 percent of that seen during the 2007-09 global financial crisis. In the first scenario, advanced-economy stress does not lead to major spillovers, and the global economy avoids recession as central banks loosen policy, with inflation declining more rapidly than the baseline. In the second scenario, substantial spillovers lead to global financial stress. This pushes the global economy into recession, with inflation falling below target in many countries despite aggressive policy loosening.

A. U.S. Financial Conditions Index

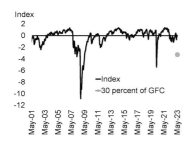

B. Global growth under different scenarios

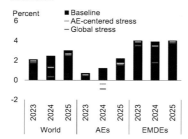

C. Global short-term interest rates

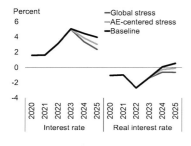

D. Global inflation

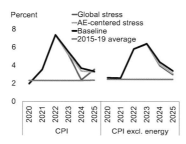

Sources: Bloomberg; Consensus Economics; Oxford Economics; World Bank.
Note: AEs = advanced economies; EMDEs = emerging market and developing economies. CPI = consumer price index. Scenarios produced using the Oxford Economics *Global Economic Model.* Unless otherwise indicated, aggregate growth rates are calculated using real U.S. dollar GDP weights at average 2010-19 prices and market exchange rates. Data are estimates for 2022 and forecasts for 2023-25.
A. GFC = 2007-09 global financial crisis. Figure shows the 14-day moving average of the Bloomberg US Financial Conditions Index. Last observation is May 25, 2023.
B. Global growth aggregate is computed by Oxford Economics using 2015 market exchange rates and prices.
C. Global nominal short-term interest rate is measured as GDP-weighted averages of national rates. Real policy rate is computed as nominal short-term rate minus GDP-weighted consumer price inflation excluding energy.
D. Model-based projection of annual global year-on-year CPI inflation using Oxford Economics *Global Economic Model.* Projection embeds global oil price forecast presented in table 1.1.

be generally limited, with a modest rise in risk-off sentiment, weaker confidence, and capital outflows.

Under this risk scenario, global GDP would grow 1.9 percent in 2023 and 1.3 percent in 2024—below baseline projections in both years (figure 1.13.B). As a result, global GDP would be 1.3 percent below baseline by 2024. This weakness would be concentrated in advanced economies,

where the gap relative to the baseline is 1.8 percent, compared with 0.5 percent for EMDEs. The response of fiscal policy to the slowdown in activity would be muted given limited fiscal space. However, central banks would start cutting policy rates in a synchronous manner in the second half of this year, such that the nominal global aggregate policy rate would be 0.6 percentage point lower than the baseline next year (figure 1.13.C). Monetary policy accommodation, which occurs endogenously in the model, would not be sufficient to offset the impact of weaker demand on prices. Global headline CPI inflation would fall to 3.4 percent in 2024—0.3 percentage point below the baseline forecast (figure 1.13.D). Both core and energy price disinflation would contribute to the decline, with oil prices falling to $77 per barrel in 2024, $5 below the baseline.

Second scenario: Global financial stress. In the second scenario, banking stress would propagate globally to a far greater degree. As in the first scenario, financial conditions in advanced economies would worsen by 30 percent as much as seen during the global financial crisis. Unlike the first scenario, however, spillovers to EMDEs would interact with some pre-existing vulnerabilities in these economies, such as banks' undercapitalization, the sovereign-bank nexus, and high levels of public and private debt. EMDEs would suffer from weakening consumer and business confidence, and increases in corporate and consumer borrowing spreads equivalent to about a third of the shock observed in the global financial crisis, along with a significant weakening in international trade. Global trade would be affected by the contraction of demand in advanced economies as well as a lack of trade credit, as large parts of the global financial system struggle to maintain liquidity flows.[3]

In this scenario, global growth would be 1.8 percent in 2023 and 0.3 percent in 2024. This scenario would entail a contraction in per capita global GDP next year, implying a global recession.

---

[3] Lack of trade credit explains about half of the overall impact on trade in the scenario. This channel is proxied by a confidence shock specific to international trade in the Oxford Economics' Global Economic Model.

Global trade would also suffer a disproportionate impact, contracting in 2024 and 2025. Central banks would reduce nominal policy rates on average by a full percentage point, with those in advanced economies lowering rates to a greater extent. Governments would also provide fiscal support, with more stimulus in advanced economies relative to EMDEs given differences in fiscal space. Widespread weakness in activity would result in a faster decline in inflation, with the global headline CPI inflation averaging 2.4 percent in 2024, 1.3 percentage point below the baseline and just above the 2015-19 average of 2.3 percent. Because of widespread weakness in demand and increased uncertainty around the global outlook, oil prices would decline sharply in this scenario to average $47 in 2024, $35 below the baseline.

Persistently high inflation, additional monetary tightening, and escalation of financial stress

Inflation forecasts have been revised up considerably in recent years, and additional inflationary pressures remain possible (figure 1.14.A). While headline inflation has started to decelerate in most countries, primarily due to falling energy prices, core inflation generally remains well above central bank targets. Despite ongoing global monetary tightening and slowing growth, core inflation could continue to prove more persistent than expected as a result of surprisingly resilient labor markets and consumer spending, or an upward drift in expectations in response to above-target inflation.

In addition, negative supply shocks could raise commodity prices. A significant disruption to oil supplies caused by geopolitical disturbances could have a persistent impact on global markets, since OPEC+ has limited spare capacity to offset a major shortfall in oil production. Higher energy prices would pass through to core consumer prices, and further increase the risk of inflation expectations becoming unanchored. A similar dynamic could take hold if China's demand for commodities proved stronger than expected. Metal prices would respond strongly, for example, if the government provided substantial stimulus through infrastructure investment and support for residential construction. Ramped-up production of clean energy equipment—especially of electric vehicles—would tighten the markets for various metals, such as copper, nickel, and cobalt.

An upside shock to global inflation would cause central banks to tighten monetary policy more than is currently expected, and keep policy rates higher for longer. This would result in a more severe growth slowdown. The global implications of additional tightening in the United States to rein in inflation would be particularly important, given the scale of international spillovers from policy actions by the Federal Reserve. Increases in the perceived hawkishness of the Federal Reserve—policy "reaction-function" shocks—have empirically driven a disproportionate share of the recent hiking cycle (figures 1.14.B and 1.14.C; chapter 3). A renewed period of rapid policy tightening would make borrowing in international markets essentially unaffordable for an even larger number of countries (figure 1.14.D).

EMDEs are particularly vulnerable to spillovers from sharply higher policy rates in the United States and other advanced economies as well as persistent domestic inflation pressure. Further tightening abroad could put additional strains on the financial systems of many EMDEs, including currency depreciation pressures, increasing the chance of capital outflows and currency crises in more vulnerable countries. Increased debt financing costs could cause corporate or even sovereign defaults, particularly in EMDEs already facing substantial sovereign risk spreads. Accumulated risks on banks' balance sheets, including those related to sovereigns, could endanger financial stability in these countries. Elevated borrowing costs, along with credit tightening due to financial stress, could further hinder investments needed to address development and climate-related goals in EMDEs (World Bank 2023c).

Weaker-than-expected long-term growth

Global potential growth is expected to fall to a three-decade low of 2.2 percent over the remainder of the 2020s—0.4 percentage point below the average from 2011-21 and continuing a long-running downward trend. This trend has multiple

FIGURE 1.14 Other risks to the outlook

Inflation forecasts have been repeatedly revised up—further such revisions could lead to more monetary tightening. Spillovers to emerging market and developing economies (EMDEs) from rising U.S. rates are especially severe when they reflect a more hawkish Federal Reserve, an important feature of the latest tightening cycle. Further increases in bond yields would make borrowing unaffordable for many EMDEs. Global potential growth may decline more than expected. On the upside, continued resilience in advanced-economy labor markets could boost consumption.

A. Inflation forecasts for 2023

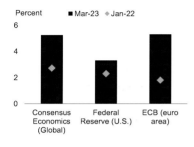

B. Contributions of shocks during Fed hiking cycles, cumulative

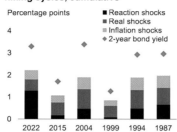

C. Impact of 25-basis-point reaction shock on EMDE financial variables after one quarter

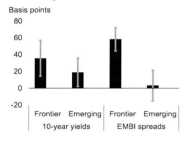

D. EMDEs with sovereign spreads above 10 percentage points

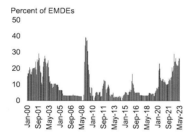

E. Global potential growth, adjusted for risks

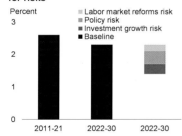

F. Unemployment rate

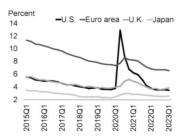

Sources: Arteta, Kamin, and Ruch (2022); BIS (database); Consensus Economics, Federal Reserve; European Central Bank; Haver Analytics; J.P. Morgan; Kose and Ohnsorge (2023a); MSCI; World Bank.

Note: ECB = European Central Bank; EMBI = emerging market bond index; EMDEs = emerging market and developing economies; FED = Federal Reserve.

A. Figure shows 2023 inflation expectations as of December 2021 and March 2023 from the Federal Reserve and the ECB, and January 2022 and March 2023 from Consensus Economics.

B. Shocks estimated from a Bayesian vector autoregression model. Inflation shocks are prompted by rising expectations of U.S. inflation, and real shocks by anticipation of improving U.S. activity. Reaction-function shocks are prompted by a hawkish shift by the Federal Reserve. Current episode is January 2022 to mid-May 2023.

C. Estimated with panel non-linear local projection model with fixed effects and robust standard errors. Sample includes up to 9 frontier markets and 19 emerging markets, using 2022 MSCI classification. Whiskers reflect 90 percent confidence bands. "EMBI spreads" based on EMBI global.

D. Figure shows share of countries with EMBI spread above 10 percentage points. Unbalanced sample includes 69 EMDEs. Last observation is May 23, 2023.

E. Baseline assumes investment growth will match consensus forecasts. Correction for investment growth risk assumes investment growth falls by the country-specific average forecast error; correction for policy risk assumes health and education outcomes repeat the smallest increase on record over any 10-year period; correction for labor market reforms risk assumes that female labor force participation rate will repeat the smallest increase.

F. Last observation is 2023Q1.

causes: the global labor force is aging and growing more slowly, and the growth rates of investment and total factor productivity are declining. This negative trend could be even worse than assumed in this baseline if labor market, education, or health outcomes disappoint, if investment is weaker than expected, or if new recessions or climate disasters cause lasting damage (figure 1.14.E).

The rising number of restrictions on international trade suggests that long-term growth could also be weakened by growing geopolitical and economic fragmentation. Further increases in geopolitical tensions could result in finance, trade, labor, and commodity markets being increasingly segmented into regional blocks. By reducing technological diffusion and the efficiency of capital and resource allocation, this would lower productivity, raise prices, and make export-led development more challenging to achieve. It could also make the financial sector more volatile by reducing the scope for risk diversification (IMF 2023a).

The global economy is increasingly vulnerable to shocks arising from climate change. Extreme weather events that inflict significant economic damage—including droughts, floods, wildfires, and windstorms—are becoming more frequent. In the near term, increased prevalence and severity of climate-related disasters would inflict substantial human costs, through failed harvests, damaged infrastructure, generalized disruptions to activity, and worsened government fiscal positions. Changes in climate may further increase food insecurity in regions with large numbers of subsistence farmers, who lack the resources to easily adjust production.

Upside risk: Stronger consumption alongside falling inflation in major economies

Labor markets in many economies—including the United States and the euro area—have shown resilience in the face of tightening monetary policy, with unemployment rates in some cases at historic lows (figure 1.14.F). Labor market strength may persist even as activity slows if rising wages cause labor force participation to rise, or a continued period of excess labor demand drives up productivity. Just as resilient labor markets in advanced economies have contributed to the current strength of consumption spending, unexpected increases in employment would further boost consumption. This would yield stronger-than-expected growth domestically and, through trade spillovers, for EMDEs as well.

In the baseline forecast, the reopening of China's economy provides a temporary boost to consumer spending, which fades over the course of 2023. It is possible that the boost will be both stronger and more persistent than envisaged. For example, household balance sheets might prove healthier than expected. Another possibility for upside surprises is that potential output might be less affected by the pandemic, and by the declining return on investment, than assumed in the baseline. If labor market strength or stronger growth in China were the result of higher-than-expected potential output, it would also have a beneficial impact on global inflation.

Policy challenges

Recent bank collapses and bouts of financial instability underline the importance of sound international financial regulation. Central bank credibility is critical amid high inflation and heightened financial risks. Depleted fiscal buffers can be restored through increased expenditure effectiveness and domestic revenue mobilization. Many sovereigns are already under stress and more are at risk, highlighting the need for globally coordinated debt relief. To reverse a projected decline in EMDE potential growth, it will be critical to implement reforms to bolster physical and human capital, labor-supply growth, productivity of services, and international trade. Continued cooperation is necessary to tackle climate change and support populations affected by crises and hunger.

Key global challenges

The collapse of multiple banks amid sharply higher interest rates has highlighted potential trade-offs between the goals of price and financial stability, which are likely to be more acute in the presence of high debt levels. While policy makers' interventions have been successful at stabilizing the global financial system for now, the recent

bank failures have important implications for international financial regulation going forward.

Among the issues to be considered are the reach and calibration of stress tests, the risks of over-reliance on binary capital and liquidity thresholds, the causes of occasional illiquidity in markets for essential collateral, and the treatment of government liabilities in risk assessments. While recent stress emerged in advanced economies, negative cross-border spillovers could emanate from further bouts of financial instability, underscoring the need for regulatory principles that reinforce the stability of the global financial system. The reforms enacted after the global financial crisis to strengthen the framework of regulation and supervision have generally worked well, but need to be strengthened. Recent financial turmoil also highlights the stress that could emerge from gaps in financial supervision—including in the supervision of non-bank financial institutions (Aramonte, Schrimpf, and Shin 2022; Carstens 2021).

The stress generated by rising global borrowing costs and slower growth has adversely affected sovereigns, particularly those with limited fiscal space. The international community needs to bolster efforts to reduce debt distress and attenuate the risk of EMDEs being unable to finance debt at sustainable rates. At least 50 percent of the world's poorest countries are already in debt distress or at high risk of distress (IMF 2023b). This challenge has been made more difficult by the increasing diversity of lenders relative to previous rounds of debt relief as well as the lower transparency of their lending (figure 1.15.A; Horn et al. 2023). In EMDEs with unsustainable levels of debt, relief efforts by the international community can help generate fiscal space. In particular, G20 creditors need to accelerate debt restructurings when needed. It is also critical that private sector creditors grant debt relief on terms comparable to the G20 Common Framework.

Addressing climate change and mitigating its consequences is a critical global development challenge. Climate change is resulting in more frequent and severe natural disasters and is set to exacerbate extreme poverty and inequality by worsening health outcomes, reducing agricultural

FIGURE 1.15 Global policy challenges

Debt of low-income countries (LICs) is held by an increasingly diverse group of creditors, which may complicate relief efforts. More generally, emerging market and developing economies (EMDEs) have become more vulnerable to rising interest rates given their increased share of market-financed debt. Low-income and lower-middle-income countries need substantial investments to achieve a robust, resilient, and low-carbon growth trajectory. Food price inflation picked up further in 2023 across EMDE regions, highlighting the need for global efforts to mitigate food insecurity. Violence and conflict remain pervasive in many EMDEs.

A. Composition of external debt, by creditor

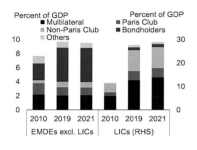

B. Additional investment needs for a resilient and low-carbon pathway, 2022-30

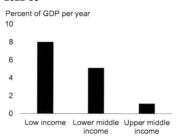

C. Food inflation, by region

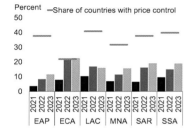

D. Violence and conflict

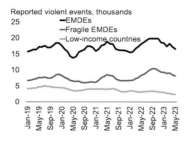

Sources: ACLED (database); IDS (database); WDI (database); World Bank (2022a); World Bank.
Note: EMDEs = emerging market and developing economies; LICs= low-income countries; EAP = East Asia and Pacific, ECA = Europe and Central Asia, LAC = Latin America and the Caribbean, MNA = Middle East and North Africa, SAR = South Asia, SSA = Sub-Saharan Africa.
A. Figure shows the U.S. dollar GDP-weighted average of public and publicly guaranteed external debt. "Others" includes multiple lenders. Sample includes 119 EMDEs, of which 24 are LICs.
B. Bars show the annual investment needs to build resilience to climate change and reduce emissions by 70 percent by 2050. Depending on availability, estimates include investment needs for transport, energy, water, urban adaptations, industry, and landscape. In some Country Climate and Development Reports, especially those for low-income and lower-middle-income countries, estimated investments include development needs and cannot be considered entirely "additional" to pre-existing financing needs.
C. Figure shows annual averages of food consumer price inflation. Sample includes 134 EMDEs. Regional inflation rates are based on averages across countries.
D. Figure shows 3-month rolling averages. Reported violent events include battles, explosions, violence against civilians, riots, and protests. Sample includes 149 EMDEs, out of which 35 are fragile EMDEs and 27 are low-income countries. Last observation is May 2023.

productivity, increasing food prices, and aggravating food and water insecurity in EMDEs (Jafino et al. 2020; World Bank 2022a). Low-income and lower-middle-income countries will need substantial investments to build a pathway to resilient, low-carbon-emission growth (figure 1.15.B). Decarbonization can also provide other benefits.

For example, reducing air pollution, including from fossil fuels, could save 7 million lives every year, mostly in EMDEs where most people exposed to poor air quality live (Peszko et al. 2022).

While the transition to low-carbon sources of energy is already underway, sustained international cooperation is needed to accelerate it. To that end, energy-related policies, fiscal regimes, and energy sector structures can be adjusted in such a way as to move energy production away from a reliance on fossil fuels and toward the use of renewables (IRENA 2022). Electricity generation from renewables has been growing, boosted by disruptions to fossil fuel distribution resulting from Russia's invasion of Ukraine, and is expected to reach 38 percent of the power mix in 2027 (IEA 2023c). Introducing carbon pricing instruments and reducing fuel subsidies can help continue this transition while adding to fiscal space.

Food price inflation remains high across all EMDE regions (figure 1.15.C). LICs tend to use more cash transfers than other EMDEs and advanced economies to mitigate the social impact of higher food and energy prices, which highlights the need to strengthen their social safety nets (Björn et al. 2022). The international community needs to safeguard the global commodity trading system by avoiding and phasing out restrictive trade measures, such as export bans on food and fertilizers. Furthermore, food shortages can be attenuated by making agriculture more productive and climate-resilient.

Greater international efforts are needed to mitigate humanitarian crises stemming from rising incidents of war and conflict (figure 1.15.D). Besides their direct toll on human life and welfare, war and conflict have substantially impaired living standards through their adverse effects on output and productivity (Dieppe, Celik, and Okou 2021). Violent conflict destroys physical assets and institutions, disrupts labor markets, provokes capital flight, and causes resources to be diverted away from productive uses and toward weaponry and defense (Collier 1999; Hutchinson and Margo 2006; Mueller 2013).

Challenges in emerging market and developing economies

EMDE monetary and financial policy challenges

In many countries, elevated core inflation has proved stickier than expected, which may lead central banks to further tighten monetary policy and maintain restrictive stances for longer than previously envisaged. At the same time, slowing growth and the risk of financial distress may lead to pressure for loosening policy. To ward off any drift in inflation expectations, safeguarding central bank independence and credibility remains critical.[4] The increase in central bank credibility in many EMDEs in recent decades has been an important policy accomplishment, as it can make monetary policy more effective, shield the economy from cross-border spillovers, and keep inflation expectations anchored (Ha, Kose, and Ohnsorge 2019). A loss of credibility at a critical juncture could cause a sudden change in investors' risk perception and trigger capital outflows.

Another way EMDEs can bolster their resilience to capital flow fluctuations and exchange rate volatility is by properly replenishing foreign currency reserves following sizable drawdowns, such as those that occurred among EMDE energy importers last year (figure 1.16.A). EMDEs can strengthen their reserve buffers, for instance by improving domestic investment conditions to attract foreign capital and reducing dependence on volatile sources of funding. Funding volatility may also affect EMDE financial institutions, for example through spillovers from stress in advanced economies' financial markets or lower risk tolerance. These institutions can also be made more resilient through regulatory reforms. Reforms implemented after the global financial crisis have strengthened banks' capital and liquidity buffers, which have recently been tested by the exception-

FIGURE 1.16 Monetary policy challenges in emerging market and developing economies

Many emerging market and developing economies (EMDEs), especially energy importers, need to continue to rebuild foreign exchange reserve buffers to attenuate vulnerability to capital outflows and currency volatility. Corporate leverage continues to rise, both in absolute terms and as a share of total EMDE debt.

A. Inflation, change in foreign exchange reserves, and currency depreciation

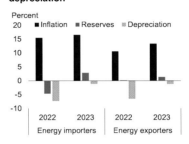

B. Non-financial corporations' debt in EMDEs

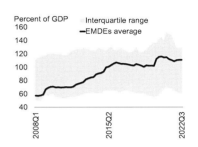

Sources: BIS (database); Haver Analytics; World Bank.
Note: EMDEs = emerging market and developing economies.
A. Figure shows changes in inflation, reserves, and exchange rates since 2021; for 2023, available data as of data cut-off. Aggregates are calculated as simple averages. Sample includes 77 EMDEs, excluding Argentina, Belarus, Lebanon, Russian Federation, Türkiye, and Ukraine. Last observation is April 2023.
B. Figure shows the share of GDP-weighted averages. Sample includes 16 EMDEs. Last observation is 2022Q3.

ally steep global monetary policy tightening. However, non-bank corporations in EMDEs have become highly leveraged, after extensive borrowing, which makes them particularly vulnerable to rising interest rates (figure 1.16.B; Koh and Yu 2020). Accurate, timely, and transparent reporting of credit quality and nonperforming loan balances is essential to ensure that prompt corrective action can be taken, if needed. Furthermore, EMDEs can strengthen bank resolution frameworks to limit the impact of potential shocks on the financial sector.

Where necessary, banking sector resilience can be bolstered through a combination of increased regulatory capital buffers; strengthened macroprudential measures, such as tighter loan-to-value ratios and loan service-to-income ratios, and enhanced safeguarding against market risks, such as currency and maturity mismatches, through hedging and diversification. Moreover, attenuating the overreliance of some EMDE governments on domestic bank financing can help limit the extent to which financial sectors amplify external shocks

---

[4] The special liquidity support measures introduced by central banks during the COVID-19 pandemic mean that their balance sheets carry assets at very low interest rates, even as the rates they pay on their liabilities have risen. Central bank balance earnings statements have in consequence shown declines in net income, and in some cases losses. This unusual situation need not compromise their ability to achieve and maintain low inflation (Bell et al. 2023).

(Deghi et al. 2022). Recent experience in the United States underlines that governments need to be mindful of gaps in the coverage of regulation and supervision, especially during times of tightening financial conditions.

EMDE fiscal policy challenges

Fiscal space in EMDEs continues to be limited, with government debt higher than its pre-pandemic level in more than three-quarters of EMDEs (figure 1.17.A; Kose et al. 2023). High inflation and the ensuing increases in nominal GDP did contribute to a decline in government debt as a share of GDP in 2021 and 2022 in many EMDEs (Kose et al. 2023). However, this only partially reversed the substantial rise in the debt ratio that occurred in 2020. The rising cost of servicing this debt, alongside slowing growth, is increasing the risk of debt distress among EMDEs and LICs (figure 1.17.B). Moreover, a further tightening of advanced-economy monetary policy could increase borrowing costs and worsen fiscal positions and debt sustainability (Arteta, Kamin, and Ruch 2022).

Policy makers need to strike a balance between ensuring fiscal sustainability and meeting spending needs. The aggregate EMDE fiscal stance is expected to remain almost unchanged this year but tighten in 2024 (figure 1.17.C). In fiscally constrained EMDEs, redirecting spending to better target support for vulnerable households can help maintain necessary spending without eroding sustainability. Improving spending efficiency is critical in EMDEs with limited fiscal space and can be achieved through strengthened institutions and domestic governance. Bolstering fiscal and public financial management and improving the effectiveness of fiscal rules and expenditure reviews can also strengthen spending efficiency and help boost investor confidence. Long-run fiscal positions can be improved through investments committed to development needs, such as infrastructure, education, and climate change adaptation, as they support growth prospects.

At the same time, countries will need to mobilize additional domestic revenue, which may be more difficult given the current context of high borrow-ing costs, slowing growth, and a declining pace of potential growth (Kose and Ohnsorge 2023b). Revenue collection has proven to be a challenge for many EMDEs and LICs, with government revenues expected to be lower than the pre-pandemic levels (figure 1.17.D). EMDEs can improve domestic revenue mobilization and make collection mechanisms more efficient by broadening tax bases, simplifying tax systems, closing loopholes in revenue collection, and improving tax administration. Tax avoidance can be mitigated through international coordination in taxation rules.

The composition of government debt poses another fiscal policy challenge. In 2022, in the median EMDE, foreign-currency-denominated debt accounted for nearly 50 percent of government debt, as did debt held by nonresidents (figure 1.17.E). This makes EMDEs vulnerable to rising debt service costs through currency depreciation or through increased sovereign risk premia (IMF 2023c). In some EMDEs, especially those with lower income levels, rising external public debt on non-concessional terms presents an additional debt service burden.

Fiscal policy poses a particularly difficult challenge for LICs, which have seen rapid growth in debt over the past decade. The debt-reducing effects of rapid growth were more than offset by the sizable fiscal deficits that resulted from persistent revenue weakness and rising spending pressures (chapter 4). Total revenue in LICs is about 10 percentage points of GDP lower than in overall EMDEs, largely reflecting broader underdevelopment and weaker institutions. The composition of government expenditures in LICs has shifted toward public sector wages, with spending efficiency remaining low (figure 1.17.F). In addition, LICs spend less on social protections that benefit the vulnerable relative to other countries: social benefit expenditures in LICs average about 3 percent of total government spending, compared with 26 percent in EMDEs and more than 40 percent in advanced economies. Amid the current steep increase in borrowing costs and tight global monetary policy, debt service—especially on external public debt—is becoming costlier. LICs will need to allocate additional revenues to service their debt repayments, which could make it more difficult to secure spending on health and education. Improving LIC debt positions is likely to require debt restructuring in some cases alongside better domestic governance and institutional arrangements.

EMDE structural policy challenges

The major shocks to the global economy over the past three years—including the pandemic, Russia's invasion of Ukraine, and a substantial rise in inflation that led to the sharpest tightening of global monetary policy in four decades—have compounded an underlying, longer-term trend weakening of potential growth (that is, the growth rate that can be sustained over the longer term at full employment and full capacity). Policy makers need to implement decisive structural reforms to reverse the potential growth slowdown currently underway. These would foster investments in physical and human capital, boost labor-supply growth, improve investment conditions, bolster services sector growth, and promote international trade.

Boosting the key drivers of potential growth

EMDE potential growth is projected to fall to an annual average of 4 percent a year during 2022-30, about one percentage point below the average of the previous decade (figure 1.18.A). Weaker long-term growth poses serious challenges for EMDEs (Kilic Celik et al. 2023b). It slows the pace of poverty reduction, reduces the resources available to invest in addressing global challenges such as climate change, limits job creation and wage growth, and adds to the difficulty of servicing elevated debt burdens.

A number of policies could help reverse the projected weakening of global potential growth. Reforms associated with higher physical capital investment, enhanced human capital, and faster labor-supply growth could raise annual potential growth by 0.7 percentage point over the period 2022-30, both globally and in EMDEs. This would offset the 0.4 percentage point decline in potential growth between 2011-21 and 2022-30 projected in the baseline scenario for the global

FIGURE 1.17 Fiscal policy challenges in emerging market and developing economies

In more than three-quarters of emerging market and developing economies (EMDEs), fiscal positions have worsened since the pandemic. Rising debt service costs have increased the risk of debt distress, especially for low-income countries (LICs). The aggregate EMDE fiscal stance is expected to tighten in 2024, and revenue collection remains a challenge. A substantial share of government debt is still held in forms susceptible to heightened volatility. In LICs, the share of government spending on public sector wages tends to be higher than in other countries at the expense of spending on social protection.

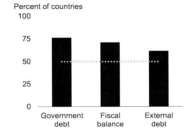

A. EMDEs with worse debt and fiscal positions than at end-2019

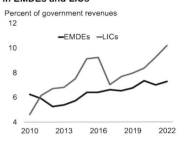

B. Government net interest payments in EMDEs and LICs

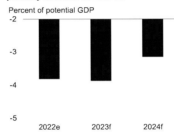

C. Aggregate cyclically adjusted primary balance in EMDEs

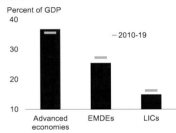

D. Expected government revenues in 2023

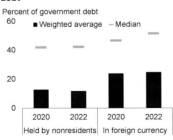

E. Composition of EMDE government debt

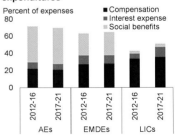

F. Composition of government expenditures

Sources: Haver Analytics; International Monetary Fund; Kose et al. (2022); World Bank.
Note: AEs = advanced economies; EMDEs = emerging market and developing economies; LICs = low-income countries.
A. Figure shows share of EMDEs with higher government or total external debt or with worse fiscal balances (all in percent of GDP) in the latest quarter with data than in 2019Q4. Fiscal balances are a 4-quarter moving sum. Debt and fiscal data are for central governments in some countries. Sample includes 59, 68, and 62 EMDEs for government debt, fiscal balance, and external debt, respectively. Dotted line indicates 50 percent.
B. Net interest payments are the difference between primary balances and overall fiscal balances. Aggregates computed with government revenues in U.S. dollars as weights, based on 150 EMDEs, including 27 LICs.
C. Aggregates calculated using potential GDP as weights. Sample includes 44 EMDEs. Data for 2023-24 are forecasts.
D. Aggregates computed with GDP in U.S. dollars as weights, based on 41 advanced economies and 147 EMDEs, including 25 LICs.
E. Weighted averages computed using government debt in U.S. dollars as weights. Sample includes 43 EMDEs for debt held by nonresidents and 32 EMDEs for debt in foreign currency.
F. "Compensation" of employees and includes wages and salaries, and social contributions. In some countries, data are for central governments. Sample includes 38 advanced economies and 116 EMDEs, including 18 LICs.

FIGURE 1.18 Structural policy challenges in emerging market and developing economies

The slowdown in potential growth over the past decade can be reversed by well-designed reforms. These reforms include additional investments in physical and human capital, as well as increases in labor force participation to offset the declining growth of working-age populations. The current limited role of services trade in emerging market and developing economies (EMDEs), compared with advanced economies, indicates substantial scope for expansion.

A. Contributions to potential growth

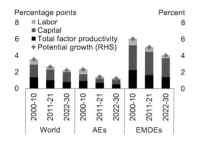

B. Global potential growth under reform scenarios

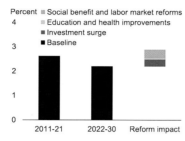

C. Working-age population

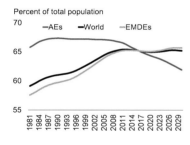

D. Composition of global trade, 2010-19

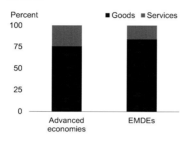

Sources: Kose and Ohnsorge (2023a); UN World Population Prospects 2022; World Bank staff estimates.
Note: AEs = advanced economies; EMDEs = emerging market and developing economies.
A. Figure shows GDP-weighted averages of production function-based potential growth estimates for a sample of 29 advanced economies and 53 EMDEs as described in Kose and Ohnsorge (2023a). Data for 2022-30 are forecasts.
B. Figure shows period averages of annual GDP-weighted averages. Scenarios assume a repeat of each country's best 10-year improvement as described in Kose and Ohnsorge (2023a). Data for 2022-30 are forecasts.
C. Figure shows population-weighted averages. The working-age population is defined as people aged 15-64 years. Data for 2023-29 are forecasts.
D. Figure shows the 2010-19 average of shares of global goods and services trade in global trade as described in Kose and Ohnsorge (2023a).

economy, and most of the 1 percentage point slowdown projected for EMDEs (figure 1.18.B).

Higher physical capital investment is key to boosting potential output growth. Investment growth slowed over the past decade and may remain muted for some time as a result of slow growth and continuing effects of the pandemic, Russia's invasion of Ukraine, tightening financial conditions, and limited fiscal policy space. Invest-

ment growth slowed during the past decade in all six EMDE regions (Kasyanenko, Kenworthy, Ruch et al. 2023a). Addressing gaps between current spending on infrastructure and the level needed to meet development goals can contribute to a sustained rise in per capita incomes while also bolstering activity in the short term (Vagliasindi and Gorgulu 2021). In particular, investment in green infrastructure projects with high economic returns and the widespread adoption of environmentally sustainable technologies can support economic growth, while contributing to tackling climate change. Sound investments, including by the private sector, that are aligned with climate goals in key areas—such as transport and energy, climate-smart agriculture and manufacturing, and land and water systems—can all boost long-term growth.

Human capital in EMDEs would benefit from strengthening education systems, in particular by improving learning outcomes. Increasing investment in human capital can help reverse the losses caused by the overlapping adverse shocks of recent years—especially the pandemic (Schady et al. 2023). Improvements in education would also boost labor force participation, as better-educated workers tend to be more firmly attached to labor markets (Kose and Ohnsorge 2023b). Furthermore, since high-productivity technologies often require complementary skilled human capital, better-quality education systems can foster private investment (Kasyanenko, Kenworthy, Ruch et al. 2023b).

The working-age population in EMDEs has started to stagnate (figure 1.18.C). The negative effect of slowing working-age population growth is expected to be sizable, though with wide variation across regions (Kasyanenko, Kenworthy, Kilic Celik et al. 2023). Policies can help maintain the size of the labor force, in particular those that engage discouraged workers or groups with historically low participation rates, such as women and older workers. Improvements to health and education, in particular, are crucial to boost overall labor force participation, since better-educated workers are more likely to remain attached to labor markets, while also increasing productivity. Raising female labor force participation is particularly important given high female unemployment rates and a continued gap in female labor force participation relative to men. In some regions, female labor force participation is about half the EMDE average, underscoring ample opportunities for improvement. Relevant policies include job training programs specifically aimed at women such as vocational training, as well as the promotion of childcare services. They also include expanded access to financial products to foster female entrepreneurial capacity.

Total factor productivity growth can be promoted by reforms that buttress institutional quality, such as by strengthening the rule of law and reining in corruption; that foster greater political stability; and that improve the business environment. Given that institutions and governance remain weak in many EMDEs, there is considerable scope for higher productivity through institutional reforms (World Bank 2018a). Such reforms can encourage private sector investment and innovation by establishing enforceable property rights, minimizing expropriation risk, promoting competition and limiting market concentration, creating a stable policy environment, lowering the costs of doing business, and encouraging participation in the formal sector where productivity tends to be higher (World Bank 2018b, 2019).

Promoting trade and fostering productivity of services

Global trade, facilitated by trade liberalization and falling transport costs, has historically been an important engine of productivity and output growth in EMDEs. A large part of the gains from trade can be attributed to the expansion of global value chains (World Bank 2020). While participation in global value chains generates efficiency gains and boosts productivity via the transfer of knowledge, capital, and other inputs across countries, it also increases sensitivity to external shocks (Constantinescu, Mattoo, and Ruta 2020). As technological innovation tends to occur in a limited number of countries, advances globally depend on international spillovers (Keller 2004). International trade is one of the primary channels of diffusion of new technology as it makes available to importers processes and products that

embody foreign knowledge and that would otherwise be unavailable or very costly (Grossman and Helpman 1991; Helpman 1997).

This role of trade as an engine of output and productivity growth is now under threat as policy interventions have adversely affected trade relations in recent years. Following Russia's invasion of Ukraine, some countries introduced food trade restrictions, which distorted the functioning of global food markets. Tariffs have risen over the past five years as trade tensions have mounted, contributing to concerns about a protectionist turn among some major economies (World Bank 2021). Geopolitical tensions have led to the imposition of a widening range of restrictions on trade in goods. The growth of global trade in goods and services was almost twice as fast as global output growth during 1970-2008, but only half as fast during 2011-19. Goods trade accounted for 75 percent of global trade in goods and services during 2010-19, with a higher share in EMDEs compared with that in advanced economies (figure 1.18.D).

To reduce elevated trade costs in EMDEs, comprehensive reforms are needed. Trade agreements can reduce trade costs and promote trade, especially if they lower both tariff and non-tariff barriers and generate momentum for further domestic reforms—including reforms that foster private sector development and domestic competition. Trade costs are still often inflated by costly administrative border and customs procedures (Moïsé and Le Bris 2013). Policy-related nontariff barriers that can be standardized include sanitary, phytosanitary, and other standards (often aimed at protecting consumer health and safety), pre-shipment inspections, licensing requirements, and quotas. Trade costs can be lowered significantly by streamlining trade and customs compliance procedures and processes (Staboulis et al. 2020). In addition, end-to-end supply chain digitalization would allow EMDEs to shorten port delays (Arvis at al. 2023). Finally, regulatory restrictions on services trade can add to trade costs. This reflects to a large extent regulations that create market entry barriers—especially with respect to the entry of foreign firms in EMDEs (Ohnsorge and Quaglietti 2023).

Services could emerge as a new engine of global growth. Future growth opportunities linked to greater digitalization could boost productivity in EMDE services sectors. Increased digitalization has improved prospects for economies of scale and innovation in the services sector that previously required face-to-face interactions. Policies to support the diffusion of digital technologies in EMDEs can bring particularly high returns, given the low starting level of digitalization in the services sector. For instance, the share of firms using email to communicate with clients was less than one-third in several EMDEs as recently as 2018 (Nayyar, Hallward-Driemeier, and Davies 2021).

Investing in information and communication technology infrastructure, updating regulatory frameworks, and strengthening management capabilities and worker skills, can boost the adoption of digital technologies. Policies to improve market access for, and skills in, ICT and professional services could ease constraints on growth.

TABLE 1.2 Emerging market and developing economies[1]

Commodity exporters[2]		Commodity importers[3]	
Algeria*	Kyrgyz Republic	Afghanistan	Samoa
Angola*	Lao PDR	Albania	Serbia
Argentina	Liberia	Antigua and Barbuda	Sri Lanka
Armenia	Libya*	Bahamas, The	St. Kitts and Nevis
Azerbaijan*	Madagascar	Bangladesh	St. Lucia
Bahrain*	Malawi	Barbados	St. Vincent and the Grenadines
Belize	Mali	Belarus	Syrian Arab Republic
Benin	Mauritania	Bosnia and Herzegovina	Thailand
Bhutan*	Mongolia	Bulgaria	Tonga
Bolivia*	Mozambique	Cambodia	Tunisia
Botswana	Myanmar*	China	Türkiye
Brazil	Namibia	Djibouti	Tuvalu
Burkina Faso	Nicaragua	Dominica	Vanuatu
Burundi	Niger	Dominican Republic	Vietnam
Cabo Verde	Nigeria*	Egypt, Arab Rep.	
Cameroon*	Oman*	El Salvador	
Central African Republic	Papua New Guinea	Eswatini	
Chad*	Paraguay	Georgia	
Chile	Peru	Grenada	
Colombia*	Qatar*	Haiti	
Comoros	Russian Federation*	Hungary	
Congo, Dem. Rep.	Rwanda	India	
Congo, Rep.*	São Tomé and Príncipe	Jamaica	
Costa Rica	Saudi Arabia*	Jordan	
Côte d'Ivoire	Senegal	Kiribati	
Ecuador*	Seychelles	Lebanon	
Equatorial Guinea*	Sierra Leone	Lesotho	
Eritrea	Solomon Islands	Malaysia	
Ethiopia	South Africa	Maldives	
Fiji	South Sudan*	Marshall Islands	
Gabon*	Sudan	Mauritius	
Gambia, The	Suriname	Mexico	
Ghana*	Tajikistan	Micronesia, Fed. Sts.	
Guatemala	Tanzania	Moldova	
Guinea	Timor-Leste*	Montenegro	
Guinea-Bissau	Togo	Morocco	
Guyana*	Uganda	Nauru	
Honduras	Ukraine	Nepal	
Indonesia*	United Arab Emirates*	North Macedonia	
Iran, Islamic Rep.*	Uruguay	Pakistan	
Iraq*	Uzbekistan	Palau	
Kazakhstan*	West Bank and Gaza	Panama	
Kenya	Yemen, Rep.*	Philippines	
Kosovo	Zambia	Poland	
Kuwait*	Zimbabwe	Romania	

* Energy exporters.

1. Emerging market and developing economies (EMDEs) include all those that are not classified as advanced economies and for which a forecast is published for this report. Dependent territories are excluded. Advanced economies include Australia; Austria; Belgium; Canada; Cyprus; Czechia; Denmark; Estonia; Finland; France; Germany; Greece; Hong Kong SAR, China; Iceland; Ireland; Israel; Italy; Japan; the Republic of Korea; Latvia; Lithuania; Luxembourg; Malta; the Netherlands; New Zealand; Norway; Portugal; Singapore; the Slovak Republic; Slovenia; Spain; Sweden; Switzerland; the United Kingdom; and the United States. Since Croatia became a member of the euro area on January 1, 2023, it has been removed from the list of EMDEs, and related growth aggregates, to avoid double counting.

2. An economy is defined as commodity exporter when, on average in 2017-19, either (1) total commodities exports accounted for 30 percent or more of total exports or (2) exports of any single commodity accounted for 20 percent or more of total exports. Economies for which these thresholds were met as a result of re-exports were excluded. When data were not available, judgment was used. This taxonomy results in the classification of some well-diversified economies as importers, even if they are exporters of certain commodities (for example, Mexico).

3. Commodity importers are EMDEs not classified as commodity exporters.

References

ACLED (The Armed Conflict Location & Event Data Project) database. Accessed May 26, 2023. https://acleddata.com/data-export-tool

Agénor, P. R., and L. A. P. da Silva. 2018. "Financial Spillovers, Spillbacks, and the Scope for International Macroprudential Policy Coordination." Bank for International Settlement, Basel, Switzerland.

Aiyar, S., J. Chen, C. H. Ebeke, R. Garcia-Saltos, T. Gudmundsson, A. Ilyina, and A. Kangur. 2023. "Geoeconomic Fragmentation and the Future of Multilateralism." Staff Discussion Note SDN/2023/001, International Monetary Fund, Washington, DC.

Alfano, M., and T. Cornelissen. 2022. "Spatial Spillovers of Conflict in Somalia." IZA Discussion Paper 15761, IZA Institute of Labor Economics, Bonn, Germany.

Anderson, D., B. Hunt, M. Kortelainen, M. Kumhof, D. Laxton, D. Muir, S. Mursula, and S. Snudden. 2013. "Getting to Know GIMF: The Simulation Properties of the Global Integrated Monetary and Fiscal Model." IMF Working Paper 13/55, International Monetary Fund, Washington, DC.

Aramonte, S., A. Schrimpf, and H. S. Shin. 2022. "Non-Bank Financial Intermediaries and Financial Stability." BIS Working Paper 972, Bank for International Settlement, Basel, Switzerland.

Arteta, C., S. Kamin, and F. U. Ruch. 2022. "How Do Rising U.S. Interest Rates Affect Emerging and Developing Economies? It Depends." Policy Research Working Paper 10258, World Bank, Washington, DC.

Arvis, J. F., L. Ojala, B. Shepherd, D. Ulybina, and C. Wiederer. 2023. "Connecting to Compete 2023: Trade Logistics in an Uncertain Global Economy." The Logistics Performance Index and Its Indicators, World Bank, Washington, DC.

Bell, S., M. Chui, T. Gomes, P. Moser-Boehm, and A. P. Tejada. 2023. "Why Are Central Banks Reporting Losses? Does It Matter?" BIS Papers 68, Bank for International Settlement, Basel, Switzerland.

Berger, D., V. Guerrieri, G. Lorenzoni, and J. Vavra. 2017. "House Prices and Consumer Spending." NBER Working Paper 21667, National Bureau of Economic Research, Cambridge, MA.

Berger, D., K. Milbradt, F. Tourre, and J. Vavra. 2021. "Mortgage Prepayment and Path-Dependent Effects of Monetary Policy." *American Economic Review* 111 (9): 2829-78.

Bernanke, B., and O. Blanchard. 2023. "What Caused the U.S. Pandemic-Era Inflation?" Hutchins Center on Fiscal and Monetary Policy, Brookings Institution, Washington, DC.

BIS (Bank for International Settlements) database. Accessed on April 3, 2023. https://bis.org/statistics/

Björn, R., S. Sosa, D. Kim, L. Kohler, G. Pierre, N. Kato, M. Debbich, et al. 2022. "Tackling the Global Food Crisis: Impact, Policy Response, and the Role of the IMF." IMF Note 2022/004, International Monetary Fund, Washington, DC.

Blagrave, P., C. Godbout, J. D. Guénette, R. Lalonde, and N. Perevalov. 2020. "IMPACT: The Bank of Canada's International Model for Projecting Activity." Technical Report 116, Canadian Economic Analysis Department Bank of Canada, Ottawa, Ontario.

Boissay, F., and R. Cooper. 2016. "The Collateral Trap." BIS Working Papers 565, Bank for International Settlement, Basel, Switzerland.

Borio, C., M. J. Lombardi, J. Yetman, and E. Zakrajšek. 2023. "The Two-Regime View of Inflation." BIS Papers 133, Bank for International Settlement, Basel, Switzerland.

Böninghausen, B., G. Kidd, and R. de Vincent Humphreys. 2018. "Interpreting Recent Developments in Market Based Indicators of Longer Term Inflation Expectations." ECB Economic Bulletin, Issue 6/2018, European Central Bank, Frankfurt.

Brayton, F., T. Laubach, and D. Reifschneider. 2014. "The FRB/US Model: A Tool for Macroeconomic Policy Analysis." FEDS Notes, Board of Governors of the Federal Reserve System, Washington, DC.

Carstens, A. 2021. "Non-Bank Financial Sector: Systemic Regulation Needed." BIS Quarterly Review, Bank for International Settlement, Basel, Switzerland.

Collier, P. 1999. "On the Economic Consequences of Civil War." *Oxford Economic Papers* 51 (1): 168-83.

Constantinescu, C., A. Mattoo, and M. Ruta. 2020. "The Global Trade Slowdown: Cyclical or Structural?" *World Bank Economic Review* 34 (1): 121-42.

Deghi, A., S. Fendoglu, T. Iyer, H. R. Tabarraei, Y. Xu, and M. Yenice. 2022. "The Sovereign-Bank Nexus in Emerging Markets in the Wake of the COVID-19 Pandemic." Working Paper 22/223, International Monetary Fund, Washington, DC.

Dieppe, A., S. K. Celik, and C. Okou. 2021. "What Happens to Productivity During Major Adverse

Events." In *Global Productivity: Trends, Drivers, and Policies*. Washington, DC: World Bank.

Duval, R., D. Furceri, R. Lee, and M. M Tavares. 2021. "Market Power and Monetary Policy Transmission." IMF Working Paper 21/184, International Monetary Fund, Washington, DC.

EBRD (European Bank for Reconstruction and Development). 2023. "Transition Report 2022-23: Business Unusual." European Bank for Reconstruction and Development, London.

Elliot, D., C. Jackson, M. Raczko, and M. Roberts-Sklar. 2015. "Does Oil Drive Financial Market Measures of Inflation Expectations?" *Bank Underground* (blog). October 20, 2015. https://bankunderground.co.uk/2015/10/20/does-oil-drive-financial-market-inflation-expectations

Engel, J., Y. Hirano, H. Nur, and Y. Nyirenda. 2023. "In 7 charts: The Urgent Need for Macroeconomic Stabilization in Malawi." *World Bank Blog*. January 31, 2023. https://blogs.worldbank.org/africacan/7-charts-urgent-need-macroeconomic-stabilization-malawi

Federal Reserve. 2023. "2023 Stress Test Scenarios." Board of Governors of the Federal Reserve System, Washington, DC.

Feyen, E., N. Fiess, A. C. Bertay, and I. Z. Huertas. 2022. "Cross-Border Banking in EMDEs: Trends, Scale, and Policy Implications." In *Handbook of Banking and Finance in Emerging Markets*, edited by D. Nguyen. Northampton, MA: Edward Elgar Publishing.

Feyen, E., and I. Zuccardi. 2019. "The Sovereign-Bank Nexus in EMDEs: What Is It, Is It Rising, and What Are the Policy Implications?" Policy Research Working Paper 8950, World Bank, Washington, DC.

FinStats (Finance, Competitiveness, and Innovation) 2023 database. Accessed on April 3, 2023. https://worldbank.org/en/about/unit/fci

Gagnon, J., and M. Sarsenbayev. 2022. "25 Years of Excess Unemployment in Advanced Economies: Lessons for Monetary Policy." Working Paper 22-17, Peterson Institute for International Economics, Washington, DC.

Góes, C., and E. Bekkers. 2022. "The Impact of Geopolitical Conflicts on Trade, Growth, and Innovation." WTO Staff Working Paper ERSD-2022-9, World Trade Organization, Geneva.

Gropp, R., T. Mosk, S. Ongena, and C. Wix. 2019. "Banks Response to Higher Capital Requirements: Evidence from a Quasi-Natural Experiment." *The Review of Financial Studies* 32 (1): 266-99.

Grossman, G., and E. Helpman. 1991. "Trade, Knowledge Spillovers, and Growth." *European Economic Review* 35 (2-3): 517-26.

GSE (Gas Infrastructure Europe) database. Accessed on May 5, 2023. https://gie.eu/transparency/databases/

GTA (Global Trade Alert) database. Accessed on May 5, 2023. https://globaltradealert.org/data_extraction

Guha Sapir, D., R. Below, and Ph. Hoyois. 2023. "EM-DAT: The CRED/OFDA International Disaster Database." Université Catholique de Louvain, Brussels, Belgium.

Ha, J., M. A. Kose, and F. Ohnsorge, eds. 2019. *Inflation in Emerging and Developing Economies: Evolution, Drivers, and Policies*. Washington, DC: World Bank.

Hardy, B., and S. Zhu. 2023. "Covid, Central Banks and The Bank-Sovereign Nexus." BIS Quarterly Review, Bank for International Settlement, Basel, Switzerland.

Helpman, E. 1997. "R&D and Productivity: The International Connection." NBER Working Paper 6101, National Bureau of Economic Research, Cambridge, MA.

Hofmann, B., T. Park, and A. P. Tejada. 2023. "Commodity Prices, the Dollar and Stagflation Risk." BIS Quarterly Review, Bank for International Settlement, Basel, Switzerland.

Horn, S., B. C. Parks, C. M. Reinhart, and C. Trebesch. 2023. "China as an International Lender of Last Resort." World Bank, Washington, DC.

Hutchinson, W., and R. A. Margo. 2006. "The Impact of the Civil War on Capital Intensity and Labor Productivity in Southern Manufacturing." *Explorations in Economic History* 43 (4): 689-704.

IDS (International Debt Statistics) database. Accessed on April 3, 2023. https://worldbank.org/en/programs/debt-statistics/ids

IEA (International Energy Agency). 2023a. "Oil Market Report." May. International Energy Agency, Paris.

IEA (International Energy Agency). 2023b. "Fossil Fuels Consumption Subsidies 2022." International Energy Agency, Paris.

IEA (International Energy Agency). 2023c. "Renewables 2022: Analysis and Forecast to 2027." International Energy Agency, Paris.

IIF (Institute of International Finance) database. Accessed on May 20, 2023. https://iif.com/Research/Download-Data

IMF (International Monetary Fund). 2023a. *Global Financial Stability Report: Safeguarding Financial Stability amid High Inflation and Geopolitical Risks.* Washington, DC: International Monetary Fund.

IMF (International Monetary Fund). 2023b. "Debt Sustainability Analysis: List of LIC DSAs for PRGT-Eligible Countries." February, International Monetary Fund, Washington, DC.

IMF (International Monetary Fund). 2023c. *Fiscal Monitor: On the Path to Policy Normalization.* April. Washington, DC: International Monetary Fund.

IPCC (The Intergovernmental Panel on Climate Change). 2023. *AR6 Synthesis Report: Climate Change 2023.* Geneva: World Meteorological Organization.

IRENA (International Renewable Energy Agency). 2022. *World Energy Transitions: Outlook 2022.* Abu Dhabi: International Renewable Energy Agency.

Jafino, B., B. Walsh, J. Rozenberg, and S. Hallegatte. 2020. "Revised Estimates of the Impact of Climate Change on Extreme Poverty by 2030." Policy Research Working Paper 9417, World Bank, Washington, DC.

Kamber, G., M. Mohanty, and J. Morley. 2020. "What Drives Inflation in Advanced and Emerging Market Economies?" BIS Papers 111, Bank for International Settlement, Basel, Switzerland.

Kasyanenko, S., P. G. Kenworthy, F. U. Ruch, E. T. Vashakmadze, C. M. Wheeler, and D. Vorisek. 2023a. "Investment in Emerging Market and Developing Economy Regions: Trends, Prospects, and Policy Options." Policy Research Working Paper 10369, World Bank, Washington, DC.

Kasyanenko, S., P. G. Kenworthy, F. U. Ruch, E. T. Vashakmadze, C. M. Wheeler, and D. Vorisek. 2023b. "Regional Dimensions of Investment: Moving in the Right Direction?" In *Falling Long-Term Growth Prospects: Trends, Expectations, and Policies,* edited by M. A. Kose and F. Ohnsorge. Washington, DC: World Bank.

Kasyanenko, S., P. G. Kenworthy, S. Kilic Celik, F. U. Ruch, E. T. Vashakmadze, and C. M. Wheeler. 2023. "The Past and Future of Regional Potential Growth: Hopes, Fears, and Realities." Policy Research Working Paper 10369, World Bank, Washington, DC.

Keller, W. 2004. "International Technology Diffusion." *Journal of Economic Literature* 42 (3): 752-82.

Kilic Celik, S., M. A. Kose, F. Ohnsorge, and F. U. Ruch. 2023a. "Potential Growth: A Global Database." Policy Research Working Paper 10354, World Bank, Washington, DC.

Kilic Celik, S., M. A. Kose, F. Ohnsorge, and F. U. Ruch. 2023b. "Potential Not Realized: An International Database of Potential Growth." In *Falling Long-Term Growth Prospects: Trends, Expectations, and Policies,* edited by M. A. Kose and F. Ohnsorge. Washington, DC: World Bank.

Koh, W. C., and S. Yu. 2020. "Macroeconomic and Financial Sector Policies." In *A Decade After the Global Recession: Lessons and Challenges for Emerging and Developing Economies,* edited by M. A. Kose and F. Ohnsorge. Washington, DC: World Bank.

Kose, M. A., S. Kurlat, F. Ohnsorge, and N. Sugawara. 2022. "A Cross-Country Database of Fiscal Space." World Bank, Washington, DC.

Kose, M. A., P. Nagle, F. Ohnsorge, and N. Sugawara. 2021. *Global Waves of Debt: Causes and Consequences.* Washington, DC: World Bank.

Kose, M. A., and F. Ohnsorge, eds. 2023a. *Falling Long-Term Growth Prospects: Trends, Expectations, and Policies.* Washington, DC: World Bank.

Kose, M. A., and F. Ohnsorge. 2023b. "Overview." In *Falling Long-Term Growth Prospects: Trends, Expectations, and Policies.* Washington, DC: World Bank.

Kose, M. A., F. Ohnsorge, K. Stamm, and N. Sugawara. 2023. "Government Debt Has Declined but Don't Celebrate Yet." *Brookings* (blog). February 21, 2023. https://brookings.edu/blog/future-development/2023/02/21/government-debt-has-declined-but-dont-celebrate-yet/

Laeven, L., and F. Valencia. 2018. "Systemic Banking Crises Revisited." IMF Working Paper No. 18/206, International Monetary Fund, Washington, DC.

Lane, P. R. 2023. "Underlying Inflation." Speech, European Central Bank, Frankfurt.

Lee, D., J. Park, and Y. Shin. 2023. "Where Are the Workers? From Great Resignation to Quiet Quitting." NBER Working Paper 30833, National Bureau of Economic Research, Cambridge, MA.

Metivier, J., M. Bacchetta, E. Bekkers, and R. Koopman. 2023. "International Trade Cooperation's Impact on the World Economy." Staff Working Paper ERSD-2023-02, World Trade Organization, Geneva, Switzerland.

Moïsé, E., and F. Le Bris. 2013. "Trade Costs—What Have We Learned? A Synthesis Report." OECD Trade Policy Paper 150, Organisation for Economic Co-operation and Development, Paris.

Mueller, H. 2013. "The Economic Cost of Conflict." Working Paper, International Growth Centre, London.

Nayyar, G., M. Hallward-Driemeier, and E. Davies. 2021. *At Your Service? The Promise of Services-Led Development*. Washington DC: World Bank.

Ohnsorge, F., and L. Quaglietti. 2023. "Trade as an Engine of Growth: Sputtering but Fixable." In *Falling Long-Term Growth Prospects: Trends, Expectations, and Policies*. Washington, DC: World Bank.

Ohnsorge, F., and S. Yu, eds. 2021. *The Long Shadow of Informality: Challenges and Policies*. Washington, DC: World Bank.

Oxford Economics. 2019. "Global Economic Model." July, Oxford Economics, Oxford, UK.

Peszko, G., M. Amann, Y. Awe, G. Kleiman, and T. S. Rabie. 2022. "Air Pollution and Climate Change: From Co-Benefits to Coherent Policies. International Development in Focus." World Bank, Washington, DC.

Pill, H. 2023. "Inflation Persistence and Monetary Policy." Speech, Bank of England, London.

Schady, N., A. Holla, S. Sabarwal, J. Silva, and A. Y. Chang. n.d. *Collapse and Recovery: How the COVID-19 Pandemic Eroded Human Capital and What to Do about It*. Washington, DC: World Bank.

Staboulis, C., D. Natos, E. Tsakiridou, and K. Mattas. 2020. "International Trade Costs in OECD Countries." *Operational Research* 20 (3): 1177-87.

UNCTAD (United Nations Conference on Trade and Development). 2022. *The Low-Carbon Transition and its Daunting Implications for Structural Transformation. The Least Developed Countries Report 2022*. Geneva: United Nations.

UNICEF 2023. *From Insight to Action: Examining Mortality in Somalia*. March 2023. New York: UNICEF.

UNWTO (United Nations World Tourism Organization). 2023. "Tourism Set to Return to Pre-Pandemic Levels in Some Regions in 2023." World Tourism Organization, Madrid.

Vagliasindi, M., and N. Gorgulu. 2021. "What Have We Learned about the Effectiveness of Infrastructure Investment as a Fiscal Stimulus? A Literature Review." Policy Research Working Paper 9796, World Bank, Washington, DC.

WDI (World Development Indicators) database. Accessed on April 3, 2023. https://databank. worldbank.org/source/world-development-indicators

WEO (World Economic Outlook) database. April 2023. Accessed on April 3, 2023. https://imf.org/en/ Publications/WEO/weo-database/2023/April

WFP and FAO (World Food Programme and Food and Agriculture Organization of the United Nations). 2022. *Hunger Hotspots. FAO-WFP Early Warnings on Acute Food Insecurity: October 2022 to January 2023 Outlook*. Rome: World Food Programme.

World Bank. 2018a. *World Development Report 2018: Learning to Realize Education's Promise*. Washington, DC: World Bank.

World Bank. 2018b. *Global Economic Prospects: The Turning of the Tide?* June. Washington, DC: World Bank.

World Bank. 2019. *Global Economic Prospects: Darkening Skies*. January. Washington, DC: World Bank.

World Bank. 2020. *World Development Report: Trading for Development in the Age of Global Value Chains*. Washington, DC: World Bank.

World Bank. 2021. *Global Economic Prospects*. January. Washington, DC: World Bank.

World Bank. 2022a. *Climate and Development: An Agenda for Action—Emerging Insights from World Bank Group 2021-22 Country Climate and Development Reports*. Washington, DC: World Bank.

World Bank. 2022b. *G5 Sahel Region Country Climate and Development Report*. Washington, DC: World Bank.

World Bank. 2023a. *Food Security Update*. April 20. Washington, DC: World Bank.

World Bank. 2023b. "Macro Poverty Outlook: Sub-Saharan Africa." World Bank, Washington, DC.

World Bank. 2023c. *Global Economic Prospects*. January. Washington, DC: World Bank.

CHAPTER 2

REGIONAL OUTLOOKS

EAST ASIA and PACIFIC

Growth in the East Asia and Pacific (EAP) region is projected to strengthen to 5.5 percent in 2023 from 3.5 percent in 2022, as a recovery in China offsets slowing activity in most other regional economies. Projected growth in China this year has been revised upward following a faster-than-expected reopening of the economy, which is bolstering near-term consumer spending, particularly on services. Growth in the region excluding China is set to slow to 4.8 percent in 2023 from 5.8 percent in 2022, as the boost from earlier reopening fades in several large economies. Regional trade growth will remain subdued amid weak global demand and domestic services-led growth in China. In 2024, growth in EAP is projected to ease to 4.6 percent as the effects of China's reopening fade. Downside risks to the outlook include tighter-than-expected global financial conditions; stubbornly high inflation; protracted weakness in China's property sector; geopolitical tensions; and, particularly for smaller economies, natural disasters, including climate-change-related extreme weather events.

Recent developments

Following a sharp slowdown in 2022, growth in the East Asia and Pacific (EAP) region is recovering, supported by strong activity in China following the reopening of the economy and a rapid decline in COVID-19 infections. Growth in China recovered strongly in early 2023, underpinned by a release of pent-up demand that bolstered consumption (figure 2.1.1.A). Retail sales surged alongside a more modest uptick in industrial production growth (figure 2.1.1.B). Activity was supported by a rebound in contact-intensive services sectors and strong Chinese New Year-related spending and travel, and the rapid return of migrant workers to workplaces. Investment has continued to be supported by infrastructure-related stimulus, which ramped up in 2022, helping to offset property sector weakness (figure 2.1.1.C). More recently, the property sector, burdened by high debts, has shown tentative signs of emerging from a protracted slump. Policies to ensure the completion of unfinished projects and restore confidence have helped lift prices in an increasing number of cities (figure 2.1.1.D).

Elsewhere in EAP, growth slowed around the turn of the year in a number of economies as the boost from earlier reopening faded (Malaysia, Philippines, Vietnam; figure 2.1.2.A). While consumption growth remained firm, goods trade decelerated before stabilizing, reflecting weak global demand and tepid activity in goods-trade-intensive sectors in China (figure 2.1.2.B). However, services trade benefited from a continued recovery in global tourism, boosted by tourists from China taking advantage of the reopening of borders.

Headline consumer price inflation has declined from recent highs in most countries and is lower than in other emerging market and developing economy (EMDE) regions, partly reflecting spare capacity along with price controls and subsidies. Moderating global food and energy prices and declining shipping costs have also helped cool inflation. However, inflation remains above central bank targets in some countries (figure 2.1.2.C). In some cases, local food production disruptions and supply bottlenecks have added to price pressures, notably in Mongolia, Myanmar, and the Philippines. Exchange rates have been broadly stable against the U.S. dollar in early 2023, with some central banks supporting currencies in the face of the spike in global investor risk aversion that accompanied the recent advanced-

---

Note: This section was prepared by Samuel Hill.

FIGURE 2.1.1 China: Recent developments

Growth in China slowed in late 2022 due to COVID-19-related disruptions. However, the reopening of the economy and a rapid decline in infections subsequently spurred a rebound, supported by household spending, especially on services. The recovery in industrial production has been relatively slower. Fixed investment growth has been supported by government infrastructure spending, helping offset weakness in the property sector. More recently, the property sector has shown signs of emerging from a protracted slump, with property prices rising.

A. China: Contributions to growth

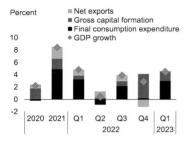

B. China: Retail sales and industrial production growth

C. China: Fixed-asset-investment growth

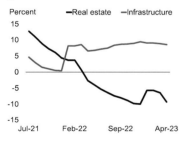

D. China: Shares of cities with changing property prices

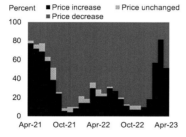

Sources: Haver Analytics; National Bureau of Statistics of China; World Bank.
A. Year-on-year real GDP growth and expenditure contributions. Last observation is 2023Q1.
B. Year-on-year growth of nominal retail sales and real industrial production. Last observation is April 2023.
C. Year-on-year growth of year-to-date real estate and infrastructure investment. Last observation is April 2023.
D. Shares of cities with increasing, unchanged, and falling month-on-month existing residential building prices. Sample includes 70 major cities. Last observation is April 2023.

economy banking turmoil. However, in the Lao People's Democratic Republic, sharp currency depreciation associated with broad domestic macroeconomic instability pushed up import prices and added to inflationary pressures. In response to persistently high inflation, some central banks hiked interest rates further in early 2023—albeit to lower levels than in other EMDE regions—to help ensure that inflation expectations remain well anchored (Malaysia, Philippines, Thailand). However, elsewhere central banks have signaled a pause to tightening (Indonesia) or have begun cutting policy rates (Vietnam).

The region's recovery from the pandemic-induced recession is now well advanced, with output exceeding pre-pandemic levels in many countries (figure 2.1.2.D). However, activity is yet to recover fully in most Pacific Island economies, where recessions were more severe and reopening was delayed, particularly in tourism-dependent economies (Fiji, Palau). Natural disasters (Tonga, Vanuatu), political instability (Myanmar), and civil unrest (Solomon Islands) have also held back recovery.

Outlook

Growth in the EAP region is projected to strengthen to 5.5 percent in 2023, with a recovery in China offsetting moderating growth in several other economies. In 2024 and 2025, growth in EAP is expected to edge down to 4.6 percent and 4.5 percent, respectively, as growth in China slows alongside broadly stable growth in the rest of the region. Compared with January projections, growth in EAP is expected to be 1.2 percentage points higher in 2023 and 0.3 percentage point lower in 2024. The revisions primarily reflect the earlier-than-expected reopening of China, where growth has been revised up by 1.3 percentage points in 2023 but down by 0.4 percentage point in 2024.

In China, growth is projected to rebound to 5.6 percent in 2023, as the reopening, together with accumulated excess savings, supports household spending, particularly on contact-intensive services. Growth is then projected to moderate to 4.6 percent in 2024 and 4.4 percent in 2025, as reopening effects fade (figure 2.1.3.A). Investment growth is expected to pick up only modestly this year, supported by infrastructure-related stimulus and a gradual recovery in the property sector. Inflation is expected to remain below target due to existing economic slack, including in labor markets.

In EAP excluding China, growth is expected to moderate to a still-strong 4.8 percent this year as the tailwinds from reopening and pent-up demand fade. Positive spillovers from China's recovery are expected to be limited given its concentration on domestic services activity. Furthermore, these positive spillovers are likely to be outweighed in some cases by domestic headwinds, particularly elevated inflation and the continued effects of domestic monetary policy tightening. While both core and headline inflation are expected to ease through 2023, in the near-term headline inflation is likely to remain above central bank targets in some countries (Mongolia, Philippines) due to the delayed pass-through of increases in global commodity prices and domestic supply shocks. Moderating commodity prices will help reduce headline inflation this year but it will also weaken the terms of trade of commodity exporters, including Indonesia.

As in China, growth in the rest of EAP will be driven primarily by domestic demand, particularly consumption where buoyant labor markets are expected to help offset the drag from increased interest rates and debt-servicing costs. Investment growth is expected to remain solid, albeit somewhat dampened by high interest rates.

This year lackluster growth in global goods trade—a key engine of the region's growth in recent decades—is also expected to weigh on activity, notably in Malaysia and Vietnam where growth is projected to moderate. For the economies most dependent on tourism, however, the continued recovery in global tourism, boosted by an increase in tourists from China, will support growth (Fiji, Palau, Thailand; figure 2.1.3.B). Mongolia is expected to benefit from the end of border disruptions with China, its primary trading partner, which is anticipated to support a recovery in mining activity.

In all, growth in EAP excluding China is expected to remain at 4.8 percent in 2024 and 2025, largely unchanged from January forecasts, as inflation moderates further, supporting consumption and investment growth. In tandem, exports are expected to pick up as global growth recovers.

This year, fiscal policy stances in most major East Asian countries are expected to be either broadly neutral or mildly contractionary (figure 2.1.3.C). Fiscal consolidation in some countries (Philippines, Thailand) is expected to be underpinned by lower public spending, including the phasing out of pandemic- and cost-of-living-

FIGURE 2.1.2 EAP excluding China: Recent developments

Growth in the region excluding China slowed sharply in late 2022 and early 2023 as the boost from earlier reopening waned. Goods trade has been muted by weak external demand owing to modest growth in major advanced economies and a services sector-centered recovery in China. Inflation has declined from high levels in 2022 but remains above target in some countries. While a growing number of countries have regained pre-pandemic levels of output, recoveries from very deep recessions remain incomplete in most Pacific Island economies.

A. Growth in selected East Asian economies

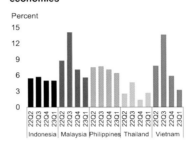

B. Growth of goods exports

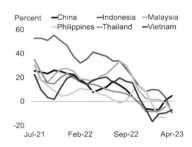

C. Consumer price inflation

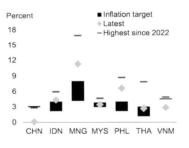

D. Deviation of 2022 GDP from pre-pandemic levels

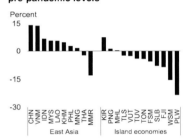

Sources: Haver Analytics; World Bank.
Note: In East Asia, CHN = China, IDN = Indonesia, LAO = Lao PDR, KHM = Cambodia, MMR = Myanmar, MNG = Mongolia, MYS = Malaysia, PHL = the Philippines, THA = Thailand, VNM = Vietnam. In Island economies, FJI = Fiji, FSM = Micronesia, Fed. Sts, KIR = Kiribati, MHL = Marshall Islands, PLW = Palau, PNG = Papua New Guinea, SLB = Solomon Islands, TLS = Timor-Leste, TON = Tonga, TUV = Tuvalu, VUT = Vanuatu, WSM = Samoa.
A. Year-on-year real GDP growth. Last observation is 2023Q1.
B. Figure shows 3-month moving average of year-on-year growth in the value of goods exports in U.S. dollars. Last observation is March 2023 for the Philippines and Thailand. Last observation is April 2023 for China, Indonesia, Malaysia and Vietnam.
C. Year-on-year consumer price inflation. "Highest" refers to the highest inflation rate since January 2022. "Inflation target" refers to the targets set by the respective central banks. Last observation is March 2023 for Malaysia. Last observation is April 2023 for China, Indonesia, Mongolia, the Philippines, Thailand, and Vietnam.
D. Figure shows the percent change in real GDP from 2019 to 2022.

related support measures, and lower public investment. This will exert modest headwinds on growth in 2023, but the impact is projected to diminish in 2024. While monetary policy tightening cycles appear to have mostly peaked, transmission lags suggest that high interest rates will continue to weigh on activity in the near term. Monetary policy easing is likely to be slow due to persistently elevated inflation. Moreover, in some

FIGURE 2.1.3 EAP: Outlook

Growth in the region is projected to strengthen to 5.5 percent in 2023, buoyed by a consumption-led rebound in China, before easing to 4.6 percent in 2024 and 4.5 percent in 2025. For most of the region, weakness in global goods trade is a headwind; however, tourism-dependent economies will see a boost from the continued recovery in global tourism, including that from China. Macroeconomic policy headwinds are expected to intensify this year as fiscal consolidation proceeds and central banks hold back easing in the face of persistent inflation, resulting in higher real interest rates.

A. China: Contributions to growth

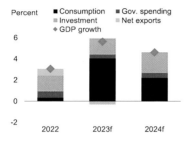

B. Tourist arrivals

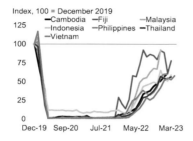

C. Fiscal impulse

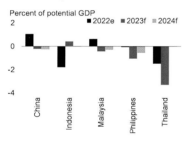

D. Real policy interest rates

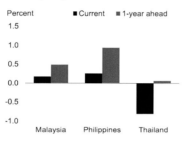

Sources: Bloomberg; Consensus Economics; Haver Analytics; International Monetary Fund; World Bank.

Note: e = estimate; f = forecast.

A. Annual real GDP growth and expenditure contributions to real GDP growth. 2023 and 2024 are projected by World Bank. Last observation is 2022.

B. Index of tourist arrivals. Last observation is April 2023 for Vietnam. Last observation is March 2023 for Fiji, Indonesia, and Thailand. Last observation is February 2023 for Cambodia and the Philippines. Last observation is December 2022 for Malaysia.

C. Bars denote change in general government structural balance. World Bank staff calculations based on IMF estimates. A positive value indicates a positive fiscal impulse to GDP.

D. Current real rate is the current policy rate minus the Consensus Economics 2023 inflation forecast; "1-year ahead" is the 30-day rolling average of the one-year-ahead market implied policy rate minus the Consensus Economics 2024 inflation forecast. Last observation is May 25, 2023.

countries, real interest rates are expected to increase over the coming year as headline inflation moderates, adding to the drag from higher nominal rates (figure 2.1.3.D). In China, monetary policy is expected to remain broadly accommodative amid modest inflationary pressures reflecting spare capacity.

Growth in EAP is expected to moderate over the longer term, in line with waning potential growth. Absent reforms, potential growth is expected to average 4.8 percent a year over the remainder of this decade, down from an average of 6.2 percent

a year in the decade to 2021, the largest decline of any EMDE region (Kose and Ohnsorge 2023). This primarily reflects slower capital accumulation and total factor productivity growth, especially in China. Population aging is also expected to exert a drag on EAP potential growth, as low fertility rates and rising longevity see working age populations in the region peak at lower income levels than in advanced economies (World Bank 2023a).

Risks

The baseline projection for the region is subject to several downside risks, including tighter-than-expected domestic and global financial conditions, persistently high inflation, continued weakness in China's property sector, and a faster-than-anticipated fading of the post-pandemic rebound in China. An intensification of geopolitical tensions presents a further downside risk, as do natural disasters, including extreme weather events related to climate change, which can impose particularly large costs on the small Pacific Island economies.

Tighter-than-expected global financial conditions, which could stem from a combination of further global banking sector turmoil and heightened investor risk aversion, or from tighter-than-expected monetary policy in major advanced economies, could have widespread adverse effects on the EAP region. Tighter global financial conditions could weigh on global growth and external demand and further dampen regional trade and activity (figure 2.1.4.A). It could also reduce capital inflows and lead to currency depreciations, which could be particularly costly for countries with large external borrowing needs or where external debt is high by EMDE standards (Cambodia, Mongolia). Currency depreciations, possibly associated with slowing capital inflows, could also give additional impetus to domestic inflation, forcing central banks to raise interest rates, compounding the drag on growth from existing policy tightening.

While external borrowing in EAP is generally lower than in other EMDE regions, overall debt levels have ratcheted up over the past decade due to increased borrowing by governments, households, and non-financial corporations (figure 2.1.4.B). Modest deleveraging over the past two years has done little to reverse the sharp run-up in debt during the initial phase of the COVID-19 pandemic. Elevated debt loads make debt distress more likely, particularly in the face of adverse shocks that lead to increased risk aversion and borrowing costs, and ultimately slower growth. This risk was highlighted by the jump in sovereign risk premia in less creditworthy EAP countries in response to bank failures in Europe and the United States in March. Reduced fiscal space also weakens the ability of governments to delay planned consolidation or provide support in the event of a renewed weakening of demand.

While the baseline forecast assumes that inflation will continue to gradually moderate across the region, there is a risk that it remains elevated. Higher input costs in the presence of robust demand, or smaller output gaps with tightening labor markets, could lead firms to increase prices further. Also, if global commodity prices do not decline as expected this would add to inflationary pressures across EAP.

China's property sector is subject to particular downside risks. While the authorities have provided liquidity support to property developers, there has been only modest progress in restructuring debts in a way that could restore the health of the sector. Moreover, while the sector's shares of investment and GDP have declined through the recent slump they remain high by historical standards, even though the growth of the urban population has slowed sharply (figure 2.1.4.C). Further adjustments may be necessary, particularly in smaller and lower-income cities, which account for sizeable shares of the housing stock and economic activity (Rogoff and Yang 2022).

The outlook for consumption in China is subject to both downside and upside risks. Possible future disruptive COVID-19 waves could heighten caution among households, prompting them to hoard savings. This could hold back consumer spending and weigh on growth. In the decade before the pandemic, consumption grew strongly, supporting output growth (figure 2.1.4.D). However, in the last few years, as the pandemic curtailed spending, increased uncertainty, and

FIGURE 2.1.4 EAP: Risks

Trade and growth in the region could be dampened by tighter-than-expected financial conditions due to additional monetary policy rate hikes, domestically or in major advanced economies; renewed global financial instability; or heightened investor risk aversion. Increased debt in the region adds to the risk of debt distress and also reduces fiscal space, limiting policy room to maneuver in the event of deteriorating conditions. Against a backdrop of slowing urban population growth, weakness in China's property sector could endure. Heightened uncertainty in China in response to further disruptive COVID-19 waves could hold back consumption.

A. Manufacturing exports

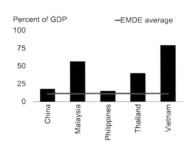

B. Debt

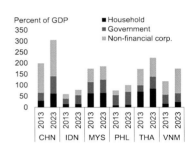

C. China: Real estate investment and urban population growth

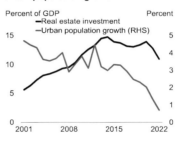

D. China: Consumption and investment shares of GDP

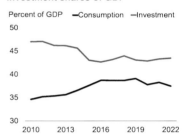

Sources: Haver Analytics; Institute of International Finance (database); National Bureau of Statistics of China; World Bank.
Note: EMDEs = emerging market and developing economies. CHN = China; IDN = Indonesia; MYS = Malaysia; PHL = the Philippines; THA = Thailand; VNM = Vietnam.
A. Manufacturing exports as a share of GDP in 2021. Line is the simple average of 99 EMDEs.
B. Components of countries' debt as a share of GDP. Observation for 2013 is 2013Q1 and for 2023 is 2023Q1. Last observation is 2023Q1.
C. Figure shows investment completed in real estate development as share of GDP (left axis) and annual growth of urban population (right axis). Last observation is 2022.
D. Figure shows consumption and investment shares of GDP. Last observation is 2022.

weakened labor markets, households increased their savings. As a result, consumption growth faltered, and this could continue. Conversely, a robust economic recovery underpinned by strong productivity and employment growth, and brighter prospects in the property market, could boost sentiment and sustain stronger-than-projected consumption growth.

Geopolitical tensions could intensify, increasing uncertainty, disrupting trade, and holding back investment, both in China and the region more broadly. For China, tensions have already disrupted access to some forms of high-technology manufacturing products, notably semiconductors and related materials. Other countries in the region are vulnerable to heightened tensions between China and the United States, given their strong trade and financial linkages with these two economies and their extensive integration in global value chains (World Bank 2023a).

Finally, natural disasters, including extreme weather events related to climate change, present downside risks to the outlook. Extreme weather events can cause economic harm by damaging infrastructure and disrupting activity, reducing domestic agricultural output—which can stoke food inflation—and weakening government finances through lower revenues and higher outlays associated with reconstruction. The twin cyclones and earthquake that hit Vanuatu earlier this year underscore the vulnerability of the Pacific Island economies to natural disasters, given their remoteness, reliance on imported goods and international tourism, and weak public finances (World Bank 2023b).

TABLE 2.1.1 East Asia and Pacific forecast summary

(Real GDP growth at market prices in percent, unless indicated otherwise)

Percentage point differences from January 2023 projections

	2020	2021	2022e	2023f	2024f	2025f	2023f	2024f
EMDE EAP, GDP [1]	1.2	7.5	3.5	5.5	4.6	4.5	1.2	-0.3
GDP per capita (U.S. dollars)	0.8	7.1	3.2	5.2	4.4	4.2	1.1	-0.2
(Average including countries that report expenditure components in national accounts) [2]								
EMDE EAP, GDP [2]	1.2	7.6	3.5	5.5	4.6	4.5	1.1	-0.3
PPP GDP	0.8	7.3	3.7	5.4	4.7	4.5	1.0	-0.2
Private consumption	-2.0	9.5	2.1	9.6	5.4	5.3	4.3	-0.7
Public consumption	3.1	3.3	3.6	2.5	3.3	2.7	-2.0	-0.7
Fixed investment	2.2	3.1	3.5	3.7	4.7	4.6	-0.3	0.2
Exports, GNFS [3]	-1.5	16.6	3.2	2.2	3.4	3.4	-0.9	-0.3
Imports, GNFS [3]	-3.9	12.4	0.7	3.0	3.9	3.9	-1.7	-1.1
Net exports, contribution to growth	0.5	1.2	0.6	-0.1	0.0	0.0	0.1	0.1
Memo items: GDP								
China	2.2	8.4	3.0	5.6	4.6	4.4	1.3	-0.4
East Asia excluding China	-3.7	2.6	5.8	4.8	4.8	4.8	0.1	0.1
Indonesia	-2.1	3.7	5.3	4.9	4.9	5.0	0.1	0.0
Thailand	-6.1	1.5	2.6	3.9	3.6	3.4	0.3	-0.1
Commodity exporters	-1.8	2.0	5.1	4.7	4.7	4.7	0.0	0.1
Commodity importers excl. China	-5.3	3.1	6.3	4.9	4.8	4.8	0.2	0.0
Pacific Island Economies [4]	-5.3	-0.9	5.0	3.8	4.2	3.2	0.0	0.9

Source: World Bank.

Note: e = estimate; f = forecast; PPP = purchasing power parity; EMDE = emerging market and developing economy. World Bank forecasts are frequently updated based on new information and changing (global) circumstances. Consequently, projections presented here may differ from those contained in other Bank documents, even if basic assessments of countries' prospects do not differ at any given moment in time.

1. GDP and expenditure components are measured in average 2010-19 prices and market exchange rates. Excludes the Democratic People's Republic of Korea and dependent territories.
2. Subregion aggregate excludes the Democratic People's Republic of Korea, dependent territories, Fiji, Kiribati, the Marshall Islands, the Federated States of Micronesia, Myanmar, Palau, Papua New Guinea, Samoa, Timor-Leste, Tonga, and Tuvalu, for which data limitations prevent the forecasting of GDP components.
3. Exports and imports of goods and non-factor services (GNFS).
4. Includes Fiji, Kiribati, the Marshall Islands, the Federated States of Micronesia, Nauru, Palau, Papua New Guinea, Samoa, the Solomon Islands, Tonga, Tuvalu, and Vanuatu.

TABLE 2.1.2 East Asia and Pacific country forecasts [1]

(Real GDP growth at market prices in percent, unless indicated otherwise)

Percentage point differences from January 2023 projections

	2020	2021	2022e	2023f	2024f	2025f	2023f	2024f
Cambodia	-3.1	3.0	5.2	5.5	6.1	6.3	0.3	-0.2
China	2.2	8.4	3.0	5.6	4.6	4.4	1.3	-0.4
Fiji	-17.0	-5.1	16.1	5.0	4.1	3.5	-0.4	0.7
Indonesia	-2.1	3.7	5.3	4.9	4.9	5.0	0.1	0.0
Kiribati	-1.4	7.9	1.2	2.5	2.4	2.3	0.2	0.3
Lao PDR	0.5	2.5	2.7	3.9	4.2	4.4	0.1	0.0
Malaysia	-5.5	3.1	8.7	4.3	4.2	4.2	0.3	0.3
Marshall Islands	-2.2	1.1	1.5	1.9	2.1	2.3	-0.3	-0.4
Micronesia, Fed. Sts.	-1.8	-3.2	-0.6	2.9	2.8	1.3	-0.1	0.3
Mongolia	-4.4	1.6	4.7	5.2	6.3	6.8	-0.1	-0.1
Myanmar [2]	3.2	-18.0	3.0	3.0	..	..	0.0	..
Nauru	0.7	1.5	3.0	1.0	2.0	2.5	-0.9	-0.8
Palau	-8.9	-13.4	-2.8	12.3	9.1	4.7	-5.9	4.6
Papua New Guinea	-3.2	0.1	4.5	3.7	4.4	3.1	0.2	1.1
Philippines	-9.5	5.7	7.6	6.0	5.9	5.9	0.6	0.0
Samoa	-3.1	-7.1	-6.0	5.0	3.4	3.3	1.0	-0.1
Solomon Islands	-3.4	-0.6	-4.1	2.5	2.4	3.0	-0.1	0.0
Thailand	-6.1	1.5	2.6	3.9	3.6	3.4	0.3	-0.1
Timor-Leste	-8.3	2.9	3.5	3.0	3.2	3.2	0.0	0.2
Tonga	0.5	-2.7	-2.0	2.5	2.8	2.6	-0.8	-0.4
Tuvalu	-4.9	0.3	0.6	4.2	3.1	2.6	0.7	-0.9
Vanuatu	-5.0	0.6	1.9	0.5	4.0	3.9	-2.9	0.5
Vietnam	2.9	2.6	8.0	6.0	6.2	6.5	-0.3	-0.3

Source: World Bank.

Note: e = estimate; f = forecast. World Bank forecasts are frequently updated based on new information and changing (global) circumstances. Consequently, projections presented here may differ from those contained in other Bank documents, even if basic assessments of countries' prospects do not significantly differ at any given moment in time.

1. Data are based on GDP measured in average 2010-19 prices and market exchange rates. Values for Timor-Leste represent non-oil GDP. For the following countries, values correspond to the fiscal year: the Marshall Islands, the Federated States of Micronesia, Myanmar, and Palau (October 1– September 30); Nauru, Samoa, and Tonga (July 1–June 30).
2. Forecast for Myanmar beyond 2023 are excluded because of a high degree of uncertainty.

EUROPE and CENTRAL ASIA

Economic prospects in Europe and Central Asia (ECA) continue to be held back by the Russian Federation's invasion of Ukraine. Growth in ECA is projected to remain weak in 2023, edging up to a modest 1.4 percent, as the effects of the invasion, high inflation, tight monetary policies, and subdued external demand weigh on activity. Regional growth is forecast to pick up to 2.7 percent in 2024, as inflation gradually recedes and demand firms. Risks to the outlook are tilted to the downside and include an intensification of Russia's invasion in Ukraine, rising geopolitical tensions elsewhere in the region, higher and more sustained inflation, a sharper economic slowdown than expected in the region's main trading partners, and further financial sector turmoil.

Recent developments

Growth in Europe and Central Asia (ECA) plummeted to 1.2 percent in 2022—the slowest growth among the six EMDE regions. Even after excluding Russia and Ukraine, regional growth still softened last year to 4.8 percent. The slowdown was broad-based, including most of the region's economies, reflecting disruptions from Russia's invasion, reduced business and consumer confidence, a surge in inflation, marked monetary tightening, and energy supply disruptions. Output fell by 20.2 percent in Eastern Europe, with contractions mainly in Ukraine, but also elsewhere in the subregion. In Central Europe and the Western Balkans, which are more closely integrated into European Union (EU) value chains, growth was dampened by steep energy price increases, energy supply disruptions, and monetary policy tightening. In contrast, growth was more resilient in the South Caucasus and Türkiye, amid inflows of trade, migrants, and finance from Russia and Ukraine—factors that also supported growth in Central Asia. The slowdown in commodity exporters other than Russia was limited by higher global commodity prices (figure 2.2.1.A; World Bank 2023c).

Output in Ukraine fell by about 29 percent last year, somewhat less dramatically than expected

earlier. The reopening of Ukraine's Black Sea ports and the resumption of grain trade offset some of the impact of Russia's invasion on activity. As of May 2023, more than 30 million tons of grain and other foodstuffs had been exported via the Black Sea Grain Initiative, which has been extended until mid-July. External official financing also helped to mitigate some of the invasion's impact. By the end of 2022, the destruction of critical energy infrastructure had affected about 40 percent of the power grid, and it continues to weigh on activity. However, there are indications that firms and households have somewhat adapted to the outages.

In Russia, ECA's largest economy, output contracted 2.1 percent in 2022, amid international sanctions imposed in response to Russia's invasion of Ukraine. The recession was less severe than projected earlier, due to higher oil production, the redirection of oil exports away from traditional markets, and more government fiscal support than initially assumed. Clear signs of trade diversion emerged following the invasion, with the value of Russian fuel exports to the EU declining by over 40 percent last year, while exports to India and China increased (figure 2.2.1.B). Russian imports from Türkiye more than doubled. Those trends were also reinforced since the beginning of the year, with Russia's fuel exports to the EU falling by 87 percent in March from a year earlier (Darvas, Martins, and McCaffrey 2023; World

---

Note: This section was prepared by Marie Albert.

FIGURE 2.2.1 **ECA: Recent developments**

Regional growth slowed to 1.2 percent, in 2022, with divergences among the subregions. Contraction in the Russian Federation's economy last year was less severe than initially expected, partly due to the diversification of trade flows. Türkiye suffered major earthquakes in February 2023. Inflation increased significantly over the last year, accompanied by hikes in monetary policy interest rates in most countries of the region.

A. Growth in 2022

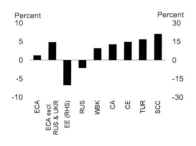

B. Destination of Russia's mineral fuels exports

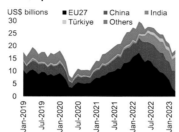

C. Impact of the earthquake in Türkiye in the most affected regions

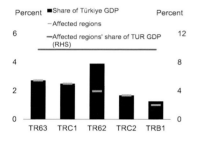

D. Changes in inflation and policy rates since April 2021 by country

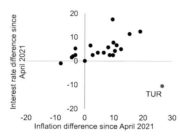

Sources: Darvas, Martins, and McCaffrey (database); Haver Analytics; Turkish Statistical Institute; World Bank.
Note: CA = Central Asia; CE = Central Europe and Baltic Countries; ECA = Europe and Central Asia; EE = Eastern Europe; EU27 = European Union (27 members); RUS = Russian Federation; SCC = South Caucasus; TR62 = Adana Subregion; TR63 = Hatay Subregion; TRB1 = Malatya Subregion; TRC1 = Gaziantep Subregion; TRC2 = Şanlıurfa Subregion; TUR = Türkiye; WBK = Western Balkans. Unless otherwise indicated, GDP aggregates are calculated using real U.S. dollar GDP weights at average 2010-19 prices and market exchange rates.
A. Columns show GDP growth for 2022 (observed if available, otherwise estimated).
B. Monthly data from January 2019 to March 2023 on the total Russian Federation's mineral fuel exports among 36 countries. "Others" include Brazil, Japan, Norway, the Republic of Korea, Switzerland, the UK, and the U.S.
C. Columns show 2021 data on each of the affected NUTS-2 regions' GDP (basic regions for the application of regional policies), as a share of Türkiye GDP. Yellow lines show the affected NUTS-3 regions' GDP (small regions for specific diagnoses), as a share of Türkiye GDP. The red line shows the aggregated value of the affected NUTS-3 regions GDP, as a share of Türkiye GDP.
D. X-axis shows CPI inflation difference between April 2021 and April 2023. Y-axis is the monetary policy interest rate difference between April 2021 and April 2023. Blue circles correspond to ECA economies. The red circle corresponds to Türkiye.

Bank 2023d). Broader regional trade patterns changed as a result of the invasion, with more Western countries exporting to Central Asia and the Caucasus. Simultaneously, there was a rise in exports from those countries to Russia. However, this apparent "intermediated trade" is only a fraction of what was previously exported directly to Russia (Chupilkin, Javorcik, and Plekhanov 2023; Darvis, Matins, and McCaffrey 2023). An

extension of the voluntary oil production cut of 500,000 bpd until the end of this year was announced in April, as part of an agreement by the members of OPEC+. Russian activity contracted by 1.9 percent year on year in the first quarter of 2023.

Türkiye was hit by two major earthquakes in early February, with direct losses estimated at 4 percent of 2021 GDP. However, the full costs of recovery and reconstruction could be twice as high (figure 2.2.1.C; World Bank 2023e). The evolution of macroeconomic policies is uncertain against the backdrop of high inflation, which has been met with further interest rate cuts by the central bank, alongside the general elections that took place last May. Exchange rate depreciation, as well as a high current account deficit and low net forex reserves also present significant challenges. Despite these headwinds, the country remains a key contributor to ECA growth, and the economy remained resilient in the first quarter of 2023.

Inflation remains high in ECA, especially in Türkiye. While nominal wage increases have generally lagged inflation, real wages dropped by as much as 3.3 percent in Eastern Europe in the first half of 2022, with Central Asia and South Caucasus the exceptions (ILO 2023). In those two subregions, diversion flows from Russia boosted domestic demand, which contributed to higher inflation. Recent signs of deceleration in 12-month inflation rates in some ECA countries, can be attributed to base effects and because of the decline in energy prices from last year's record highs. Core inflation remains elevated. To rein in the above-target inflation, 17 central banks in the region raised policy rates in 2022, and 6 have raised them further so far in 2023 (figure 2.2.1.D).

Outlook

Growth in ECA is projected to edge up slightly in 2023, to 1.4 percent; however the outlook remains particularly uncertain due to Russia's invasion of Ukraine and its repercussions. The baseline assumes that the invasion continues throughout the forecast period but with no escalation in its intensity. Excluding Russia and Ukraine, growth in ECA is projected to nearly halve in 2023, to 2.4 percent. The 1.3 percentage points forecast upgrade since January for the region is mainly because of an upward revision for Russia (figure 2.2.2.A). Regional growth is projected to rebound to 2.7 percent a year in 2024-2025, driven by stronger external and domestic demand, in a context of fading adverse growth shocks. Divergences in growth rates within the region should fade as migrant and capital flows from Russia ease, and growth improves in the EU. After declining in 2023, the projected increase in oil prices in 2024-2025 should benefit oil exporters.

The dual shocks of the COVID-19 pandemic and Russia's invasion had a significant impact on regional growth, which is expected to remain below its potential rate during the forecast horizon. This dampening is attributed to tighter financial conditions and gradual fiscal consolidation in many countries. Potential growth in the region is projected to slow to an annual average pace of 3 percent in 2022-30, down from 3.6 percent in 2011-21. Potential growth is expected to depend increasingly on capital accumulation as the growth rates of both the labor force, including of women, and total factor productivity are set to weaken (figure 2.2.2.B; Kilic Celik, Kose and Ohnsorge 2023).

Output in *Russia* is projected to contract slightly, by 0.2 percent in 2023, a 3.1 percentage point upgrade from the January 2023 forecast.[1] This change mainly reflects the unexpected resilience of oil production and higher-than-expected growth momentum from 2022. Continued contraction in export volumes, weak domestic demand, policy uncertainty, and sanctions due to Russia's invasion of Ukraine will continue to weigh on activity. In 2024, growth is expected to turn positive, but remain modest at only 1.2 percent, which is lower than the average pace of growth in the 2010s. The economy is expected to confront persistent structural problems, including unfavorable

---

[1] Growth forecasts for Russia are subject to a high degree of uncertainty due to the significant changes to the economy associated with the Russia's invasion in Ukraine. Moreover, the decision by Russia to limit publication of economic data, notably related to external trade, and the financial and monetary sectors, adds to the uncertainty.

FIGURE 2.2.2 ECA: Outlook

Growth in ECA is projected to firm modestly in 2023, as activity stabilizes in the Russian Federation and Ukraine. Potential growth in the region is expected to slow further in the current decade following the trend decline since 2000. In Ukraine, large-scale emigration and significant disruptions in education exacerbate long-term damage to the country's human capital and potential output. Central Europe will benefit from funding from the EU Recovery and Resilience Facility (RRF).

A. Contributions to ECA GDP growth

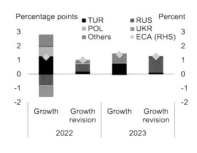

B. Contributions to potential output growth

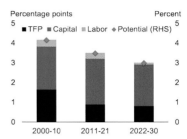

C. Refugees from Ukraine

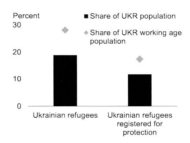

D. Amount of RRF and NGEU impact

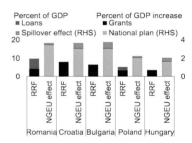

Sources: Kilic Celik, Kose, and Ohnsorge (2023); NGEU tracker; Pfeiffer, Varga, and in 't Veld (2021); UNHCR; World Bank.
Note: ECA = Europe and Central Asia; NGEU = NextGenerationEU; POL = Poland; RRF = Recovery and Resilience Facility; RUS = Russian Federation; TFP = total factor productivity; TUR = Türkiye; UKR = Ukraine.
A. Figure shows the contributions to ECA GDP growth and the growth revisions compared with January 2023 (World Bank 2023b).
B. Period averages of annual GDP-weighted averages. Estimates based on production function approach. The sample includes 9 ECA countries (Türkiye, 2 in Central Asia, 4 in Central Europe, 1 in South Caucasus, and 1 in Western Balkans). The Russian Federation and Ukraine are excluded.
C. Columns show the number of refugees from Ukraine recorded across Europe and registered for Temporary Protection or similar national protection schemes in Europe. Data as of May 2023.
D. Blue and red columns denote loans and grants given to European Union member states from the Recovery and Resilience Facility as a share of member states' GDP in 2022. Orange and yellow columns show the percent of GDP increase of NextGenerationEU (NGEU) until 2024 in a high productivity scenario (Max effect NGEU) and is decomposed into the National plan and spillover effects of other plans.

demographic trends, and a low investment rate and productivity.

In *Ukraine*, Russia's invasion continues to take a heavy human and economic toll. The outlook is marked by pronounced uncertainty. Output is anticipated to expand by 2 percent in 2023. This represents a downgrade of 1.3 percentage points since January, mostly to take account of the economic disruptions caused by the destruction of energy infrastructure in the fourth quarter of 2022. Public finances will remain under pressure despite official external support, including the recently agreed IMF financing of $15.6 billion under the Extended Fund Facility (IMF 2023a). Reconstruction and recovery costs have been estimated at 2.6 times the 2022 level of GDP and more than 8 million refugees have been recorded across Europe (figure 2.2.2.C; World Bank 2023f).

Growth in *Türkiye* is anticipated to slow to 3.2 percent in 2023 before rebounding to 4.3 percent in 2024, assuming normalization in macroeconomic policies with a tightening of the policy mix, with domestic demand remaining the key driver.[2] Despite the damage caused by the earthquakes in early 2023, forecasted growth in both years is slightly higher than previously projected, partly owing to positive momentum from strong growth in late 2022 and additional government support to households. Reconstruction efforts are expected to support investment.

In *Central Europe*, growth is anticipated to experience a significant further decline to 1.1 percent this year, as a result of the slowdown in the euro area and the tightening of domestic monetary policies. Growth is expected to gather pace in 2024-25, partly owing to increased use of funding from the EU Recovery and Resilience Facility (RRF), including by Bulgaria and Croatia, a new member of the euro area since January 2023 (figure 2.2.2.D; Pfeiffer, Varga, and in't Veld 2021).

In the *Western Balkans*, growth is forecast to decelerate to 2.6 percent in 2023, reflecting spillovers from Russia's invasion of Ukraine, lower private consumption, tight global financial conditions, and weaker growth of demand from the euro area. Fiscal consolidation should be limited, with higher fiscal spending expected in several economies. Growth should pick up moderately in 2024-2025, driven partly by strengthening growth in the EU (World Bank 2023g).

In the *South Caucasus*, growth in 2023 is projected to slow to 3 percent, as growth weakens in the EU and migrant and capital flows from Russia ease. Private sector growth remains constrained by poor connectivity and infrastructure, skills mismatch, and weaknesses in the business environment. Growth in the subregion is projected to pick up somewhat, to an annual average of 3.5 percent, in 2024-25.

Growth in *Central Asia* is anticipated to remain flat at 4 percent in 2023. Slower growth in the Kyrgyz Republic, Tajikistan, and Uzbekistan, due to lower remittances from Russia, is offset by robust, energy sector-driven growth in Kazakhstan. Growth is expected to increase modestly in 2024-25, as investment growth strengthens thanks to FDI in mining, and inflation returns to pre-pandemic rates in tandem with global inflation, mainly reflecting lower energy prices. Energy access remains an important challenge for countries like the Kyrgyz Republic and Tajikistan. Structural reforms to increase international competitiveness and boost the private sector are likely to increase potential growth in the longer term. In Uzbekistan, the government aims to partially privatize state-owned enterprises (SOEs) and state-owned banks, while in Kazakhstan, a new independent competition agency and a privatization plan for 2021-2025 should help to reduce the role of SOEs.

Risks

Risks to the regional outlook remain tilted to the downside. These include the possibility of a more intense or prolonged Russia's invasion of Ukraine, a protracted period of tighter monetary policies amid elevated inflation, and weaker-than-expected external demand. Downside risks also include financial sector stress, the possibility of an escalation in geopolitical tensions in other parts of the region, and greater dislocations from possible adverse weather events associated with climate change. An escalation of the invasion of Ukraine could increase the risk of energy insecurity, as the region continues to be vulnerable to supply disruptions and its dependency on Russia.

A steeper-than-expected slowdown in the euro area could further dampen external demand.

---

[2] As for other countries, the "errors and omissions" in the balance of payments data has increased, reflecting large unexplained financial flows.

Countries in Central Europe and the Western Balkans would be hardest hit since the euro area accounts for a relatively high proportion of their exports—about 52 percent on average for 2010-19 (World Bank 2023h).

The costs of sending remittances from Russia have been raised significantly by international sanctions in response to the invasion (IMF 2023b). Such remittances could grow more slowly than projected this year, especially in Central Asia and South Caucasus, where remittances from Russia accounted for 57 percent in 2021 and were equivalent on average to 12 percent of the GDP of the two subregions during 2010-19 (figure 2.2.3.A; World Bank 2022a).

More sustained inflation than expected would erode real disposable incomes and consumer confidence. A resurgence in food or energy prices would heighten concerns for the food or energy security of vulnerable households, particularly in countries where fiscal space is lacking (World Bank 2023d). Inflation could be more persistent as tensions have been observed in some real estate markets, with rental prices increasing due to a higher demand, also associated with migrant inflows in the Eastern part of the ECA region. Inflation may not decline to the target levels of some central banks over the next year (figure 2.2.3.B).

Central banks could hike policy rates by more than currently expected if inflation remains persistently high; however the potency of monetary policy transmission to bank lending remains weak in some countries, especially in the East of the region. Further monetary policy tightening would increase borrowing costs and lead to a more pronounced slowdown. Financial stress among sovereigns, banks, and non-bank financial institutions may result not only from additional monetary tightening but also from concerns associated with a possible weaker growth in an environment of elevated debt. Moreover, further stress in the banking sectors of advanced economies could spill over to the region and lead to exchange rate pressures, increasing foreign exchange credit and liquidity risks, especially in the Caucasus and Central Asia, characterized by high levels of

FIGURE 2.2.3 ECA: Risks

Risks to the regional outlook remain tilted to the downside, including lower remittances and more persistent inflation than projected in the baseline. Financial sector stress could affect already-fragile banking systems. Climate-change-related extreme weather events could also increase in frequency or severity and exacerbate the already-high welfare costs of pollution.

A. Remittances inflows

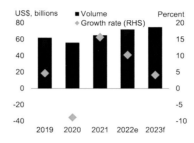

B. Inflation expectations and targets

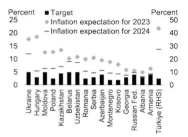

C. Dollarization in South Caucasus and Central Asia

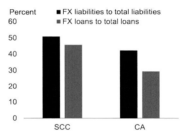

D. Welfare costs of pollution

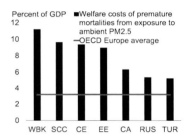

Sources: Consensus Economics; IMF financial soundness indicators; national sources; OECD Stats; World Bank.
Note: e = estimate; f = forecast; PM2.5 = fine particulate matter of size 2.5 micrometers. CA = Central Asia; CE = Central Europe and Baltic Countries; ECA = Europe and Central Asia; EE = Eastern Europe; RUS = Russian Federation; SCC = South Caucasus; TUR = Türkiye; WBK = Western Balkans.
A. Blue bars represent estimates and projections of remittance volume, represented in billions of U.S. dollars, in the ECA region. The yellow diamond represents estimates and projections of the growth rate of remittance flows.
B. Figure shows the median Consensus Economics forecast of headline CPI inflation for 2023-24 based on the May 2023 surveys of 16 ECA economies. Inflation targets as of May 2023.
C. Blue columns show the average foreign currency-denominated liabilities to total liabilities ratio for the countries of the subregion. Red columns show the foreign currency-denominated loans to total loans ratio for the countries of the subregion. Annual data as of 2022 when available (2021 or 2020 data used otherwise).
D. Blue columns represent the welfare costs of premature mortalities to ambient PM2.5 pollution, in percent of GDP. Red line represents the OECD Europe average. This indicator uses estimates of premature mortality and morbidity attributable to ambient PM2.5 air pollution to value the economic cost in dollar terms. Data as of 2020.

dollarization (figure 2.2.3.C; Khandelwal et al. 2022).

Political uncertainty remains significant in the region. There are questions in several countries about prospects for progress with structural reforms that are assumed in the baseline (Bosnia and Herzegovina, Montenegro, North Macedonia). There is still no agreement to form a coalition government in Bulgaria, following April's parliamentary election (the 5th in two years). In Georgia, authorities dropped a controversial foreign agent law after mass protests. In Türkiye, macroeconomic policies may change following the elections last month. Border tensions threaten a resumption of further escalation of tensions between Armenia and Azerbaijan, while tensions between Kosovo and Serbia have reduced in the context of the recent advances in the dialogue on the implementation of an EU-sponsored plan to normalize relations.

Finally, natural disasters, illustrated recently by the earthquakes in Türkiye but also by several extreme weather events, could disrupt economic activity. Without further action to mitigate or adapt to climate change, economic damage from droughts and floods in Central Asia is projected to amount to the equivalent of 1.3 percent of GDP per year (World Bank 2022b). About 96 percent of the ECA population is exposed to levels of pollution exceeding World Health Organization guideline values. The welfare costs of premature deaths due to PM2.5 pollution have been estimated at the equivalent of between 5 to 11 percent of GDP in the subregions, well above the European average of 3 percent (figure 2.2.3.D; OECD 2022).

TABLE 2.2.1 Europe and Central Asia forecast summary

(Real GDP growth at market prices in percent, unless indicated otherwise)

Percentage point differences
from January 2023 projections

	2020	2021	2022e	2023f	2024f	2025f	2023f	2024f
EMDE ECA, GDP [1]	-1.7	7.1	1.2	1.4	2.7	2.7	1.3	-0.1
GDP per capita (U.S. dollars)	-1.9	7.0	1.3	1.4	2.6	2.5	1.2	0.0
EMDE ECA excl. Russian Federation, Türkiye, and Ukraine, GDP	-2.7	6.4	4.3	1.8	3.2	3.4	0.1	0.1
EMDE ECA excl. Russian Federation and Ukraine, GDP	-1.0	8.3	4.8	2.4	3.6	3.7	0.3	0.2
EMDE ECA excl. Türkiye, GDP	-2.7	5.9	-0.1	0.8	2.2	2.3	1.5	-0.2
(Average including countries that report expenditure components in national accounts) [2]								
EMDE ECA, GDP [2]	-1.7	7.2	0.9	1.2	2.6	2.6	1.4	-0.1
PPP GDP	-1.7	7.2	0.3	1.2	2.7	2.6	1.3	0.0
Private consumption	-2.5	10.1	5.0	1.4	2.7	2.9	0.5	-0.5
Public consumption	2.5	3.2	1.5	3.6	1.6	2.2	1.2	-0.4
Fixed investment	-1.1	6.3	3.3	3.4	5.0	3.4	5.0	0.9
Exports, GNFS [3]	-6.5	10.3	0.5	0.5	4.5	5.0	0.7	0.1
Imports, GNFS [3]	-4.5	12.6	1.8	4.1	5.9	5.8	-0.5	-0.8
Net exports, contribution to growth	-1.0	-0.4	-0.4	-1.3	-0.5	-0.3	0.3	0.2
Memo items: GDP								
Commodity exporters [4]	-2.6	5.5	-2.5	0.6	1.8	1.6	2.4	-0.4
Commodity exporters excl. Russian Federation and Ukraine	-2.1	5.4	4.5	3.8	4.1	4.0	0.0	0.0
Commodity importers [5]	-0.8	8.7	4.8	2.2	3.5	3.6	0.3	0.2
Central Europe [6]	-2.9	6.7	4.8	1.1	2.9	3.3	0.0	0.2
Western Balkans [7]	-3.1	7.7	3.1	2.6	3.1	3.6	0.1	0.0
Eastern Europe [8]	-3.1	3.6	-20.2	1.5	2.8	4.5	0.4	-0.7
South Caucasus [9]	-5.2	6.7	7.0	3.0	3.4	3.6	-0.3	-0.1
Central Asia [10]	-1.4	5.2	4.2	4.0	4.4	4.2	0.1	0.1
Russian Federation	-2.7	5.6	-2.1	-0.2	1.2	0.8	3.1	-0.4
Türkiye	1.9	11.4	5.6	3.2	4.3	4.1	0.5	0.3
Poland	-2.0	6.9	5.1	0.7	2.6	3.2	0.0	0.4

Source: World Bank.

Note: e = estimate; f = forecast; PPP = purchasing power parity; EMDE = emerging market and developing economy. World Bank forecasts are frequently updated based on new information and changing (global) circumstances. Consequently, projections presented here may differ from those contained in other Bank documents, even if basic assessments of countries' prospects do not differ at any given moment in time. The World Bank is currently not publishing economic output, income, or growth data for Turkmenistan owing to a lack of reliable data of adequate quality. Turkmenistan is excluded from cross-country macroeconomic aggregates. Since Croatia became a member of the euro area on January 1, 2023, it has been added to the euro area aggregate and removed from the ECA aggregate in all tables to avoid double counting.

1. GDP and expenditure components are measured in average 2010-19 prices and market exchange rates, thus aggregates presented here may differ from other World Bank documents.
2. Aggregates presented here exclude Azerbaijan, Bosnia and Herzegovina, Kazakhstan, Kosovo, the Kyrgyz Republic, Montenegro, Serbia, Tajikistan, Turkmenistan, and Uzbekistan, for which data limitations prevent the forecasting of GDP components.
3. Exports and imports of goods and nonfactor services (GNFS).
4. Includes Armenia, Azerbaijan, Kazakhstan, the Kyrgyz Republic, Kosovo, the Russian Federation, Tajikistan, Ukraine, and Uzbekistan.
5. Includes Albania, Belarus, Bosnia and Herzegovina, Bulgaria, Georgia, Hungary, Moldova, Montenegro, North Macedonia, Poland, Romania, Serbia, and Türkiye.
6. Includes Bulgaria, Hungary, Poland, and Romania.
7. Includes Albania, Bosnia and Herzegovina, Kosovo, Montenegro, North Macedonia, and Serbia.
8. Includes Belarus, Moldova, and Ukraine.
9. Includes Armenia, Azerbaijan, and Georgia.
10. Includes Kazakhstan, the Kyrgyz Republic, Tajikistan, and Uzbekistan.

TABLE 2.2.2 Europe and Central Asia country forecasts [1]

(Real GDP growth at market prices in percent, unless indicated otherwise)

Percentage point differences from January 2023 projections

	2020	2021	2022e	2023f	2024f	2025f	2023f	2024f
Albania	-3.3	8.9	4.8	2.8	3.3	3.3	0.6	-0.1
Armenia	-7.2	5.7	12.6	4.4	4.8	5.0	0.3	0.0
Azerbaijan	-4.2	5.6	4.6	2.2	2.5	2.6	-0.6	-0.1
Belarus	-0.7	2.4	-4.7	0.6	1.4	1.3	2.9	-1.1
Bosnia and Herzegovina[2]	-3.0	7.4	3.9	2.5	3.0	3.5	0.0	0.0
Bulgaria	-4.0	7.6	3.4	1.5	2.8	3.0	-0.2	-0.5
Croatia	-8.6	13.1	6.3	1.9	3.1	3.3	1.1	0.0
Georgia	-6.8	10.5	10.1	4.4	5.0	5.0	0.4	0.0
Hungary	-4.7	7.2	4.6	0.6	2.6	2.6	0.1	0.4
Kazakhstan	-2.6	4.1	3.3	3.5	4.0	3.6	0.0	0.0
Kosovo	-5.3	10.7	3.5	3.7	4.4	4.2	0.0	0.2
Kyrgyz Republic	-8.4	6.2	7.0	3.5	4.0	4.0	0.0	0.0
Moldova	-7.4	13.9	-5.9	1.8	4.2	4.1	0.2	0.0
Montenegro	-15.3	13.0	6.1	3.4	3.1	2.9	0.0	0.0
North Macedonia	-4.7	3.9	2.1	2.4	2.7	2.9	0.0	0.0
Poland	-2.0	6.9	5.1	0.7	2.6	3.2	0.0	0.4
Romania	-3.7	5.8	4.7	2.6	3.9	4.1	0.0	-0.3
Russian Federation	-2.7	5.6	-2.1	-0.2	1.2	0.8	3.1	-0.4
Serbia	-0.9	7.5	2.3	2.3	3.0	3.8	0.0	0.0
Tajikistan	4.4	9.4	8.0	6.5	5.0	4.5	1.5	1.0
Türkiye	1.9	11.4	5.6	3.2	4.3	4.1	0.5	0.3
Ukraine[3]	-3.8	3.4	-29.1	2.0	..	..	-1.3	..
Uzbekistan	2.0	7.4	5.7	5.1	5.4	5.8	0.2	0.3

Source: World Bank.

Note: e = estimate; f = forecast. World Bank forecasts are frequently updated based on new information and changing (global) circumstances. Consequently, projections presented here may differ from those contained in other Bank documents, even if basic assessments of countries' prospects do not significantly differ at any given moment in time. The World Bank is currently not publishing economic output, income, or growth data for Turkmenistan owing to a lack of reliable data of adequate quality. Turkmenistan is excluded from cross-country macroeconomic aggregates.

1. Data are based on GDP measured in average 2010-19 prices and market exchange rates, unless indicated otherwise.
2. GDP growth rate at constant prices is based on production approach.
3. Forecasts beyond 2023 are excluded.

LATIN AMERICA and THE CARIBBEAN

Growth in Latin America and the Caribbean is expected to slow sharply from 3.7 percent in 2022 to 1.5 percent in 2023. With core and headline inflation above most central bank targets across the region, monetary policy is likely to remain tight in the near term, dampening growth. Policy uncertainty in some countries is damaging business and consumer confidence. Downside risks to the baseline forecast include slower growth in major trading partners, as well as tighter monetary policies and renewed financial stress in advanced economies, which would have adverse spillovers in the region through weaker trade or more restrictive financial conditions. Climate change poses a significant risk as well given the increasing frequency of extreme weather events.

Recent developments

Growth slowed in all major Latin American economies in 2022 from the unusually high rates experienced in the initial post-pandemic recoveries of 2021. The slowdown extended into the latter half of 2022, reflecting weaker external demand growth and both global and domestic monetary policy tightening (figure 2.3.1.A). GDP in Argentina and Brazil contracted in the last quarter of 2022, quarter-over-quarter, while growth softened in other economies. The associated carryover effect weighs on projected growth in 2023.

Purchasing managers' indexes, which are survey-based measures of business conditions, have indicated weak but improving growth in private sector activity across the major Latin American countries since late 2022. Consumer confidence has been mixed across the region, with a low and stagnant trend observed in Colombia, similar to business confidence in Chile. However, consumer confidence has been on the rise in Brazil and Mexico (figures 2.3.1.B and 2.3.1.C). Consumer spending has, nevertheless, shown some resilience, but investment growth has generally remained weak, largely on account of increased borrowing costs as well as economic and political uncertainties. Countries that are popular tourism

destinations for the United States have benefitted from solid external demand for related services, though tourism has not yet reached pre-pandemic levels (Maloney et al. 2023). Prices of the main export commodities (copper, iron ore, maize, and soybeans) partly recovered in the first quarter of 2023 after declines in late 2022 (Baumeister, Verduzco-Bustos, and Ohnsorge 2022; World Bank 2023c). A major drought in Argentina has severely damaged agricultural output and exports in recent months.

Several central banks in the region began to raise their policy interest rates in 2021 to combat rising inflation, acting ahead of central banks in most advanced economies. Although headline inflation has declined somewhat as key commodity prices, including energy prices, have retreated, persistent high core inflation has remained a challenge, with several unexpected upside movements in recent months (figure 2.3.1.D). Food price inflation has declined from its peak but remains high, posing threats to food security in poorer countries. Overall headline inflation and short-term inflation expectations, as well as core inflation, have remained above most central banks' targets, leading them to maintain high policy rates. Fiscal balances have improved significantly in 2022, providing additional support to contractive monetary efforts.

Social unrest and political uncertainty have persisted in several LAC countries, dampening

---

Note: This section was prepared by Francisco Arroyo Marioli.

FIGURE 2.3.1 **LAC: Recent developments**

Growth weakened significantly in all major LAC countries in the second half of 2022, but purchasing managers' indexes suggest a stabilization of private sector activity more recently. Consumer confidence has been buoyant in Brazil and Mexico but weaker in Argentina and Colombia, like business confidence in Chile. Headline inflation has fallen from its peaks but remains above central bank targets in most countries, while core

A. Annualized GDP growth

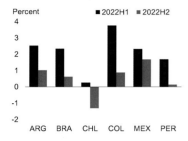

B. Confidence indicators

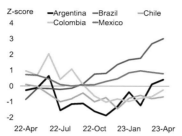

C. Purchasing managers' indexes

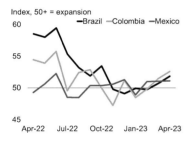

D. Consumer price inflation year-on-year

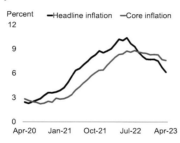

Sources: Haver Analytics; World Bank.
Note: ARG = Argentina, BRA = Brazil; CHL = Chile; COL = Colombia; MEX = Mexico; PER = Peru.
A. Annualized growth rates. 2022H1 is seasonally adjusted GDP growth in the first half of 2022 compared with the second half of 2021. 2022H2 is seasonally adjusted GDP growth in the second half of 2022 compared with the first half of 2022.
B. Figure shows the z-score of business confidence for Chile and consumer confidence for Argentina, Brazil, Colombia, and Mexico. Last observation is April 2023.
C. A Purchasing Managers' Index (PMI) of 50 or higher (lower) indicates expansion (contraction). Composite PMI for Brazil and manufacturing PMI for Colombia and Mexico. Last observation is April 2023.
D. Aggregate is GDP-weighted average and includes five major economies in the region (Brazil, Chile, Colombia, Mexico, and Peru). Last observation is April 2023.

consumer and investor confidence. At the start of this year, significant protests took place in Peru after the ousting of the previous president, while Chile is currently discussing a new constitutional reform after a previous proposal was rejected in a referendum. Argentina, where annual consumer price inflation has recently risen significantly, is facing possible policy adjustments amid the drought, while Brazil is debating changes in its fiscal rules, including possible adjustments to caps on spending. At the time of writing, in Colombia

significant changes to health and pension systems are being discussed.

Outlook

Growth in LAC is projected to slow further in 2023, to 1.5 percent. Weak growth in advanced economies is expected to weigh on export demand, while continuing tight monetary policies in those economies, together with persistently high domestic inflation, are likely to prevent any material near-term easing of financial conditions. However, domestic monetary policy easing is expected to commence toward the end of the year, allowing growth to pick up to 2 percent in 2024. Projected growth implies only limited per capita growth, and therefore marginal reductions in poverty in the region.

U.S. dollar prices for LAC's main export commodities are expected to fall, on average, in 2023, beyond the decline that was already expected in January. Metal prices are expected to remain broadly stable, while agriculture and energy prices are projected to be lower than last year, with a particularly large drop in the case of energy. Although activity in China, LAC's largest trading partner, is projected to accelerate this year, the services-focused nature of China's recovery will limit beneficial spillovers to commodity exporters in LAC. Movements in terms of trade are unlikely to support investment in the region in 2023; in recent decades, terms of trade and investment have moved together closely (figure 2.3.2.A).

In *Brazil,* growth is expected to slow to 1.2 percent in 2023, and then pick up slightly to 1.4 percent in 2024. Headline and core inflation have declined from their peaks and have recently fallen below the upper bound of the central bank's target range. Policy rates are expected to ease in the second half of the year as inflation recedes further, allowing recovery in 2024. Uncertainty about fiscal policy continues to harm business confidence and investment. Although agricultural exports are projected to grow strongly this year because of robust soybean and corn harvests, external demand is not expected to support growth significantly in 2023.

Mexico's growth rate is expected to slow slightly to 2.5 percent this year, amid tighter monetary policy. With inflation having fallen from its peak last year, the central bank has paused the monetary contraction. This comes after a series of rate hikes, from 4 percent in mid-2021, and reaching 11.25 percent in April 2023. Growth is expected to continue expanding in 2024, rising by 1.9 percent as monetary policy eases. Fiscal policy is not expected to support growth in 2023 given its focus on the completion of landmark public investment projects and social programs. Investment and consumption, which were stronger than expected in late 2022, are expected to be somewhat subdued this year as a result of high interest rates and inflation.

Output in *Argentina* is projected to fall 2 percent in 2023 and then grow by 2.3 percent in 2024 as the economy recovers from this year's major drought. The drought has caused declines in the harvests of soybeans and maize—the major export commodities—equivalent to 3 percent of GDP. The drought has also badly affected wheat production. Meanwhile, this year's economic slowdown in Brazil, Argentina's main trading partner, will weigh on the country's non-commodity exports. The resulting scarcity of foreign exchange will create difficulties for importers, notably those in non-agricultural industries . Additionally, inflation has continued to rise, surging somewhat above 100 percent on a 12-month base.

Colombia's growth is projected to weaken from 7.5 percent in 2022 to 1.7 percent in 2023. The central bank began raising interest rates later than those of other LAC countries, which has contributed to a delayed peak in core inflation. Given high inflation and interest rates, consumption is expected to grow at a weak pace of 0.7 percent in 2023. As inflation subsides in response to monetary tightening and falling global energy and food prices, and as external demand gradually recovers, growth is expected to pick up to 2 percent in 2024.

Output in *Chile* is projected to contract by 0.4 percent in 2023. The projected full-year recession in 2023 is a result of the carry-over effects from three quarters of negative growth in 2022. This

FIGURE 2.3.2 LAC: Outlook

The region's terms of trade are expected to remain fairly stable, providing limited support to investment. As core inflation remains stubborn across the region, markets continue to expect above-target inflation in 2023. This implies elevated real interest rates throughout the year. Given limited fiscal space, fiscal policy is not expected to support growth over the next two years.

A. Investment and terms of trade changes

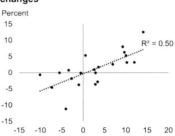

B. Market-implied real policy rates

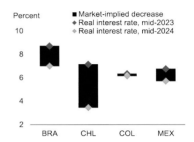

C. One-year inflation expectations

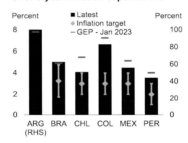

D. Fiscal impulse

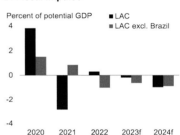

Sources: Bloomberg; Consensus Economics; Haver Analytics; International Monetary Fund; World Bank.
Note: ARG = Argentina; BRA = Brazil; CHL = Chile; COL = Colombia; MEX = Mexico; PER = Peru.
A. Horizontal axis refers to year-on-year growth of fixed investment. Vertical axis refers to year-on-year growth of net barter term of trade. Last observation is 2020.
B. Real interest rate is the policy rate minus the one-year-ahead inflation expectation from Consensus Economics, transformed to a constant time horizon using a weighted average of expectations from 2023 and 2024. Market-implied change is the 30-day rolling average of one-year-ahead market implied policy rate, minus the Bloomberg private forecasters composite consumer price inflation forecast, transformed to a constant time horizon using a weighted average of expectations from 2024 and 2025. Last observation is May 25, 2023.
C. Bars show the latest one-year-ahead inflation forecasts from Consensus Economics. Fixed-horizon forecasts are linearly transformed to one-year-ahead forecasts using a weighted average of months in the current and following year. Orange diamonds and whiskers denote the upper and lower bounds of inflation targets set by authorities in respective countries. Red lines denote the one-year-ahead inflation expectations in the January 2023 Global Economic Prospects report. Last observation is April 2023.
D. Figure shows the negative of the regionwide GDP-weighted change in the structural primary balance (calculated as the structural balance net of projected interest costs). A positive value indicates a positive impulse to GDP growth.

downturn can be primarily attributable to the abrupt withdrawal of substantial monetary, fiscal, and quasi-fiscal stimulus. Inflation peaked last year, but core inflation has been more persistent and has increased in recent months, leading the central bank to maintain a restrictive stance. The price of copper, Chile's main export, is forecast to fall modestly in 2023, with little effect on growth. Growth is expected to increase to 1.8 percent in 2024 as monetary policy eases.

FIGURE 2.3.3 LAC: Risks

External financing needs are elevated in many LAC countries, exposing them to unexpected market turbulence. This could be triggered by additional increases in advanced-economy policy rates or a deterioration in risk appetite. In either case, domestic currencies may depreciate, as has occurred in the past—for example, 2013. A further weakening of China's real estate sector could reduce metal and other global commodity prices, as demand for these would fall. Climate change is imposing more frequent and rising costs in the region.

A. Exchange rate against U.S. dollar

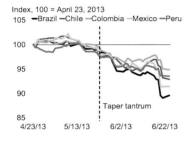

B. External financing needs

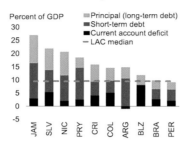

C. Metal prices and Chinese new construction

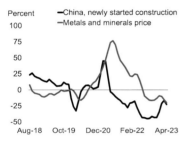

D. Natural disasters and economic costs

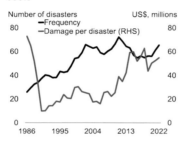

Sources: EM-DAT (database); Haver Analytics; International Monetary Fund; national sources; World Bank.
Note: ARG = Argentina; BLZ = Belize; BRA = Brazil; COL = Colombia; CRI = Costa Rica; JAM = Jamaica; NIC = Nicaragua; PER = Peru; PRY = Paraguay; SLV = El Salvador.
A. Daily exchange rate—U.S. dollars per unit of local currency—one month before and after the taper tantrum (May 23, 2013).
B. Figure shows current account balance and debt obligations coming due in 2023. Debt obligations coming due are the sum of short-term and long-term debt principal payments and interest payments (the latter being within the current account). Short-term external debt in 2023 is estimated. GDP and current account balance in 2023 are projections. Blue dashed line denotes the regional median which excludes member economies in the Organization of Eastern Caribbean States.
C. Three-month moving averages of year-on-year growth in the nominal U.S. dollar price of metals and minerals, and in the floor space area of newly started construction in China. Last observation is April 2023.
D. Five-year moving averages of frequency and damage per disaster. Disasters refers to droughts, floods, and extreme temperatures. Last observation is end-2022.

Peru's growth in 2023 is projected at 2.2 percent, slightly weaker than in 2022, with increased government consumption partly offsetting a weakening in investment. Monetary policy interest rates are likely to remain elevated throughout the year due to persistent, above-target core inflation. Despite output disruptions caused by protests at copper mines at the beginning of this year, exports are expected to continue growing by about 5 percent a year. However, political uncertainty is

adversely affecting consumer and business confidence, particularly with regard to investment. Growth in 2024 is expected to reach 2.6 percent, but this is contingent on social tensions subsiding and investment recovering modestly.

Growth in *Central America* is projected to slow to 3.6 percent in 2023 from 5.4 percent in 2022. Recoveries in remittances, helped by the tight labor market in the United States, and in tourism are expected to support activity this year. Panama's strong growth is expected to continue, driven by services exports and investment. In El Salvador, growth is expected to moderate to 2.3 percent but remain above historical averages, fueled by private consumption, public investment, and tourism. Inflation remains high in the sub-region, particularly in countries such as Honduras and Nicaragua where food price inflation remains high. Growth in Central America is projected to pick up slightly to 3.8 percent in 2024 as advanced economies rebound and monetary policy eases.

Following strong growth of 7.9 percent in 2022, output in the *Caribbean* economies is set to expand by 5.1 percent in 2023. The subregion's outlook partly reflects the oil boom in Guyana, where GDP is expected to grow by 25.2 percent this year and 21.2 percent in 2024 as production at new oil fields continues to ramp up. Output in the rest of the subregion's countries is expected to grow at an average rate of 3.3 percent in 2023, boosted by continued recovery in tourism and buoyant remittances. The Dominican Republic's economy is expected to grow by 4.1 percent in 2023 amid strong export growth. In contrast, Haiti's economy is expected to continue to contract amid increased violence and instability. This will further worsen the country's food security situation, as almost half of households have recently experienced limitations in accessing food (FAO 2022). For 2024, aside from Guyana, the Caribbean is expected to grow by 3.9 percent as external demand from advanced economies recovers.

Potential output growth in LAC weakened in the past decade, 2010-2019. In the current decade, it is expected to be the lowest among emerging market and developing economy (EMDE) regions as a result of below-average growth of both total factor productivity and the labor force (Kose and Ohnsorge 2023). As LAC economies move on from pandemic-driven recessions and subsequent recoveries, low potential growth underlies the generally weak growth prospects for the region.

Risks

The outlook is subject to various downside risks. Persistent inflation in advanced economies may require their central banks to maintain tighter monetary policies than assumed in the baseline, resulting in adverse trade, commodity prices, and financial spillovers to the region. In particular, LAC currencies may depreciate against those of advanced economies, increasing debt-service costs and further pushing up local inflation (figure 2.3.3.A). Currency depreciations could also occur if global market risk appetite were to deteriorate, reducing capital inflows to LAC.

If such developments were to occur, they would likely require further domestic monetary tightening, which could lead to a protracted period of even weaker growth. The negative effect on growth would likely be exacerbated by the high levels of public and private debt in several LAC economies, which could impose restrictions on the ability of governments to absorb a fall in revenue (figure 2.3.3.B). The lack of financial resources could force governments to adopt more restrictive fiscal stances, weakening demand and output growth (Arroyo Marioli and Vegh 2023). Investor outflows from EMDE bond markets, possibly given impetus by elevated current account deficits,

could also force unplanned budgetary consolidation, further reducing growth.

China is the main destination for the region's metal exports—mostly copper and iron—which are primary inputs to its construction sector. Despite China's growth rebound this year, its property sector has remained weak, held back by structural headwinds. If it were to deteriorate further, this could affect global metal prices significantly (figure 2.3.3.C). This downside risk is particularly relevant to Brazil, Chile, and Peru (de la Torre, Filippini, and Ize 2016).

Climate change poses particularly significant risks for countries heavily relying on agriculture and mining sectors, Caribbean island economies, and Central America (Kenworthy, Kirby, and Vorisek 2023). As the drought in Argentina ends and heavy rains hit Colombian populations after three years of La Niña, other extreme weather events could significantly affect agricultural production across the region (figure 2.3.3.D). Hurricanes and extreme storms frequently impact Caribbean and Central American economies. Global warming increases the probability of extreme events of both El Niño and La Niña (Cai et al. 2015; Wang et al. 2019), which can cause both severe droughts and floods. The damage caused by such events tends to be exacerbated by inadequate infrastructure. In the medium to long term, economic growth seems likely to be significantly affected as shifting climate patterns adversely impact the productivity of key sectors and regions (Dellink et al. 2014; Kahn et al 2021).

TABLE 2.3.1 Latin America and the Caribbean forecast summary

(Real GDP growth at market prices in percent, unless indicated otherwise)

Percentage point differences from January 2023 projections

	2020	2021	2022e	2023f	2024f	2025f	2023f	2024f
EMDE LAC, GDP [1]	**-6.2**	**6.9**	**3.7**	**1.5**	**2.0**	**2.6**	**0.2**	**-0.4**
GDP per capita (U.S. dollars)	-7.1	6.1	3.0	0.8	1.3	1.9	0.2	-0.4
(Average including countries that report expenditure components in national accounts) [2]								
EMDE LAC, GDP [2]	-6.2	6.9	3.6	1.4	2.0	2.5	0.2	-0.3
PPP GDP	-6.5	7.0	3.7	1.5	2.0	2.5	0.2	-0.4
Private consumption	-7.5	7.6	5.6	1.3	2.5	2.7	-0.4	-0.2
Public consumption	-1.9	4.0	1.5	0.9	0.6	0.6	0.3	-0.3
Fixed investment	-11.8	17.3	4.6	0.0	2.4	2.7	0.5	0.0
Exports, GNFS [3]	-9.0	8.3	7.1	3.1	4.4	4.5	-0.5	-0.3
Imports, GNFS [3]	-14.0	18.3	7.7	1.3	4.5	4.4	-1.5	0.1
Net exports, contribution to growth	1.3	-2.1	-0.3	0.4	-0.1	0.0	0.3	-0.1
Memo items: GDP								
South America [4]	-5.4	7.2	3.6	0.8	1.8	2.5	-0.3	-0.4
Central America [5]	-7.6	10.3	5.4	3.6	3.8	3.9	0.4	0.3
Caribbean [6]	-7.4	9.7	7.9	5.1	5.6	6.7	-0.5	-0.1
Brazil	-3.3	5.0	2.9	1.2	1.4	2.4	0.4	-0.6
Mexico	-8.0	4.7	3.0	2.5	1.9	2.0	1.6	-0.4
Argentina	-9.9	10.4	5.2	-2.0	2.3	2.0	-4.0	0.3

Source: World Bank.

Note: e = estimate; f = forecast; PPP = purchasing power parity; EMDE = emerging market and developing economy. World Bank forecasts are frequently updated based on new information and changing (global) circumstances. Consequently, projections presented here may differ from those contained in other Bank documents, even if basic assessments of countries' prospects do not differ at any given moment in time. The World Bank is currently not publishing economic output, income, or growth data for República Bolivariana de Venezuela owing to a lack of reliable data of adequate quality. República Bolivariana de Venezuela is excluded from cross-country macroeconomic aggregates.

1. GDP and expenditure components are measured in average 2010-19 prices and market exchange rates.

2. Aggregate includes all countries in notes 4, 5, and 6, plus Mexico, except Antigua and Barbuda, Barbados, Dominica, Grenada, Guyana, Haiti, St. Kitts and Nevis, St. Lucia, St. Vincent and the Grenadines, and Suriname.

3. Exports and imports of goods and non-factor services (GNFS).

4. Includes Argentina, Bolivia, Brazil, Chile, Colombia, Ecuador, Paraguay, Peru, and Uruguay.

5. Includes Costa Rica, El Salvador, Guatemala, Honduras, Nicaragua, and Panama.

6. Includes Antigua and Barbuda, The Bahamas, Barbados, Belize, Dominica, the Dominican Republic, Grenada, Guyana, Haiti, Jamaica, St. Kitts and Nevis, St. Lucia, St. Vincent and the Grenadines, and Suriname.

TABLE 2.3.2 Latin America and the Caribbean country forecasts [1]

(Real GDP growth at market prices in percent, unless indicated otherwise)

Percentage point differences from January 2023 projections

	2020	2021	2022e	2023f	2024f	2025f	2023f	2024f
Argentina	-9.9	10.4	5.2	-2.0	2.3	2.0	-4.0	0.3
Bahamas, The	-23.8	13.7	11.0	4.3	2.0	1.9	0.2	-1.0
Barbados	-13.7	0.7	10.0	4.9	3.9	3.1	0.1	0.0
Belize	-13.4	15.2	9.6	2.4	2.0	2.0	0.4	0.0
Bolivia	-8.7	6.1	3.1	2.5	2.0	2.0	-0.6	-0.7
Brazil	-3.3	5.0	2.9	1.2	1.4	2.4	0.4	-0.6
Chile	-6.0	11.7	2.4	-0.4	1.8	2.2	0.5	-0.5
Colombia	-7.3	11.0	7.5	1.7	2.0	3.2	0.4	-0.8
Costa Rica	-4.3	7.8	4.3	2.9	3.0	3.2	0.0	-0.1
Dominica	-16.6	6.9	5.8	4.7	4.6	4.2	0.1	0.0
Dominican Republic	-6.7	12.3	4.9	4.1	4.8	5.0	-0.7	-0.2
Ecuador	-7.8	4.2	2.9	2.6	2.8	2.8	-0.5	0.0
El Salvador	-8.2	10.3	2.8	2.3	2.1	2.1	0.3	0.1
Grenada	-13.8	4.7	5.8	3.6	3.3	3.1	0.4	0.3
Guatemala	-1.8	8.0	4.0	3.2	3.5	3.5	0.1	0.0
Guyana	43.5	20.0	57.8	25.2	21.2	28.2	0.0	0.0
Haiti [2]	-3.3	-1.8	-1.7	-2.4	1.7	2.4	-1.3	-0.3
Honduras	-9.0	12.5	4.0	3.5	3.7	3.8	0.4	0.0
Jamaica	-9.9	4.6	4.2	2.0	1.7	1.2	0.0	0.5
Mexico	-8.0	4.7	3.0	2.5	1.9	2.0	1.6	-0.4
Nicaragua	-1.8	10.3	4.1	3.0	3.4	3.5	1.0	0.9
Panama	-17.9	15.3	10.5	5.7	5.8	5.9	1.2	1.3
Paraguay	-0.8	4.0	-0.3	4.8	4.3	4.3	-0.4	0.1
Peru	-10.9	13.4	2.7	2.2	2.6	2.8	-0.4	0.0
St. Lucia	-24.4	12.2	15.4	3.6	3.4	2.5	-0.8	0.2
St. Vincent and the Grenadines	-5.3	1.3	5.0	5.6	4.8	3.5	-0.4	0.0
Suriname	-16.0	-2.7	1.9	2.4	3.2	3.1	0.1	0.2
Uruguay	-6.1	4.4	5.0	1.8	2.8	2.4	-0.9	0.3

Source: World Bank.

Note: e = estimate; f = forecast. World Bank forecasts are frequently updated based on new information and changing (global) circumstances. Consequently, projections presented here may differ from those contained in other Bank documents, even if basic assessments of countries' prospects do not significantly differ at any given moment in time.

1. Data are based on GDP measured in average 2010-19 prices and market exchange rates.

2. GDP is based on fiscal year, which runs from October to September of next year.

MIDDLE EAST and NORTH AFRICA

Following a solid recovery in 2022, growth in the Middle East and North Africa (MNA) is forecast to slow to 2.2 percent in 2023, 1.3 percentage points below the January forecast, with growth revised downward for both oil exporters and oil importers. Growth in oil exporters is expected to slow sharply to 2.0 percent this year, reflecting lower oil prices and production, whereas growth in oil importers is projected to edge down to 3.4 percent due to high inflation, dollar shortages, and fiscal and monetary policy tightening. Risks to the outlook remain predominantly to the downside and include falling external demand due to banking stress or further policy tightening; rising violence and social tensions, perhaps arising from the high levels of unemployment in much of the region; a greater incidence of financial crises; and adverse weather events stemming from climate change.

Recent developments

The Middle East and North Africa (MNA) region entered 2023 with solid growth momentum in oil-exporting economies owing to high oil prices—which had helped these economies grow at a decade-high rate in 2022—and ongoing recoveries in services sectors. Purchasing managers' indexes in oil exporters were in expansion territory in the first half of 2023 (figure 2.4.1.A). In the region's oil-importing economies, however, growth slowed markedly at about the turn of the year as high inflation sapped the purchasing power of households and raised the import costs of productive inputs. While declines in global food and energy prices helped boost the terms of trade of oil importers and narrowed wide current account deficits, foreign exchange reserves remain low.

With the boon from high oil prices for oil exporters fading and global demand wavering, OPEC+ announced an oil production cut in April 2023 (figure 2.4.1.B). Total oil and gas production in the Gulf Cooperation Council (GCC) countries subsequently dropped to about 22.7 million barrels a day in April 2023, about 0.9 million barrels a day below its recent peak last September,

with further cuts announced. Production in Saudi Arabia was 0.5 million barrels below its peak of 12.4 million barrels a day. In other MNA oil producers, production was 11.5 million barrels a day in April, 0.4 million barrels below recent peaks.

Despite slowing oil production, output in Saudi Arabia expanded in the first quarter of 2023 owing to robust growth of 5.8 percent on a year ago in the non-oil sector. The unemployment rate also dropped to a two-decade low, with unemployment among Saudi nationals at 8.0 percent. In Qatar, economic growth slowed in early 2023 following decade-high growth in the final quarter of 2022 helped by the FIFA World Cup tournament. The country has recently signed several long-term gas supply agreements with China and Germany and started construction on projects to rapidly expand production. Despite above trend growth in oil exporters, consumer price inflation in these economies has remained below much of the world, at a median of 3.7 percent on an annual basis in April, reflecting their fixed exchange rates against the U.S. dollar and consumer subsidies.

In oil importers, economic growth was weak in early 2023 with real incomes under pressure from high inflation. Additionally, several economies faced vulnerabilities based on large current ac-

Note: This section was prepared by Franz Ulrich Ruch.

FIGURE 2.4.1 MNA: Recent developments

Economic growth in early 2023 remained solid in oil exporters, benefiting from still-high oil prices, but weak in oil importers, undermined by high inflation. Oil production in the region in early 2023 was about 1.1 million barrels below its 2022 peaks, reflecting agreed-upon production cuts. Among countries with floating exchange rates, the currencies of Morocco and Tunisia have depreciated slightly against the U.S. dollar since mid-2022, but the Egyptian pound has depreciated significantly. Consumer price inflation has remained high in several economies.

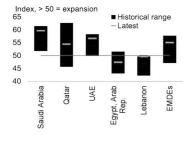

A. Purchasing managers' indexes

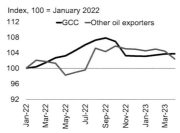

B. Oil production

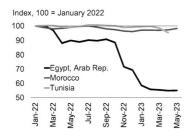

C. Nominal effective exchange rate

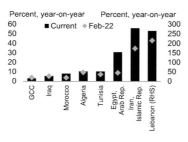

D. Consumer price inflation

Sources: Haver Analytics; International Energy Agency; International Monetary Fund; J.P. Morgan; World Bank.
Note: EMDEs = emerging market and developing economies; GCC = Gulf Cooperation Council; UAE = United Arab Emirates.
A. Historical range reflects the 5th and 95th percentile from as far back as January 2006. Latest observation is April 2023.
B. GCC includes Bahrain, Kuwait, Oman, Qatar, Saudi Arabia, and the United Arab Emirates. Latest observation is April 2023.
C. Lower numbers reflect depreciation. Latest observation is May 2023 (data through the 19th of the month).
D. GCC is median observation for Bahrain, Kuwait, Oman, Qatar, Saudi Arabia, and the United Arab Emirates. Latest observation is April 2023.

count deficits, low foreign exchange reserves, and deteriorating sentiment. In the Arab Republic of Egypt, limited access to foreign currency and shift to a more flexible exchange rate saw the pound lose about half its value against the U.S. dollar and equity prices in U.S. dollar terms fall by 26 percent between the start of 2022 and May 2023 (figure 2.4.1.C). Rising costs, difficulties securing imported inputs, and slowing global demand weighed on activity, with industrial production (excluding oil) contracting by 6.0 percent on a year ago in January 2023. Urban consumer price

inflation was 30.6 percent (year-on-year) in April 2023, reflecting the depreciation of the pound (figure 2.4.1.D). In response to rising inflation, dwindling reserves, and declining net foreign assets, the central bank more than doubled policy rates since the start of 2022.

In Morocco, the persistent drought and high inflation are weakening growth, with unemployment rising to reach 12.9 percent in March 2023, above its pandemic peak, and labor force participation falling to 43.1 percent. In Tunisia, adverse terms of trade shocks, slow reform progress and policy uncertainty held back activity in late 2022. As a result, Tunisia is one of few economies in the region whose output is still below pre-pandemic levels.

Several economies in the region continue to grapple with fragility, armed conflict, financial stress, and political crisis. In Lebanon, persistently high inflation and policy uncertainty continue to undermine growth, with output contracting further in the first quarter of 2023. In the Syrian Arab Republic, output also contracted further in early 2023, undermined by armed conflict, fuel shortages, and higher input costs; one-half of the country's oil supplies and one-third of its cereal consumption is imported (World Bank 2023i). The earthquakes that hit the northern and western parts of the country in February are estimated to have caused $5.2 billion in losses and damage (World Bank 2023j). In Yemen, output is estimated to have grown by 1.5 percent in 2022, supported by inflows of remittances and aid, a temporary truce, and reforms that improved exchange rate stability. However, oil production continues to be undermined by an export embargo, and the truce between Houthis and the internationally recognized government that expired in October has yet to be renewed.

Outlook

Growth in MNA is expected to slow to 2.2 percent in 2023, with downward revisions from January projections for both oil exporters and importers (figure 2.4.2.A; table 2.4.1). Growth in the region is expected to rebound in 2024, to 3.3 percent, as inflation and global headwinds subside, and oil production rises. The growth outlook for oil exporters in 2024 has improved since January, reflecting an assumed rebound in oil production, the expected effects of reform initiatives, and investment drives in Saudi Arabia and the United Arab Emirates.

In Saudi Arabia, oil production cuts are expected to result in stagnant industrial output and exports. Growth is forecast to decelerate from 8.7 percent in 2022 to 2.2 percent in 2023, with the oil sector experiencing a contraction this year. Growth is projected to rebound to 3.3 percent in 2024, supported by a government investment drive and continued solid activity in the services sector. In the United Arab Emirates, constrained oil production and tightening financial conditions are envisaged to dampen growth to 2.8 percent in 2023 from 7.9 percent in 2022. Growth is expected to slow in the Islamic Republic of Iran to 2.2 percent in FY2023/24, from 2.9 percent the previous fiscal year, as oil exports and government consumption growth slows. In Kuwait, growth is forecast to slow to 1.3 percent in 2023 because of OPEC+ oil production limits, despite the newly established Al Zour refinery. This slowdown is further compounded by policy uncertainty caused by political deadlock that is expected to undermine the implementation of new infrastructure projects.

Oil-importing economies continue to face domestic headwinds, including high inflation and limited access to foreign currency. Thus, growth in these economies is projected to decelerate to 3.4 percent in 2023, a 0.7 percentage point downgrade from January and a 1.3 percentage point downgrade from the January 2022 forecasts made shortly before the Russian Federation's invasion of Ukraine (figure 2.4.2.B). Growth is expected to pick up through the forecast period as global and domestic headwinds subside.

In Egypt, growth is projected to slow to 4.0 percent in FY2022/23 (July-June), a 0.5 percentage point downward revision from January. Significant increases in interest rates, severe currency depreciation, high and rising inflation, limited access to foreign currency, and higher production costs are expected to continue constraining both consumption by households and

FIGURE 2.4.2 MNA: Outlook

Growth in the Middle East and North Africa is projected to slow to 2.2 percent in 2023 before picking up to 3.3 in 2024, well below its pace in the two decades before the pandemic. Growth in oil importers in 2023 has been substantially revised downward since early 2022. Potential growth in the region has slowed significantly in the past decade and is expected to remain low throughout the coming decade. While oil exporters run fiscal surpluses, oil importers face wide deficits caused partly by large debt-service bills.

A. GDP growth

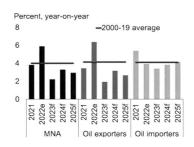

B. Growth in oil importers

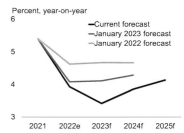

C. Fiscal balance

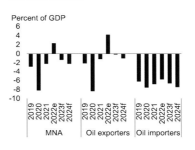

D. Contributions to potential growth

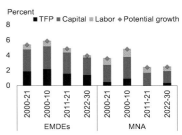

Sources: International Monetary Fund; Kilic Celik, Kose, and Ohnsorge (2023); World Bank.
Note: e = estimate; EMDEs = emerging market and developing economies; f = forecast; MNA = Middle East and North Africa; TFP = total factor productivity.
C. GDP-weighted average based on five oil importers and nine oil exporters.
D. Period averages of annual GDP-weighted averages. Estimates based on the production function approach in Kilic Celik, Kose, and Ohnsorge (2023). Sample includes 5 MNA economies and 53 EMDEs. GDP weights are calculated using average real U.S. dollar GDP (at average 2010-19 prices and market exchange rates) for the period 2011-21. Data for 2022-30 are forecasts.

production by firms. In Morocco, growth is expected to pick up to 2.5 percent in 2023 from 1.1 percent the previous year, supported by resilience in tourism and the automotive industry. The growth projection for the year, however, has been downgraded by 1.0 percentage point due to adverse climatic conditions which will postpone the normalization of agricultural output after consecutive years of drought. In Tunisia, policy uncertainties amid limited structural reforms are expected to reduce growth in 2023, to 2.3 percent.

Fiscal and monetary policies have tightened across the region over the past year; however,

FIGURE 2.4.3 MNA: Risks

Government debt levels remain elevated among oil-importing economies, limiting fiscal space to respond to future slowdowns. Oil remains the major source of government revenue in oil exporters, implying risks in the short term from lower oil prices and in the long term from the energy transition. High global and regional food prices and the risk of future increases could undermine growth, impart lasting scars on the population, and increase fiscal and current account deficits. The region continues to see one of the highest levels of youth not in education, employment, or training, which could become a flash point for rising social tensions.

A. Government debt

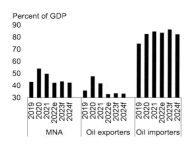

B. Oil-related government revenue in oil-exporting economies

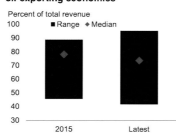

C. Global and domestic food prices

D. Share of youth not in education, employment, or training

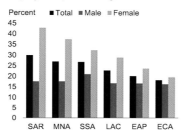

Sources: Haver Analytics; International Labour Organization; International Monetary Fund; World Bank.
Note: e = estimate; f = forecast. EAP = East Asia and Pacific; ECA = Europe and Central Asia; LAC = Latin America and the Caribbean; MNA = Middle East and North Africa; SAR = South Asia; SSA = Sub-Saharan Africa.
A. GDP-weighted average of 5 oil importers and 9 oil exporters.
B. Based on data for 7 economies. "Latest" reflects data for 2021-22 where available. "Range" reflects maximum and minimum country shares.
C. Consumer food inflation based on medians of 5 oil importers and 8 oil exporters. Latest observation is April 2023.
D. Data for 2022. Data may differ from nationally reported figures and the Global SDG Indicators Database on account of differences in sources and/or reference years. The share of youth not in education, employment or training (also known as the NEET rate) conveys the number of young persons not in education, employment, or training as a percentage of the total youth population.

stances and outlooks differ between oil exporters and importers (figure 2.4.2.C). In oil exporters, government budgets are expected to remain in or close to surplus owing to strong revenues from high oil prices and spending cuts as COVID-19 measures unwind. In oil importers, by contrast, fiscal deficits are large and forecast to increase as debt-service costs rise. Monetary policy in oil exporters with currencies pegged to the U.S. dollar

has tightened in line with the rise in the Federal Reserve's policy rate. Among oil importers, policy rates have been hiked sharply to contain increases in inflation. In Egypt, for example, the central bank has raised policy rates by 10 percentage points since the start of 2022.

MNA continues to struggle with weaker potential growth than most other EMDE regions (figure 2.4.2.D; Kose and Ohnsorge 2023). It is estimated that potential growth more than halved between the 2000s and 2010s, widening the gap with other EMDEs. Although conditions vary across MNA, potential growth in most countries is constrained by severe structural challenges, including large gender gaps in work and education, low returns to education, high youth unemployment, limited economic diversification, excessive state involvement in economic activity, and prolonged armed conflicts. Potential growth is expected to average 2.5 percent a year over the remainder of this decade (2022-30), higher in oil importers than oil exporters, mainly driven by capital accumulation amid anemic growth of total factor productivity. However, this pace would generate per capita income growth of no more than about 1 percent a year—suggesting only limited progress in poverty reduction.

Risks

Risks to the forecast remain predominantly to the downside. They include further possible falls in external demand due to banking stress or policy tightening in advanced economies; sharp changes in commodity prices; rising violence and social tensions, perhaps related to the high levels of unemployment in the region; new financial crises or the worsening of existing ones; and weather shocks related to climate change.

Oil-importing economies in the region are expected to achieve higher growth than their oil-exporting peers; however, the balance of risks among oil importers is more significantly skewed to the downside. Oil importers generally have more government debt, lower foreign exchange reserves, weaker macroeconomic management, and they generally also run both fiscal and current account deficits (figure 2.4.3.A). Several economies also have a large state-owned enterprises footprint with significant fiscal costs (IMF 2021). Further increases in borrowing costs, currency depreciations, or food and energy price spikes could jeopardize debt sustainability in several oil-importing economies and lead to significantly slower growth. Limited progress on structural reforms has perpetuated weak growth in several oil importers, increasing risks to the outlook through higher incidence of poverty and social unrest, and less favorable debt dynamics. In December, Egypt entered into a new International Monetary Fund (IMF) arrangement in support of a policy program designed to address vulnerabilities (IMF 2023c). Morocco has become the first lower middle-income economy to sign a Flexible Credit Line with the IMF. This precautionary arrangement is a testament to the country's strong policies, institutional frameworks, and economic funda-mentals (IMF 2023d).

Oil exporters remain reliant on oil production for about one-third of output, two-thirds of merchandise exports, and three-quarters of government revenue (figure 2.4.3.B). Rising geopolitical tensions could raise oil prices and renew the substantial surplus to oil exporters (chapter 1). However, if the global economy were to slow more than expected, or oil prices were to weaken for other reasons, this could put renewed economic and financial pressure on these economies. The heavy reliance on oil makes diversification a priority. In the long run, the global energy transition away from fossil fuels will also require significant diversification if these economies are to avoid economic stagnation. Any global push to hasten the green energy transition could leave these economies exposed to an unexpected drop in fossil fuel demand. The oil intensity of global output

declined by about one-third in the two decades to 2021, and this trend will likely continue.

The region continues to suffer from high levels of violence and armed conflict, with the potential for rising social tensions, which could undermine productivity and investment (EBRD 2022). Given the already-high prevalence of insufficient food consumption (especially in Syria and the Republic of Yemen) and the highest levels of youth not in employment, education, or training among EMDE regions only behind South Asia, any further increases in food and energy prices could increase the incidence of violence in the region (figures 2.4.3.C and 2.4.3.D; ILO 2022). Rising food prices, even if temporary, can cause long term damage to education, health, and income (World Bank 2023k).

Climate change presents a significant downside risk to the region. In particular, it could deepen disparities in human development because marginalized and poor members of society are often the worst affected by adverse weather events and have few resources to cope. Securing sufficient food supplies may also be an increasing challenge for the region as climate change is likely to increase the frequency and intensity of drought and other climate-change-related disasters (IMF 2022). In Egypt—the region's most populous country, which is heavily reliant on the Nile River—rising temperatures could lead to extreme drought and flooding, compromise water availability, and increase the severity, frequency, and duration of heatwaves (World Bank 2022c). The costs of climate change in Egypt could amount to 2-6 percent of GDP by 2060. In Iraq, rising temperatures could undermine water availability and crop yields, leading to a 3.9 percent decline in GDP by 2050 (World Bank 2022d).

TABLE 2.4.1 Middle East and North Africa forecast summary

(Real GDP growth at market prices in percent, unless indicated otherwise)

Percentage point differences from January 2023 projections

	2020	2021	2022e	2023f	2024f	2025f	2023f	2024f
EMDE MNA, GDP [1]	-3.8	3.8	5.9	2.2	3.3	3.0	-1.3	0.6
GDP per capita (U.S. dollars)	-5.0	2.6	4.5	0.9	2.0	1.7	-1.2	0.6
(Average including countries that report expenditure components in national accounts) [2]								
EMDE MNA, GDP [2]	-2.9	4.2	6.0	2.5	3.1	2.9	-1.0	0.4
PPP GDP	-2.1	4.4	5.6	2.6	3.1	3.0	-0.9	0.3
Private consumption	-1.0	5.5	6.4	3.3	3.1	3.0	0.2	0.1
Public consumption	0.5	3.9	1.7	2.9	2.8	2.6	0.7	0.3
Fixed investment	-8.6	7.6	11.0	4.7	3.5	3.9	-0.6	-0.2
Exports, GNFS [3]	-6.7	6.1	14.9	4.0	4.5	3.9	-1.2	0.4
Imports, GNFS [3]	-8.6	8.9	17.2	6.0	4.7	4.4	0.9	0.0
Net exports, contribution to growth	0.1	-0.4	0.5	-0.4	0.3	0.1	-1.0	0.1
Memo items: GDP								
Oil exporters [4]	-4.5	3.5	6.4	2.0	3.2	2.7	-1.3	0.9
GCC countries [5]	-4.8	3.4	7.6	2.4	3.2	2.8	-1.3	0.8
Saudi Arabia	-4.3	3.9	8.7	2.2	3.3	2.5	-1.5	1.0
Iran, Islamic Rep. [6]	1.9	4.7	2.9	2.2	2.0	1.9	0.0	0.1
Oil importers [7]	-0.8	5.4	3.9	3.4	3.9	4.1	-0.7	-0.4
Egypt, Arab Rep. [6]	3.6	3.3	6.6	4.0	4.0	4.7	-0.5	-0.8

Source: World Bank.

Note: e = estimate; f = forecast; PPP = purchasing power parity; EMDE = emerging market and developing economy. World Bank forecasts are frequently updated based on new information and changing (global) circumstances. Consequently, projections presented here may differ from those contained in other Bank documents, even if basic assessments of countries' prospects do not differ at any given moment in time.

1. GDP and expenditure components are measured in average 2010-19 prices and market exchange rates. Excludes Lebanon, Libya, the Syrian Arab Republic, and the Republic of Yemen as a result of the high degree of uncertainty.

2. Aggregate includes all economies in notes 4 and 7 except Djibouti, Iraq, Qatar, and West Bank and Gaza, for which data limitations prevent the forecasting of GDP components.

3. Exports and imports of goods and non-factor services (GNFS).

4. Oil exporters include Algeria, Bahrain, the Islamic Republic of Iran, Iraq, Kuwait, Oman, Qatar, Saudi Arabia, and the United Arab Emirates.

5. The Gulf Cooperation Council (GCC) includes Bahrain, Kuwait, Oman, Qatar, Saudi Arabia, and the United Arab Emirates.

6. Fiscal-year-based numbers. The fiscal year runs from July 1 to June 30 in the Arab Republic of Egypt, with 2020 reflecting FY2019/20. For the Islamic Republic of Iran, it runs from March 21 through March 20, with 2020 reflecting FY2020/21.

7. Oil importers include Djibouti, Egypt, Jordan, Morocco, Tunisia, and West Bank and Gaza.

TABLE 2.4.2 Middle East and North Africa economy forecasts[1]

(Real GDP growth at market prices in percent, unless indicated otherwise)

Percentage point differences from January 2023 projections

	2020	2021	2022e	2023f	2024f	2025f	2023f	2024f
Algeria	-5.1	3.4	3.2	1.7	2.4	2.1	-0.6	0.6
Bahrain	-4.6	2.7	4.9	2.7	3.2	3.1	-0.5	0.0
Djibouti	1.2	4.8	3.0	4.4	5.4	5.9	-0.9	-0.8
Egypt, Arab Rep. [2]	3.6	3.3	6.6	4.0	4.0	4.7	-0.5	-0.8
Iran, Islamic Rep. [2]	1.9	4.7	2.9	2.2	2.0	1.9	0.0	0.1
Iraq	-12.0	1.6	7.0	-1.1	6.0	3.7	-5.1	3.1
Jordan	-1.6	2.2	2.5	2.4	2.4	2.4	0.0	0.0
Kuwait	-8.9	1.3	7.9	1.3	2.6	2.4	-1.2	0.1
Lebanon [3]	-21.4	-7.0	-2.6	-0.5	..	..	..	..
Libya [3]	-29.8	31.4	-1.2	..	..	..	..	..
Morocco	-7.2	7.9	1.1	2.5	3.3	3.5	-1.0	-0.4
Oman	-3.4	3.1	4.3	1.5	2.8	2.6	-2.4	0.4
Qatar	-3.6	1.5	4.6	3.3	2.9	3.1	-0.1	0.0
Saudi Arabia	-4.3	3.9	8.7	2.2	3.3	2.5	-1.5	1.0
Syrian Arab Republic [3]	-0.2	1.3	-3.5	-5.5	..	..	-2.3	..
Tunisia	-8.8	4.4	2.5	2.3	3.0	3.0	-1.0	-0.6
United Arab Emirates	-5.0	4.4	7.9	2.8	3.4	3.4	-1.3	1.1
West Bank and Gaza	-11.3	7.0	3.9	3.0	3.0	3.0	0.0	0.0
Yemen, Rep. [3]	-8.5	-1.0	1.5	-0.5	2.0	..	-1.5	..

Source: World Bank.

Note: e = estimate; f = forecast. World Bank forecasts are frequently updated based on new information and changing (global) circumstances. Consequently, projections presented here may differ from those contained in other Bank documents, even if basic assessments of economies' prospects do not significantly differ at any given moment in time.

1. Data are based on GDP measured in average 2010-19 prices and market exchange rates.

2. Fiscal-year-based numbers. The fiscal year runs from July 1 to June 30 in the Arab Republic of Egypt, with 2020 reflecting FY2019/20. For the Islamic Republic of Iran, it runs from March 21 through March 20, with 2020 reflecting FY2020/21.

3. Forecasts for Lebanon (beyond 2023), Libya (beyond 2022), the Syrian Arab Republic (beyond 2023), and the Republic of Yemen (beyond 2024) are excluded because of a high degree of uncertainty.

SOUTH ASIA

Growth in South Asia is expected to slow marginally in 2023, to 5.9 percent, and more significantly in 2024, to 5.1 percent. Unexpected resilience in private consumption and investment, and robust growth in the services sector in India, underlie an upward revision to growth in 2023. The lagged impact of tightening domestic policy and global financial conditions, and the aftermath of crises and natural disasters in several economies, are expected to temper growth in 2024. Risks to the outlook are mainly to the downside and include adverse spillovers from possible further advanced-economy monetary policy tightening or banking sector stress, sharper-than-expected tightening of domestic macroeconomic policies to anchor inflation expectations or stabilize foreign exchange reserves, social tensions arising from food insecurity, and extreme weather events related to climate change. The materialization of such risks could worsen economic and humanitarian crises in Afghanistan and Sri Lanka and/or give rise to crises in other economies in the region.

Recent developments

In 2022, South Asia (SAR) endured significant negative spillovers from rapid monetary policy tightening in advanced economies, weak growth in China, and the Russian Federation's invasion of Ukraine. The peak impact of these shocks appears to have passed, and regional economic conditions have improved so far in 2023, however, the economic and financial consequence of these shocks persist. Terms of trade have become more favorable since the second half of 2022, and large trade deficits caused by high import commodity prices have partially receded (figure 2.5.1.A). Maldives, the region's fastest-growing economy in 2022, benefited from sustained high levels of tourists from Europe, India, and Russia, and returning tourism from China since early this year (figure 2.5.1.B). Import restrictions imposed by several economies (Bangladesh, Nepal, Pakistan, Sri Lanka), which adversely affected economic activity, have been relaxed as external imbalances have improved and exchange rate pressures have eased. Food export bans, however, are expected to

remain in place in Bangladesh, India, and Pakistan through 2023 despite falling global prices.

In India, which accounts for three-quarters of output in the region, growth in early 2023 remained below what it achieved in the decade before the pandemic as higher prices and rising borrowing costs weighed on private consumption. However, manufacturing rebounded into 2023 after contracting in the second half of 2022, and investment growth remained buoyant as the government ramped up capital expenditure. Private investment was also likely boosted by increasing corporate profits. Unemployment declined to 6.8 percent in the first quarter of 2023, the lowest since the onset of the COVID-19 pandemic, and labor force participation increased. India's headline consumer price inflation has returned to within the central bank's 2-6 percent tolerance band (figure 2.5.1.C).

In Bangladesh, continued import suppression measures and energy shortages have weighed on both industrial production and the services sector. Real household earnings are yet to recover to pre-pandemic levels despite an improvement in employment. A policy program supported by the International Monetary Fund (IMF)—approved in

Note: This section was prepared by Franz Ulrich Ruch.

FIGURE 2.5.1 SAR: Recent developments

Merchandise trade deficits in the region have narrowed since mid-2022 as terms of trade have improved on falling global oil and food commodity prices. Regional economic activity diverged widely in the latter part of 2022, with industrial production contracting in Pakistan and Sri Lanka and tourism recovering in Maldives. Consumer price inflation remains above target in most economies and is particularly high in Pakistan and Sri Lanka. Limited foreign exchange reserve cover in some economies limits access to imported intermediate goods for production.

A. Merchandise trade balance and terms of trade

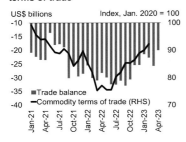

B. Manufacturing and tourism activity

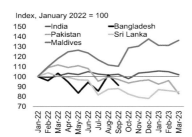

C. Consumer price inflation

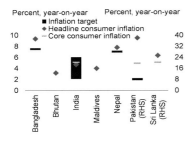

D. Foreign exchange reserves

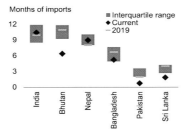

Sources: CEIC; Haver Analytics; International Monetary Fund; World Bank.
Note: EMDEs = emerging market and developing economies.
A. "Trade balance" based on Bangladesh, India, Nepal, Pakistan, and Sri Lanka. "Terms of trade" is the net export price across economies weighted by using 2022 real GDP in U.S. dollars.
B. Data for Bangladesh, India, Pakistan, and Sri Lanka are industrial production. Data for Maldives are international tourist arrivals (seasonally adjusted using X13-ARIMA-SEATS).
C. Colombo consumer price index used in Sri Lanka. Latest observations are March-May 2023.
D. Reserves are expressed in number of months of imports they could pay for. Based on monthly data from January 2000 to April 2023 or where available. "2019" reflects an average for the year.

January—aims to pre-emptively address further balance of payments pressures and help unwind import suppression measures.

Some economies in the region have suffered significant domestic shocks, and deep crises are continuing to undermine their growth—particularly Afghanistan, Pakistan, and Sri Lanka. In Sri Lanka, industrial production fell by 15.8 percent in the year to March 2023. Inadequate foreign exchange reserves hindered the import of sufficient food and energy. More recently, there have been signs of stabilization following the IMF's approval in March of a program to support economic policies and reforms (IMF 2023e). Since the start of the year, the Sri Lankan rupee has partially reversed some of its earlier losses against the U.S. dollar but remained about two-thirds its value compared with that in early March 2022, prior to its debt suspension announcement. Consumer price inflation in Colombo reached a peak of close to 70 percent in the year to September 2022, but had declined to 25.2 percent by May.

In Pakistan, the lasting effects of the August 2022 floods, along with policy uncertainty and limited foreign exchange resources to pay for imports of food, energy, and intermediate inputs, have depressed activity, with industrial production contracting by about 25 percent in the year to March 2023. With dwindling foreign exchange reserves and stagnant remittances, the government has increased exchange rate flexibility, allowing the Pakistani rupee to depreciate by 20 percent since the start of the year (figure 2.5.1.D). Consequently, headline consumer price inflation has risen sharply, reaching 38 percent in the year to May, its highest level since records began in the late 1970s.

In Afghanistan, poverty is widespread, with 92 percent of the population having insufficient food because of inadequate incomes (WFP 2023a). Consumer price inflation declined from double-digit rates in July 2022 to 1.9 percent, year-on-year, in March 2023. Income-generating opportunities for the self-employed and casual workers weakened during adverse winter weather that set back agriculture, construction, and related activities.

Outlook

Growth in the region is expected to slow marginally to 5.9 percent in 2023 and more significantly to 5.1 percent in 2024 (figure 2.5.2.A). Relative to January projections, this is a 0.4 percentage point upward revision in 2023 and a 0.7 percentage point downward revision for 2024. Greater-than-expected resilience in private consumption and investment, and a robust services sector in India, is supporting growth in 2023. The downward revision in 2024 mainly reflects the lagged impact of tightening domestic policy and global financing conditions, the aftermath of floods and policy uncertainty in Pakistan, and the humanitarian crisis in Afghanistan. As domestic and global headwinds dissipate, output growth is expected to pick up to 6.4 percent in 2025, close to the region's potential growth rate (figure 2.5.2.B). In the longer term, potential growth in SAR is forecast to remain above 6 percent over the rest of this decade—the fastest of all emerging market and developing economy (EMDE) regions (Kose and Ohnsorge 2023). However, several of SAR's economies face ongoing crises, the resolution of which is subject to significant uncertainty, which could undermine potential growth.

Growth in India is expected to slow further to 6.3 percent in FY2023/24 (April-March), a 0.3 percentage point downward revision from January. This slowdown is attributed to private consumption being constrained by high inflation and rising borrowing costs, while government consumption is impacted by fiscal consolidation. Growth is projected to pick up slightly through FY2025/26 as inflation moves back toward the midpoint of the tolerance range and reforms payoff. India will remain the fastest-growing economy (in terms of both aggregate and per capita GDP) of the largest EMDEs.

In SAR excluding India, growth is expected to slow to 2.9 percent in 2023 before rebounding to 4.3 percent in 2024. In Bangladesh, elevated inflation, policy uncertainty, and weakening external demand are expected to slow growth to 5.2 percent in FY2022/23 (July-June) from 7.1 percent in the previous fiscal year. Gains in market share in key export markets are expected to sustain export growth, offsetting the effects of weaker growth in advanced economies. Growth is projected to accelerate to 6.2 percent in FY2023/24 as inflationary pressures ease, reform implementation accelerates, and transportation and energy infrastructure megaprojects are completed.

In Pakistan, continuing effects of the August 2022 floods, compounded by worsening social tensions, high inflation, and policy uncertainty, are estimated to have limited growth to 0.4 percent in FY2022/23 (July-June), a 1.6 percentage-point downward revision from January. Agriculture

FIGURE 2.5.2 SAR: Outlook

Regional growth is projected to weaken in 2023-24 because of ongoing and lagged impacts of domestic and global policy tightening and the aftermath of crises and disasters in several economies. Growth is not expected to return to its 2000-19 average until 2025. Potential growth in South Asia is forecast to remain above 6 percent in the coming decade, in contrast to the slowdown facing other emerging market and developing economy regions. The number of poor in the region is expected to continue its downward trend in the years ahead, but at a slower pace, after the 2020-21 COVID-19-induced increase. Domestic monetary policy tightening has slowed in economies facing crisis and high inflation. Government debt burdens persist at high levels despite benefiting from fiscal policy consolidation, and high nominal growth.

A. Output growth

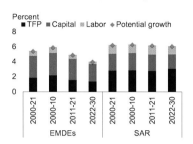

B. Contributions to potential growth

C. Macroeconomic policy indicators

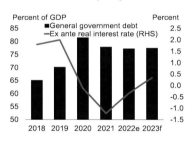

D. Poverty

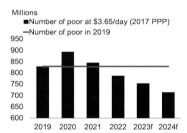

Sources: Consensus Economics; Haver Analytics; Kilic Celik, Kose, and Ohnsorge (2023); World Bank.
Note: e = estimate; EMDEs = emerging market and developing economies; f = forecast; SAR = South Asia; TFP = total factor productivity.
B. Period averages of annual GDP-weighted averages. Estimates based on the production function approach in Kilic Celik, Kose, and Ohnsorge (2023). Sample includes three SAR economies and 53 EMDEs. GDP weights are calculated using average real U.S. dollar GDP (at average 2010-19 prices and market exchange rates) for the period 2011-21. Data for 2022-30 are forecasts.
C. Ex ante real interest rate is based on one-year-ahead forecasts of consumer inflation from Consensus Economics. GDP-weighted average for Bangladesh, India, Pakistan, and Sri Lanka. 2023 is based on the first two quarters of the year. "General government debt" is GDP-weighted gross debt for SAR (Afghanistan and Sri Lanka are excluded).
D. Nowcast until 2022. For India, the latest estimates based on official data are from 2011. Estimations for later years up to 2021 are based on imputed consumption using the Consumer Pyramid Household Surveys and following Sinha Roy and van der Weide (2022). From 2022 onward, a microsimulation uses growth rates for five sectors and a pass-through factor of 0.65. As Afghanistan did not participate in the International Comparison Program exercise, the number of poor is adjusted with the rest of the region's poverty rate and Afghanistan's population projection.

output seems likely to have contracted for the first time in two decades. Economic recovery in the next two fiscal years is expected to be anemic, with growth of 2 and 3 percent, respectively, as there is limited fiscal room for the government to support a recovery from flood-related damages.

FIGURE 2.5.3 **SAR: Risks**

Further tightening of global monetary policy, and renewed banking stress, could have adverse impacts in South Asian economies. These impacts would include putting downward pressure on currency values, with further drawdowns of foreign exchange reserves or currency depreciations. Inflation expectations could de-anchor, requiring further domestic monetary policy tightening and slowing activity. High debt-service payments could limit governments' ability to respond to future emergencies. South Asia is the most vulnerable emerging market and developing economy region to shocks related to climate change.

A. Impact of a 25-basis-point increase in U.S. interest rates on exchange rates

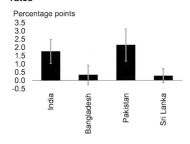

B. Inflation expectations

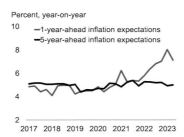

C. General government interest payments

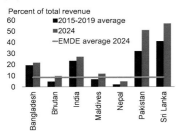

D. Climate risk index, 2022

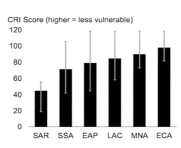

Sources: Arteta, Kamin, and Ruch (2022); Consensus Economics; Germanwatch; World Bank.
Note: EAP = East Asia and Pacific; ECA = Europe and Central Asia; LAC = Latin America and the Caribbean; MNA = Middle East and North Africa; SAR = South Asia; SSA = Sub-Saharan Africa.
A. Results from local projection models for each country, to reaction-function shocks (for example, a pivot toward a more hawkish monetary policy stance). Shocks are estimated from a sign-restricted Bayesian vector autoregression (VAR) model with stochastic volatility. Local projection models include monthly data from as long as June 2001 to September 2022 for short- and long-term interest rates, equity prices, exchange rates to the U.S. dollar, real exports, consumer inflation, and foreign exchange reserves. Dummies for the global financial crisis and COVID-19 pandemic included. Orange whiskers reflect 90 percent confidence intervals. First-month response. Exchange rate is local currency per U.S. dollar with positive values reflecting a depreciation. Official exchange rate in Bangladesh.
B. GDP-weighted based on data for Bangladesh, India, Pakistan, and Sri Lanka.
C. Based on share of interest payments of total revenue and grants.
D. Based on the average climate risk index (CRI) score by region. Orange whiskers show the interquartile range.

In Bhutan, the relaxation of entry restrictions for tourists in September and the recovery in global tourism are estimated to have boosted growth to 4.5 percent in FY2022/23 (July-June) despite a new tourist levy. Growth in Nepal in FY2022/23, undermined by import restrictions and cooled by tighter monetary policy in the face of higher inflation, has been revised down to 4.1 percent.

The outlook for the economies in crisis remains dire, with minimal expectation of reversing the recent declines in per capita income. In Sri Lanka, output is expected to contract by 4.3 percent in 2023 before a tepid recovery starts in 2024. The economic outlook in Afghanistan has stabilized on returning aid flows; output growth is expected to turn positive in the next two years.

Monetary policy tightening in the region has continued, with average real interest rates in the first half of 2023 turning positive on a GDP-weighted basis (figure 2.5.2.C). There are large differences among countries, however. In Pakistan and to a lesser extent in Sri Lanka, policy rate increases have not kept pace with expected inflation; consequently, real interest rates have turned deeply negative. In Bangladesh, while the central bank raised policy rates, transmission to the broader economy has been impaired by a cap on lending interest rates. Fiscal consolidation is expected to continue across the region, gradually in economies with fiscal space and more abruptly in economies in crisis.

While poverty has recently been increasing in economies facing severe economic pressures—notably Afghanistan, Pakistan, and Sri Lanka—it is expected that the region as a whole will resume its downward trend that was interrupted in 2020-21 (figure 2.5.2.D; World Bank 2023l). The decline, however, will not be as quick as previously expected, given the impacts of high inflation, slow recovery in employment, and withdrawal of pandemic-related food support. The number of people in SAR living on less than $3.65 a day in 2023 is expected to be well below the 2020 pandemic-induced uptick. Despite this improvement, opportunities to move out of poverty remain limited and uneven for women and other vulnerable populations (World Bank 2023l).

Risks

Risks to the outlook remain predominantly to the downside. These risks include adverse spillovers from further monetary policy tightening or banking sector stress in advanced economies, the possibility of more economies falling into crisis, sharper-than-expected tightening of domestic macroeconomic policies to contain inflation expectations or protect foreign exchange reserves, social tensions, policy uncertainty, and climate-change-related shocks. In economies already in crisis, the human toll could worsen, with possibilities of widespread starvation and disease outbreaks.

South Asian countries could face significant adverse spillovers from further global monetary tightening, although their severity would differ among countries depending on their integration into global financial markets as well as on domestic policy choices (chapter 3; World Bank 2023l). Additional increases in U.S. interest rates would likely cause foreign exchange market pressures, leading to local currency depreciations relative to the U.S. dollar, declining foreign exchange reserves, capital outflows, or broader financial stress (figure 2.5.3.A). Renewed financial sector stress in advanced economies could spill over into the region—including by undermining global growth (chapter 1).

Expected inflation one year ahead has risen sharply in the region since early 2022 in response to broad-based price increases (figure 2.5.3.B). Additionally, in several economies, economic crises have further contributed to this inflationary pressure. Medium-term inflation expectations appear thus far to have remained subdued; however, if higher inflation expectations became entrenched, additional monetary policy tightening would be required and could affect financial stability as well as economic activity in the region. Financial sector risks remain elevated in several economies, with high levels of non-performing loans, weak capital buffers, and weak bank governance. Ratios of non-performing loans to total loans are elevated and have recently been rising in Bangladesh and Sri Lanka. In Bangladesh, weak corporate governance and capital buffers also increase the risk of stress in the financial sector.

High government and external debt, low foreign exchange reserves, and socio-economic tensions heighten the risk of financial crises in several economies in the region. Such crises could significantly reduce potential as well as actual output growth (Kilic Celik et al. 2023). Rising interest payments on debt, and the need to consolidate government expenditure following pandemic-related stimulus, may undermine efforts to support vulnerable communities and economic activity in the face of global headwinds (figure 2.5.3.C). With limited ability to access international financial markets and elevated fiscal needs, many governments have been looking to borrow domestically, which could increase linkages between the banking sector and government and complicate any debt resolution. One-third of banking sector assets, on average, were claims on governments in late 2022—up from one-fourth in the decade before the pandemic. Increased government borrowing risks crowding out private sector investment and could lead to fiscal dominance, where interest rates are set too low for economic needs, to make it cheaper for the government to service its debt.

Economies in South Asia are among the most vulnerable to climate change (figure 2.5.3.D). More than half of South Asians have been affected by one or more climate-related disasters over the past two decades, with the 2022 floods in Pakistan leaving one-third of the country under water and causing damage estimated at 4.8 percent of GDP (Government of Pakistan et al. 2022). The region has been facing intensifying heatwaves, cyclones, droughts, and floods. With climate change increasing risks to economic activity and development, there is an urgent need to increase resilience. Failure to act could see climate change-related events imposing rising costs. In Nepal, for example, the economic impact from flooding could triple and the number of people affected more than double by 2030 (World Bank 2022e).

TABLE 2.5.1 South Asia forecast summary

(Real GDP growth at market prices in percent, unless indicated otherwise)

Percentage point differences from January 2023 projections

	2020	2021	2022e	2023f	2024f	2025f	2023f	2024f
EMDE South Asia, GDP[1,2]	**-4.1**	**8.3**	**6.0**	**5.9**	**5.1**	**6.4**	**0.4**	**-0.7**
GDP per capita (U.S. dollars)	-5.1	7.2	5.1	4.9	4.0	5.3	0.4	-0.7
EMDE South Asia excluding India, GDP	2.6	6.5	3.6	2.9	4.3	4.7	-0.7	-0.3
(Average including countries that report expenditure components in national accounts)[3]								
EMDE South Asia, GDP[3]	-4.0	8.3	6.0	5.9	5.1	6.4	0.4	-0.7
PPP GDP	-4.1	8.3	6.0	5.9	5.1	6.4	0.4	-0.7
Private consumption	-3.7	10.8	7.0	4.9	6.0	4.9	0.1	-0.1
Public consumption	-2.4	7.4	1.6	2.5	4.1	2.9	-4.2	-0.6
Fixed investment	-8.7	15.6	8.7	7.2	6.8	6.9	0.9	-0.8
Exports, GNFS[4]	-10.4	21.7	15.1	5.8	9.0	6.3	-1.7	1.3
Imports, GNFS[4]	-10.7	21.9	14.6	5.9	8.1	3.9	-0.4	-1.3
Net exports, contribution to growth	0.9	-1.6	-1.1	-0.5	-0.5	0.2	0.0	1.0
Memo items: GDP[2]	2019/20	2020/21	2021/22e	2022/23f	2023/24f	2024/25f	2022/23f	2023/24f
India	3.9	-5.8	9.1	7.2	6.3	6.4	0.3	-0.3
Pakistan (factor cost)	-0.9	5.8	6.1	0.4	2.0	3.0	-1.6	-1.2
Bangladesh	3.4	6.9	7.1	5.2	6.2	6.4	0.0	0.0

Source: World Bank.
Note: e = estimate; f = forecast; PPP = purchasing power parity; EMDE = emerging market and developing economy. World Bank forecasts are frequently updated based on new information and changing (global) circumstances. Consequently, projections presented here may differ from those contained in other Bank documents, even if basic assessments of countries' prospects do not differ at any given moment in time.
1. GDP and expenditure components are measured in average 2010-19 prices and market exchange rates. Excludes Afghanistan because of the high degree of uncertainty.
2. National income and product account data refer to fiscal years (FY) while aggregates are presented in calendar year (CY) terms. (For example, aggregate under 2020/21 refers to CY 2020). The fiscal year runs from July 1 through June 30 in Bangladesh, Bhutan, and Pakistan; from July 16 through July 15 in Nepal; and April 1 through March 31 in India.
3. Subregion aggregate excludes Afghanistan, Bhutan, and Maldives, for which data limitations prevent the forecasting of GDP components.
4. Exports and imports of goods and non-factor services (GNFS).

TABLE 2.5.2 South Asia country forecasts

(Real GDP growth at market prices in percent, unless indicated otherwise)

Percentage point differences from January 2023 projections

	2020	2021	2022e	2023f	2024f	2025f	2023f	2024f
Calendar year basis[1]								
Afghanistan[2]	-2.4	-20.7	..	..	..	..	..	..
Maldives	-33.5	41.7	13.9	6.6	5.3	5.9	-1.6	-2.8
Sri Lanka	-4.6	3.5	-7.8	-4.3	1.2	2.0	-0.1	0.2
Fiscal year basis[1]	2019/20	2020/21	2021/22e	2022/23f	2023/24f	2024/25f	2022/23f	2023/24f
Bangladesh	3.4	6.9	7.1	5.2	6.2	6.4	0.0	0.0
Bhutan	-2.3	-3.3	4.3	4.5	3.1	4.3	0.4	-0.6
India	3.9	-5.8	9.1	7.2	6.3	6.4	0.3	-0.3
Nepal	-2.4	4.8	5.6	4.1	4.9	5.5	-1.0	0.0
Pakistan (factor cost)	-0.9	5.8	6.1	0.4	2.0	3.0	-1.6	-1.2

Source: World Bank.
Note: e = estimate; f = forecast. World Bank forecasts are frequently updated based on new information and changing (global) circumstances. Consequently, projections presented here may differ from those contained in other Bank documents, even if basic assessments of countries' prospects do not significantly differ at any given moment in time.
1. Historical data are reported on a market price basis. National income and product account data refer to fiscal years (FY) with the exception of Afghanistan, Maldives, and Sri Lanka, which report in calendar year. The fiscal year runs from July 1 through June 30 in Bangladesh, Bhutan, and Pakistan; from July 16 through July 15 in Nepal; and April 1 through March 31 in India.
2. Data for Afghanistan beyond 2021 are excluded because of a high degree of uncertainty.

SUB-SAHARAN AFRICA

Growth in Sub-Saharan Africa is projected to slow to 3.2 percent in 2023, as external headwinds, persistent inflation, higher borrowing costs, and increased insecurity weigh on activity. Recoveries from the pandemic remain incomplete in many countries, with elevated costs of living tempering the growth of consumption. Fiscal space has narrowed further, while surging import bills and higher debt burdens have heightened financing needs. Although the baseline projection for 2024-25 envisions a pickup in growth, per capita incomes are expected to expand much more slowly than needed to make progress in reducing extreme poverty. Risks to the baseline remain tilted to the downside. These include a deeper-than-expected global economic slowdown, deteriorating terms of trade, higher inflation along with further domestic and international monetary policy tightening, renewed financial distress in advanced economies, and more adverse weather events. Materialization of these risks would not only dampen growth, but also exacerbate poverty and limit the ability of many countries to strengthen climate resilience.

Recent developments

Private sector activity in Sub-Saharan Africa (SSA) softened markedly in early 2023, reflecting various country-specific challenges and heightened external economic headwinds (figure 2.6.1.A). While many economies across the region are still coping with repercussions of earlier adverse economic and climate shocks, recoveries have been tempered by weaker external demand, further tightening of global financial conditions, domestic policy tightening, and recent flareups of violence and social unrest (Kenya, Sudan).

Elevated costs of living across SSA—partly reflecting the effects of last year's rise in global food and energy prices—have severely worsened the economic hardship of the poor and sharply increased food insecurity. Moreover, in several countries, prolonged droughts (East Africa) and armed conflicts have compounded these effects. As a result, the region entered this year with nearly 180 million people in acute food insecurity—35 million more than at the start of 2022 (WFP 2023b). Although SSA headline inflation has

recently moderated, annual food price inflation has remained above 20 percent in several large SSA economies (Ethiopia, Ghana, Rwanda), and in double digits in over 60 percent of countries—reflecting large currency depreciations and supply disruptions induced by conflict and adverse weather events (figure 2.6.1.B; World Bank 2023m).

Growth in *Nigeria*, the region's largest economy, eased further in early 2023 as a rebound in oil output remained constrained by persistent production challenges (figure 2.6.1.C). The recovery in the non-oil sector, which propelled activity last year, lost momentum early this year amid persistently high inflation, foreign exchange shortages, and shortages of banknotes caused by currency redesign.

Activity in *Angola* last year expanded at its fastest pace since 2014; however, growth lost some momentum in early 2023 as oil production—a key driver of 2022's growth performance—slowed. Meanwhile, high oil prices have boosted the current account and fiscal balances which, together with government debt falling below 65 percent of GDP last year, have helped trim external financing needs.

Note: This section was prepared by Sergiy Kasyanenko.

FIGURE 2.6.1 **SSA: Recent developments**

Private sector activity in Sub-Saharan Africa (SSA) softened in early 2023 as country-specific challenges were amplified by a less favorable global environment. Although headline inflation has receded from last year's highs, elevated food prices continue to exacerbate poverty across the region. Oil production is recovering in Nigeria, but remains well below its pre-pandemic level. Meanwhile, record-high power outages in South Africa have crippled the region's second-largest economy.

A. Purchasing managers' indexes

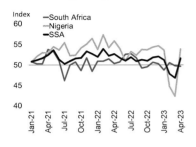

B. Food price inflation

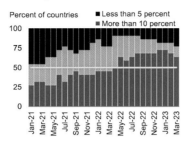

C. Oil production

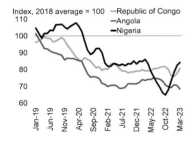

D. Energy crisis in South Africa

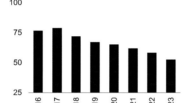

Sources: CSIR Energy Centre; Eskom; Haver Analytics; OPEC; World Bank.
Note: SSA = Sub-Saharan Africa.
A. Purchasing Managers' Index (PMI) values above 50 indicate expansion in private activity. Composite PMI covers manufacturing and services; SSA represents GDP weighted average for Ghana, Kenya, Mozambique, Nigeria, South Africa, Uganda, and Zambia. SSA average = Real GDP weighted average. Last observation is April 2023.
B. Sample include 22 countries. Last observation is March 2023.
C. Three-month moving averages. Last observation is March 2023.
D. Energy availability factor is the percentage of the time that power generating capacity is available to provide electricity to the grid. Last observation is January-March 2023.

Growth in *South Africa* decelerated sharply in early 2023, reflecting policy tightening and the impact of an intensifying energy crisis. The country's power utility, Eskom, beset by chronic unprofitability and lack of maintenance, has been struggling to meet a post-pandemic rebound in electricity demand (figure 2.6.1.D). Power outages have hit record highs this year and crippled the economy. Headline inflation has receded from its peak, but it has been above the 6 percent upper bound of the central bank's target range since April 2022, prompting even more policy tightening in the first half of this year.

Elsewhere in the region, capacity expansions in extractive sectors have boosted growth in some resource-rich countries (Democratic Republic of Congo, Niger, Senegal). In other resource-rich countries, however, recoveries have remained subdued. Several oil producers have continued to face production challenges because of aging oil fields and underinvestment (Equatorial Guinea), and disruptions owing to insecurity and weather (Chad, South Sudan). In some metal exporters, political uncertainty, policy tightening, and high inflation (Liberia, Mauritania, Sierra Leone) have weakened growth.

Recoveries in non-resource-rich countries have slowed amid deteriorating terms of trade, widening current account and fiscal deficits, and sharp cost-of-living increases. Most of these countries are agricultural commodity producers where farming activity has been curbed by high production costs, unfavorable weather, and insecurity. Increased fragility, owing to political uncertainty and intercommunal violence, has been amplifying these negative developments. Growth in small agricultural commodity producers affected by fragility (Burkina Faso, Mali) eased to just 1.2 percent last year—almost four percentage points slower than in other SSA agricultural commodity producers. Growth in Ethiopia—SSA's largest agricultural commodity producer and its most populous low-income country—is estimated at 6.4 percent for the current fiscal year ending in July, driven by stronger-than-expected activity in agriculture and services.

External financing needs across the region remain large, partly reflecting the legacy of the pandemic and last year's cost-of-living increases. Current account deficits are elevated in many countries still struggling with high import bills and increased debt and debt-service costs. Covering financing needs has become even more challenging as a result of the rapid tightening of global financial conditions, and, in some countries, shrinking foreign exchange reserves and reduced donor support. Public spending across SSA remains restrained on account of slowing growth, elevated risks of debt distress, and necessary fiscal consolidation.

Outlook

Growth in SSA is expected to slow from 3.7 percent in 2022 to 3.2 percent this year—a 0.4 percentage point downgrade from January forecasts—with a moderate improvement to 3.9 percent next year (table 2.6.1). Over half of the 2023 downgrade is attributable to an abrupt slowdown in South Africa. However, downgrades are widespread across energy and metal producers, and non-resource-rich countries. Excluding South Africa, growth in SSA is expected to slow from 4.2 percent in 2022 to 3.9 percent this year. While this represents a minor downgrade from January, this pace of expansion is still a full percentage point below the 2000-19 average.

Although the reopening of China is expected to boost exports of some countries this year, limited access to external borrowing is forecast to hold back recoveries as debt burdens and financing needs increase. More broadly, high costs of living across the region are projected to continue to restrain private consumption, while limited fiscal space and tight monetary policies are likely to weigh on investment growth. These elevated domestic vulnerabilities together with tight global financial conditions and weak global growth are expected to keep recoveries subdued over the forecast horizon.

The three largest economies in Sub-Saharan Africa—Nigeria, South Africa, and Angola—which are projected to grow by about 2.1 percent annually over 2023-24, a rate more than 2 percentage points per year below the 2000-19 average, are expected to continue to inhibit the overall growth of the region (figure 2.6.2.A). The outlook for smaller producers of metals, oil, and agricultural commodities is dimmed by an expected weakening of global commodity prices, with growth forecasts for these groups of countries downgraded for both 2023 and 2024 (figure 2.6.2.B). In addition to multiple external and domestic headwinds, many of these countries are confronted with increased fragility because of pervasive insecurity and political instability, as well as persistent poverty.

Growth in *Nigeria* is projected at 2.8 percent in 2023, revised down marginally since January, and

FIGURE 2.6.2 SSA: Outlook

Growth in SSA is projected to firm next year, although the recovery will be tempered by elevated domestic vulnerabilities, continued policy tightening, and moderating commodity prices. As a result, per capita income growth is projected to remain well below its long-term trend, further delaying the reversal of income losses and poverty increases inflicted by the pandemic and subsequent cost-of-living shocks.

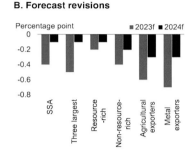

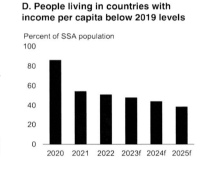

Sources: World Bank.
Note: f = forecast; SSA = Sub-Saharan Africa. Three largest countries include Nigeria, South Africa, and Angola.
A. Aggregate growth rates calculated using constant GDP weights at average 2010-19 prices and market exchange rates.
B. Revisions relative to forecast published in the January 2023 *Global Economic Prospects* report. Resource-rich countries include metal and oil producers; agricultural commodity exporters exclude Ethiopia; metal exporters exclude the Democratic Republic of Congo, South Africa, and Zambia.

is forecast to inch up to 3.0 percent in 2024. This translates to per capita income growth of only 0.4 percent a year on average in 2023-24—far slower than that needed to make significant inroads into mitigating extreme poverty. With continued structural challenges in the oil sector expected to keep oil production below the average of the last five years, growth is projected to be driven mainly by the non-oil sector. However, foreign exchange restrictions, high living costs, security challenges, and limited fiscal space are expected to constrain growth momentum. Financing needs are projected to remain elevated, due to higher borrowing costs, lower oil production and prices, and persistent fiscal and external pressures amid weak domestic revenue mobilization.

Growth in *South Africa* is projected to slow sharply to 0.3 percent this year—a 1.1 percentage point downgrade from January. The drag from the abrupt slowdown that started late last year and continued into early 2023 amid widespread power outages is expected to weigh heavily on the recovery. Growth is forecast to firm to 1.5 percent next year—still a 0.3 percentage point downward revision, as power cuts are expected to be more severe than previously projected. They are, however, assumed to gradually ease as private generation capacity expands. This subdued recovery implies that per capita incomes will stagnate. Persisting structural problems, such as high unemployment, crumbling transportation and power supply infrastructure, inefficiencies in state-owned enterprises, and slow implementation of reforms are expected to prevent a much-needed pickup in growth.

Growth in *Angola* is projected to weaken to 2.6 percent this year—a 0.2 percentage point downgrade—as lower oil prices and falling oil production reduce export and fiscal revenues. The recovery is forecast to pick up to 3.3 percent in 2024, driven by a strong performance in the non-oil sectors, particularly services and agriculture. A reduced need for aggressive fiscal consolidation will add impetus to the recovery. Growth is still projected to fall below Angola's population growth, leaving per capita income 10 percent lower than pre-pandemic levels even at the end of 2024 (figure 2.6.2.C).

Elsewhere, growth projections for SSA resource-rich countries—excluding the three largest economies and two biggest copper producers, the Democratic Republic of Congo and Zambia—have been downgraded. In several metal and oil producers, headwinds from the weaker external environment have been amplified by capacity constraints in extractive sectors (Cameroon, Equatorial Guinea, Gabon). Recovery prospects are also less favorable for many small agricultural commodity producers coping with food insecurity, increased prices and shortages of farming inputs, the lingering effects of past weather shocks, and violence (Burkina Faso, Malawi, Mali). More broadly, elevated financing needs, high levels of debt, and limited fiscal space are expected to weigh on activity and exacerbate unfavorable debt dynamics in several countries.

Per capita income in SSA is projected to grow by less than 1 percent a year on average in 2023-24—a 0.3 percentage point downgrade from the January forecast. In over a fifth of the region's economies, home to over 450 million people, average per capita income growth in 2023-24 is not expected to exceed 0.5 percent, while in over a tenth, including Angola and South Africa, it will be negative. Thus, prospects for poverty reduction in the region remain bleak, with almost 40 percent of SSA's population living in countries (including the three largest economies) with lower per capita incomes next year than at the start of the pandemic (figure 2.6.2.D).

Risks

The baseline projections remain subject to multiple downside risks amid uncertainty about developments in global commodity markets, the degree of additional global and domestic policy tightening needed to subdue persistent inflation, and the resilience of the world economy and global financial system to a prolonged period of tight monetary policies. Commodity prices may remain unusually volatile and vulnerable to further shocks if disruptions to the supply of major commodities worsen—for instance, due to intensifying geopolitical tensions or conflicts. Furthermore, global activity may decelerate faster than envisioned if the reopening of China's economy fails to generate a durable recovery.

If global and domestic inflationary pressures were to persist for longer than currently anticipated and inflation expectations become de-anchored, policy makers could be forced to raise interest rates by more than expected or keep borrowing costs elevated for longer (figure 2.6.3.A). Additional policy tightening in advanced economies could be accompanied by renewed banking stress. As a result, SSA financial conditions could tighten much more than projected in the baseline, triggering even greater deterioration in access to markets and elevating risks of financial distress and government debt defaults (figure 2.6.3.B).

Global food and energy prices have retreated from last year's peaks, but further disruptions in global or local trade and production, amid already-tight global supplies of many commodities, could reignite consumer price inflation across the region. Recent declines in prices of agricultural commodities, alongside still-elevated prices of inputs such as fuel, chemicals, and fertilizer, could also weigh on food availability and affordability if farmers were prompted to reduce output or substitute staples with cash crops.

The region remains particularly vulnerable to extreme weather events, which can seriously disrupt activity in mining and agriculture, the latter being a source of livelihood and employment for many poor and vulnerable people in SSA. Climate change-induced increases in average temperatures could significantly lower crop yields across the region, reducing exports and food supply (World Bank 2022f, 2022g, 2022h). More severe and prolonged extreme weather—such as droughts, floods, and tropical cyclones—would aggravate misery and devastation across SSA and escalate insecurity in countries already stressed by the increased frequency and severity of such events (Ethiopia, Kenya, Malawi, Mozambique, Sudan; World Bank 2022i; figure 2.6.3.C).

Many SSA economies already coping with negative consequences of climate change are also affected by fragility stemming from persistent poverty, as well as festering violence and conflict (Somalia, South Sudan, Sudan; figure 2.6.3.D). These countries lack the needed policy space to mitigate the consequences of, and adapt to, climate change because of macroeconomic vulnerabilities, such as high debt or even debt distress, reliance on food and fuel imports, and elevated inflation. Despite recent peacemaking efforts in several large countries (Democratic Republic of Congo, Ethiopia), fragility could worsen further amid high levels of insecurity (for example, in the Sahel region, especially in Sudan) as well as flare-ups of social unrest in other countries (Kenya, Senegal). Violence and conflict could depress growth more severely than in the baseline and leave the most vulnerable countries unprepared to tackle the challenges of climate change, resulting in drawn-out humanitarian crises.

FIGURE 2.6.3 SSA: Risks

The outlook is subject to multiple downside risks. Domestic and global macroeconomic policies could tighten by more than assumed if inflation pressures persist or if access to international borrowing becomes more difficult. Violence and insecurity could escalate, especially in fragile countries. More severe and frequent adverse weather events could amplify damage from domestic and global shocks. In the countries least prepared for the effects of climate change, overlapping vulnerabilities could prolong and deepen humanitarian crises.

A. Monetary policy interest rates, change since December 2020

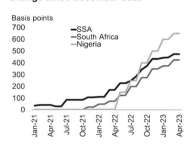

B. International bond issuance

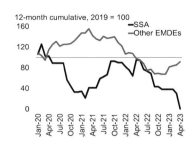

C. Violence and conflict

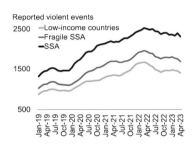

D. Overlapping vulnerabilities

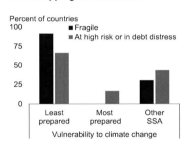

Sources: ACLED (database); Dealogic; International Monetary Fund; Notre Dame Global Adaptation Initiative (ND-GAIN), University of Notre Dame; World Bank.
Note: EMDEs = emerging market and developing economies; Fragile SSA = SSA EMDEs with fragile and conflict affected situations; SSA = Sub-Saharan Africa.
A. SSA average = simple average for 8 SSA EMDEs. Last observation is April 2023.
B. Twelve-month cumulative issuance of bonds by SSA and EMDE governments. Last observation April 2023.
C. Six-month moving averages; violent events include battles, explosions, violence against civilians, riots and protests. Last observation is April 2023.
D. Least (most) prepared SSA include countries in the bottom (top) 25 percent of ND-GAIN's vulnerability to climate change index. Debt distress assessment as of the end of February 2023.

TABLE 2.6.1 Sub-Saharan Africa forecast summary

(Real GDP growth at market prices in percent, unless indicated otherwise)

Percentage point differences from January 2023 projections

	2020	2021	2022e	2023f	2024f	2025f	2023f	2024f
EMDE SSA, GDP [1]	-2.0	4.4	3.7	3.2	3.9	4.0	-0.4	0.0
GDP per capita (U.S. dollars)	-4.5	1.8	1.2	0.6	1.3	1.5	-0.4	-0.1
(Average including countries that report expenditure components in national accounts) [2]								
EMDE SSA, GDP [2,3]	-2.0	4.4	3.7	3.2	3.9	4.0	-0.4	0.0
PPP GDP	-1.8	4.3	3.7	3.2	4.0	4.1	-0.4	0.0
Private consumption	-1.5	10.2	4.0	3.0	3.1	3.4	-0.1	-0.3
Public consumption	8.6	-2.0	2.0	-1.0	4.2	3.0	-1.7	1.4
Fixed investment	-2.0	8.6	6.1	6.3	5.7	6.6	-0.7	-1.6
Exports, GNFS [4]	-15.9	2.8	8.6	6.8	6.3	6.1	0.2	0.0
Imports, GNFS [4]	-19.8	17.2	10.9	6.2	5.9	6.0	-1.0	-1.5
Net exports, contribution to growth	1.5	-3.3	-1.0	-0.2	-0.2	-0.3	0.3	0.4
Memo items: GDP								
Eastern and Southern Africa	-2.9	4.8	3.7	3.1	3.9	4.0	-0.4	0.0
Western and Central Africa	-0.8	4.0	3.7	3.3	3.9	4.0	-0.4	-0.1
SSA excluding Nigeria, South Africa, and Angola	0.1	4.8	4.7	4.6	5.3	5.4	-0.2	0.0
Oil exporters [5]	-2.0	3.2	3.2	2.6	3.0	3.3	-0.3	0.0
CFA countries [6]	0.4	4.1	4.6	4.5	5.5	5.1	-0.7	-0.2
CEMAC	-1.6	1.1	2.9	2.7	2.8	3.0	-0.3	-0.4
WAEMU	1.7	6.0	5.6	5.5	7.0	6.2	-0.9	0.0
SSA3	-4.0	4.0	2.8	1.7	2.4	2.5	-0.6	0.0
Nigeria	-1.8	3.6	3.3	2.8	3.0	3.1	-0.1	0.1
South Africa	-6.3	4.9	2.0	0.3	1.5	1.6	-1.1	-0.3
Angola	-5.6	1.1	3.5	2.6	3.3	3.1	-0.2	0.4

Source: World Bank.

Note: e = estimate; f = forecast; PPP = purchasing power parity; EMDE = emerging market and developing economy. World Bank forecasts are frequently updated based on new information and changing (global) circumstances. Consequently, projections presented here may differ from those contained in other Bank documents, even if basic assessments of countries' prospects do not differ at any given moment in time.

1. GDP and expenditure components are measured in average 2010-19 prices and market exchange rates.

2. Subregion aggregate excludes the Central African Republic, Eritrea, Guinea, São Tomé and Príncipe, Somalia, and South Sudan, for which data limitations prevent the forecasting of GDP components.

3. Subregion growth rates may differ from the most recent edition of Africa's Pulse (https://www.worldbank.org/en/region/afr/publication/africas-pulse) because of data revisions.

4. Exports and imports of goods and non-factor services (GNFS).

5. Includes Angola, Cameroon, Chad, the Republic of Congo, Equatorial Guinea, Gabon, Ghana, Nigeria, and South Sudan.

6. The Financial Community of Africa (CFA) franc zone consists of 14 countries in Sub-Saharan Africa, each affiliated with one of two monetary unions. The Central African Economic and Monetary Union (CEMAC) comprises Cameroon, the Central African Republic, Chad, the Republic of Congo, Equatorial Guinea, and Gabon; the West African Economic and Monetary Union (WAEMU) comprises Benin, Burkina Faso, Côte d'Ivoire, Guinea-Bissau, Mali, Niger, Senegal, and Togo.

TABLE 2.6.2 **Sub-Saharan Africa country forecasts**[1]

(Real GDP growth at market prices in percent, unless indicated otherwise)

Percentage point differences from January 2023 projections

	2020	2021	2022e	2023f	2024f	2025f	2023f	2024f
Angola	-5.6	1.1	3.5	2.6	3.3	3.1	-0.2	0.4
Benin	3.8	7.2	6.0	6.0	5.9	6.1	-0.2	-0.1
Botswana	-8.7	11.8	6.5	4.0	4.0	4.0	0.0	0.0
Burkina Faso	1.9	6.9	2.5	4.3	4.8	5.1	-0.7	-0.5
Burundi	0.3	3.1	1.8	3.0	4.0	4.2	0.0	0.0
Central African Republic	1.0	1.0	0.0	3.0	3.8	3.8	0.0	0.0
Cabo Verde	-14.8	7.0	15.0	4.8	5.4	5.3	0.0	-0.3
Cameroon	0.5	3.6	3.4	3.9	4.2	4.5	-0.4	-0.4
Chad	-1.6	-1.2	2.2	3.2	3.4	3.1	-0.1	0.1
Comoros	-0.3	2.1	2.3	2.8	2.9	3.6	-0.5	-0.9
Congo, Dem. Rep.	1.7	6.2	8.6	7.7	7.6	7.5	1.3	1.0
Congo, Rep.	-6.2	-2.2	1.5	3.5	4.3	2.8	-0.2	-0.2
Côte d'Ivoire	1.7	7.0	6.7	6.2	6.5	6.5	-0.6	-0.1
Equatorial Guinea	-4.2	-2.8	2.9	-3.7	-6.0	-3.1	-1.1	-2.6
Eritrea	-0.5	2.9	2.5	2.7	2.9	2.8	0.0	0.0
Eswatini	-1.6	7.9	0.4	3.0	2.9	2.7	0.4	0.2
Ethiopia[2]	6.1	6.3	6.4	6.0	6.6	7.0	0.7	0.5
Gabon	-1.8	1.5	3.1	3.1	3.0	3.0	0.1	0.1
Gambia, The	0.6	4.3	4.3	5.0	5.5	5.8	1.0	0.0
Ghana	0.5	5.4	3.2	1.6	2.9	4.8	-1.1	-0.6
Guinea	4.9	4.3	4.7	5.6	5.8	5.6	0.3	0.2
Guinea-Bissau	1.5	6.4	3.5	4.5	4.5	4.5	0.0	0.0
Kenya	-0.3	7.5	5.2	5.0	5.2	5.3	0.0	-0.1
Lesotho	-5.6	1.6	1.8	2.6	3.1	3.3	0.3	0.2
Liberia	-3.0	5.0	4.8	4.3	5.5	5.6	-0.4	-0.2
Madagascar	-7.1	5.7	3.8	4.2	4.8	5.1	0.0	0.2
Malawi	0.8	2.8	0.9	1.4	2.4	3.0	-1.6	-1.0
Mali	-1.2	3.1	1.8	4.0	4.0	5.0	0.0	0.0
Mauritania	-0.9	2.4	5.2	4.5	5.6	6.8	-0.6	-2.3
Mauritius	-14.6	3.5	8.3	4.7	4.1	3.6	-0.8	-0.1
Mozambique	-1.2	2.3	4.1	5.0	8.3	5.3	0.0	0.3
Namibia	-8.0	2.7	3.5	2.4	1.7	2.1	0.4	-0.2
Niger	3.6	1.4	11.5	6.9	12.5	9.1	-0.2	2.4
Nigeria	-1.8	3.6	3.3	2.8	3.0	3.1	-0.1	0.1
Rwanda	-3.4	10.9	8.1	6.2	7.5	7.5	-0.5	0.5
São Tomé and Príncipe	3.1	1.9	0.9	2.1	3.4	3.7	0.0	1.0
Senegal	1.3	6.5	4.2	4.7	9.9	5.2	-3.3	-0.6
Seychelles	-8.6	5.4	8.8	3.8	3.0	3.1	-1.4	-1.8
Sierra Leone	-2.0	4.1	3.0	3.4	3.7	4.4	-0.3	-0.7
South Africa	-6.3	4.9	2.0	0.3	1.5	1.6	-1.1	-0.3
Sudan	-3.6	-1.9	-1.0	0.4	1.5	2.0	-1.6	-1.0
South Sudan[2]	9.5	-5.1	-2.3	-0.4	2.3	2.4	0.4	0.2
Tanzania	2.0	4.3	4.6	5.1	5.6	6.2	-0.2	-0.5
Togo	1.8	5.3	4.9	4.9	5.3	5.5	-0.7	-1.1
Uganda[2]	3.0	3.4	4.7	5.7	6.2	6.7	0.2	0.1
Zambia	-2.8	4.6	3.9	4.2	4.7	4.8	0.3	0.6
Zimbabwe	-7.8	8.5	3.4	2.9	3.4	3.4	-0.7	-0.2

Source: World Bank.

Note: e = estimate; f = forecast. World Bank forecasts are frequently updated based on new information and changing (global) circumstances. Consequently, projections presented here may differ from those contained in other Bank documents, even if basic assessments of countries' prospects do not significantly differ at any given moment in time.

1. Data are based on GDP measured in average 2010-19 prices and market exchange rates.
2. Fiscal-year-based numbers.

References

ACLED (Armed Conflict Location & Event Data Project) database. Accessed on May 8, 2023. https://acleddata.com/data-export-tool

Arroyo Marioli, F., and C. A. Vegh. 2023. "Fiscal Procyclicality in Commodity Exporting Countries: How Much Does It Pour and Why." Policy Research Working Paper 10428, World Bank, Washington, DC.

Arteta, C., S. B. Kamin, and F. U. Ruch. 2022. "How Do Rising U.S. Interest Rates Affect Emerging and Developing Economies? It Depends (English)." Policy Research Working Paper 10258, World Bank, Washington, DC.

Baumeister, C., G. Verduzco-Bustos, and F. Ohnsorge. 2022. "Special Focus: Pandemic, War, Recession: Drivers of Aluminum and Copper Prices." In *Commodity Markets Outlook.* October. Washington, DC: World Bank.

Chupilkin, M., B. Javorcik, and A. Plekhanov. 2023. "The Eurasian Roundabout: Trade Flows into Russia through the Caucasus and Central Asia." EBRD Working Paper 276, European Bank for Reconstruction and Development, London.

Cai, W., G. Wang, A. Santoso, M. J. McPhaden, L. Wu, F. Jin, A. Timmermann, et al. 2015. "Increased Frequency of Extreme La Niña Events under Greenhouse Warming." *Nature Climate Change* 5 (2): 132-37.

Darvas, Z., C. Martins, and C. McCaffrey. 2023. "Russian Foreign Trade Tracker." Brussels: Bruegel. https://bruegel.org/dataset/russian-foreign-trade-tracker

de la Torre, A., F. Filippini, and A. Ize. 2016. *The Commodity Cycle in Latin America: Mirages and Dilemmas.* April. Washington, DC: World Bank.

Dellink, R., E. Lanzi, J. Château, F. Bosello, R. Parrado, and K. Bruin. 2014. "Consequences of Climate Change Damages for Economic Growth: A Dynamic Quantitative Assessment." OECD Economics Department Working Paper 1135, Organisation for Economic Co-operation and Development, Paris.

EBRD (European Bank for Reconstruction and Development). 2022. *Transition Report 2022-23: Business Unusual.* London: European Bank for Reconstruction and Development.

FAO (Food and Agriculture Organization). 2022. "Haiti: Response Overview: October 2022." Food and Agriculture Organization of the United Nations, Rome.

Government of Pakistan, Asian Development Bank, European Union, United Nations Development Programme, and World Bank. 2022. *Pakistan Floods 2022: Post-Disaster Needs Assessment.* Islamabad: Ministry of Planning Development and Special Initiatives.

ILO (International Labour Organization). 2022. *Global Employment Trends for Youth 2022: Investing in Transforming Futures for Young People.* Geneva: ILO.

ILO (International Labour Organization). 2023. *Global Wage Report 2022-23: The Impact of Inflation and COVID-19 on Wages and Purchasing Power.* Geneva: ILO.

IMF (International Monetary Fund). 2021. *State-Owned Enterprises in Middle East, North Africa, and Central Asia: Size, Role, Performance, and Challenges.* DP/2021/019. Washington, DC: International Monetary Fund.

IMF (International Monetary Fund). 2022. *Feeling the Heat: Adapting to Climate Change in the Middle East and Central Asia.* Washington, DC: International Monetary Fund.

IMF (International Monetary Fund). 2023a. "Ukraine: Request for an Extended Arrangement Under the Extended Fund Facility and Review of Program Monitoring with Board Involvement. Press Release; Staff Report; and Statement by the Executive Director for Ukraine." IMF Country Report 23/132, International Monetary Fund, Washington, DC.

IMF (International Monetary Fund). 2023b. *Global Financial Stability Report.* April. Washington, DC: International Monetary Fund.

IMF (International Monetary Fund). 2023c. "Arab Republic of Egypt: Request for Extended Arrangement Under the Extended Fund Facility-Press Release; and Staff Report. IMF Country Report 23/2, International Monetary Fund, Washington, DC.

IMF (International Monetary Fund). 2023d. *Morocco: Request for an Arrangement Under the Flexible Credit Line-Press Release; Staff Report; And Statement by the Executive Director for Morocco.* Washington, DC: International Monetary Fund.

IMF (International Monetary Fund). 2023e. *Sri Lanka: Request for an Extended Arrangement Under the Extend-*

ed Fund Facility-Press Release; Staff Report; and Statement by the Executive Director for Sri Lanka. Washington, DC: International Monetary Fund.

Kahn, M. E., K. Mohaddes, R. N. C. Ng, M. H. Pesaran, M. Raissi, and J. Yang. 2021. "Long-Term Macroeconomic Effects of Climate Change: A Cross-Country Analysis." *Energy Economics* 104: 105624.

Kenworthy, P., P. Kirby, and D. Vorisek. 2023. "Small State: Overlapping Crises, Multiple Challenges." In *Global Economic Prospects.* January. Washington, DC: World Bank.

Khandelwal, P., E. Cabezon, S. Mirzayev, and R. Al-Farah. 2022. "Macroprudential Policies to Enhance Financial Stability in the Caucasus and Central Asia." IMF Departmental Paper 22/006, International Monetary Fund, Washington, DC.

Kilic Celik, S., M. A. Kose, and F. Ohnsorge. 2023. "Potential Growth Prospects : Risks, Rewards, and Policies." Policy Research Working Paper 10355, World Bank, Washington, DC.

Kilic Celik, S., M. A. Kose, F. Ohnsorge, and F. U. Ruch. 2023. "Potential Growth: A Global Database." Policy Research Working Paper 10354, World Bank, Washington, DC.

Kose, M. A., and F. Ohnsorge, eds. 2023. *Falling Long-Term Growth Prospects: Trends, Expectations, and Policies.* Washington, DC: World Bank.

Maloney, W. F., D. Riera-Crichton, E. I. Ianchovichina, G. Vuletin, and G. Beylis. 2023. *The Promise of Integration: Opportunities in a Changing Global Economy. Latin America and the Caribbean Economic Review.* April. Washington, DC: World Bank.

OECD (Organisation for Economic Co-operation and Development). 2022. *Green Economy Transition in Eastern Europe, the Caucasus, and Central Asia—Progress and Ways Forward.* Paris: OECD Publishing.

Pfeiffer, P., J. Varga, and Jan in 't Veld. 2021. "Quantifying Spillovers of Next Generation EU Investment." Discussion Paper 144, European Commission, Luxembourg.

Rogoff, K. S., and Y. Yang. 2022. "A Tale of Tier 3 Cities." NBER Working Paper 30519, National Bureau of Economic Research, Cambridge, MA.

Sinha Roy, S., and R. Van Der Weide. 2022. "Poverty in India has Declined Over the Last Decade but not as

Much as Previously Thought." Policy Research Working Paper 9994, World Bank, Washington, DC.

Wang, B., X. Luo, Y. Yang, W. Sun, M. A. Cane, W. Cai, S. Yeh, and J. Liu. 2019. "Historical Change of El Niño Properties Sheds Light on Future Changes of Extreme El Niño." *Proceedings of the National Academy of Sciences* 116 (45): 22512-17.

World Bank. 2022a. *Remittances Brave Global Headwinds, Special Focus: Climate Migration.* Migration and Development Brief 37. Washington, DC: World Bank.

World Bank. 2022b. "Climate Change in Europe and Central Asia." Europe and Central Asia brief. World Bank, Washington, DC.

World Bank. 2022c. *Egypt Country Climate and Development Report.* Washington, DC: World Bank.

World Bank. 2022d. *Iraq Country Climate and Development Report.* Washington, DC: World Bank.

World Bank. 2022e. *Nepal Country Climate and Development Report.* Washington, DC: World Bank.

World Bank. 2022f. *Angola Country Climate and Development Report.* World Bank: Washington, DC.

World Bank. 2022g. *Ghana Country Climate and Development Report.* World Bank: Washington, DC.

World Bank. 2022h. *Malawi Country Climate and Development Report.* World Bank: Washington, DC.

World Bank. 2022i. *Rwanda Country Climate and Development Report.* World Bank: Washington, DC.

World Bank. 2023a. *Reviving Growth.* East Asia and Pacific Economic Update. Apri). Washington, DC: World Bank.

World Bank. 2023b. *Global Economic Prospects.* January. Washington, DC: World Bank.

World Bank. 2023c. *Commodities Markets Outlook.* April. Washington, DC: World Bank.

World Bank. 2023d. *Weak Growth, High Inflation, and a Cost-of-Living Crisis.* Europe and Central Asia Economic Update. April. Washington, DC: World Bank.

World Bank. 2023e. *Global Rapid Post-Disaster Damage Estimation (GRADE): February 2023, Kahramanmaraş Earthquakes—Türkiye Report.* Washington, DC: World Bank.

World Bank. 2023f. *Ukraine Rapid Damage and Needs Assessment; February 2022—February 2023.* March. Washington, DC: World Bank.

World Bank. 2023g. *Western Balkans Regular Economic Report: Testing Resilience.* April. Washington, DC: World Bank.

World Bank. 2023h. *Energizing Europe.* EU Regular Economic Report. May. Washington, DC: World Bank.

World Bank. 2023i. *Syria Economic Monitor: Syria's Economy in Ruins After a Decade-long War.* Washington, DC: World Bank.

World Bank. 2023j. *Syria Earthquake 2023: Rapid Damage and Needs Assessment.* Washington, DC: World Bank.

World Bank. 2023k. *MENA Economic Update: Altered Destinies: The Long-Term Effect of Rising Prices and Food Insecurity in the Middle East and North Africa.* Washington, DC: World Bank.

World Bank. 2023l. *South Asia Economic Focus: Expanding Opportunities: Toward Inclusive Growth.* Washington, DC: World Bank.

World Bank. 2023m. *Africa's Pulse: Leveraging Resource Wealth During the Low Carbon Transition.* World Bank: Washington, DC.

WFP (World Food Programme). 2023a. "WFP Afghanistan: Situation Report." March. World Food Programme, Rome.

WFP (World Food Programme). 2023b. "WFP Global Operational Response Plan 2023. Update #7." February. World Food Programme, Rome.

CHAPTER 3

FINANCIAL SPILLOVERS OF RISING U.S. INTEREST RATES

The rapid rise in interest rates in the United States poses a significant challenge to emerging market and developing economies (EMDEs). As the Federal Reserve has pivoted toward a more hawkish stance to rein in inflation, a substantial part of the sharp increases in U.S. interest rates since early 2022 has been driven by shocks that capture changes in perceptions of the Fed's reaction function. These reaction shocks are associated with especially adverse financial market effects in EMDEs, including a higher likelihood of experiencing a financial crisis. Their effects also appear to be more pronounced in EMDEs with greater economic vulnerabilities. These findings suggest that major central banks can alleviate adverse spillovers through proper communication that clarifies their reaction functions. They also highlight that EMDEs need to adjust macroeconomic and financial policies to mitigate the negative impact of rising global and U.S. interest rates.

Introduction

The swift tightening of monetary policy in advanced economies, especially the United States, in response to high inflation poses grave challenges to emerging market and developing economies (EMDEs; figures 3.1.A and 3.1.B). Tight monetary policy by the Federal Reserve adversely affects EMDEs in several ways. It slows the U.S. economy, thereby diminishing imports from EMDEs and thus dampening their economic activity. The tightening of financial conditions in the United States and the associated increase in risk aversion spill over to EMDEs, leading to higher domestic interest rates and risk spreads as well as lower equity prices. Increases in U.S. interest rates also boost the cost of servicing dollar-denominated debt—both directly, by raising interest payments, and indirectly, by pushing up the foreign exchange value of the dollar, which increases the domestic-currency cost of repaying dollar debt. Currency depreciation may also exacerbate inflation, requiring additional monetary tightening by EMDE central banks.

These spillovers can heighten the likelihood of financial distress in EMDEs, especially in those with pre-existing vulnerabilities. Indeed, these developments have already contributed to financial strains and even default in several countries. EMDEs have become particularly exposed to rising global interest rates, as the COVID-19 pandemic gave further impetus to a broad-based surge in debt levels in EMDEs, with government debt reaching record highs (Kose et al. 2021; World Bank 2022).

The effects of rising U.S. interest rates on EMDE financial conditions are likely to be particularly injurious because of their underlying cause. This chapter distinguishes between the effects of three different types of shocks that can boost U.S. interest rates: (1) inflation shocks, which are prompted by rising expectations of U.S. inflation; (2) reaction shocks, which are prompted by investor assessments that the Federal Reserve has shifted toward a more hawkish stance; and (3) real shocks, which are prompted by anticipation of strengthening U.S. economic activity. Increases in U.S. interest rates associated with inflation or reaction shocks should lead to more adverse spillovers because rising interest rates would coincide with weakening U.S. economic activity and dampened investor sentiment. This could depress exports, capital inflows, and financial conditions in EMDEs. In contrast, positive real shocks leading to higher U.S. interest rates should have relatively benign effects on EMDEs, since the beneficial effects of strong U.S. import demand and improved investor confidence would somewhat offset the adverse effects of higher borrowing costs.

Persistently high U.S. inflation, along with the Fed's pivot toward a more aggressive tightening stance, suggests that increases in U.S. interest rates over the past year and a half have been driven predominantly by inflation and reaction shocks. That said, the recent period of turmoil in the global banking sector has further complicated the path of U.S. monetary policy. If recent banking stresses were to intensify, the Fed could pause or even reverse its tightening of monetary policy. However, insofar as that reversal would reflect prospects of deteriorating economic conditions—essentially, a negative real shock to U.S. interest rates—it, too, would likely be associated with

---

Note: This chapter was prepared by Carlos Arteta, Steven Kamin, and Franz Ulrich Ruch. It is based and expands on Arteta, Kamin, and Ruch (2022).

FIGURE 3.1 Recent financial developments in the United States and EMDEs

The Federal Reserve has embarked on its fastest and steepest hiking cycle to rein in high inflation since the early 1980s. This has resulted in adverse financial spillovers for emerging market and developing economies (EMDEs). These spillovers are particularly pronounced for countries with weaker credit ratings.

A. Federal Reserve hiking cycles, cumulative

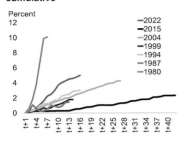

B. U.S. personal consumption expenditure inflation

C. Sovereign risk spreads

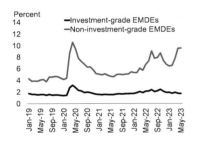

D. Change in EMDE CDS premia around advanced-economy bank failures

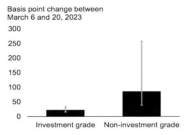

Sources: Bloomberg; Federal Reserve Bank of St. Louis; J.P. Morgan; Moody's Analytics; World Bank.
Note: EMDEs = emerging market and developing economies.
A. Based on the effective Federal Funds Rate. Monthly data. Last observation is May 2023.
B. PCE = personal consumption expenditure. Last observation is April 2023.
C. Sample includes 29 non-investment-grade and 15 investment-grade EMDEs based on Moody's long-term sovereign rating in foreign currency as of May 2023. Sample excludes Belarus, Ghana, Lebanon, the Russian Federation, Sri Lanka, Ukraine, and Zambia. Last observation is May 2023. Based on emerging market bond index global spreads.
D. Median change in 5-year U.S. dollar-denominated credit default swaps for 48 EMDEs, including 19 investment-grade and 29 non-investment-grade countries. Whiskers indicate interquartile range.

negative impacts on EMDEs. Although there is considerable uncertainty about future Fed policy action—with market participants assuming an earlier reversal of the tightening cycle than FOMC members do—most observers expect policy rates to remain elevated for some time. In particular, EMDEs with continued financial vulnerabilities and greater macroeconomic imbalances are likely to be more susceptible to the negative impacts of U.S. interest rate increases.

Against this backdrop, this chapter examines the effects of rising U.S. interest rates on financial

conditions in EMDEs, including an analysis of the role of macroeconomic and financial vulnerabilities. The chapter also provides insights into the policy implications of these findings. In particular, it aims to answer the following questions:

- What mix of real, inflation, and reaction shocks have driven changes in U.S. interest rates in recent years?

- How do reaction shocks amid aggressive Fed policy affect EMDE financial conditions and the likelihood of financial crisis?

- Are EMDEs with lingering vulnerabilities and macroeconomic imbalances particularly prone to suffer the adverse effects of rising U.S. interest rates?

- What are the policy implications?

This chapter reports the following key findings. First, rising rates since the beginning of 2022 have been driven mainly by continued increases in inflation expectations and, especially, a perceived hawkish shift in the Fed's reaction function as it focuses on reining in inflation. These increases have been only slightly reversed since the onset of the banking stress amid prospects for weaker growth. Unless banking stresses were to intensify and become more widespread, Fed policy will most likely remain tight as inflation remains well above target and the Fed continues to reaffirm that returning inflation to target is its most urgent priority at present.

Second, this chapter confirms the intuition described above that such increases in U.S. interest rates, driven by inflation expectations and changing perceptions of the Fed's reaction function, are especially detrimental to EMDEs. Inflation and especially reaction shocks boost local-currency bond yields, widen sovereign risk spreads, depress equity prices, depreciate currencies, and dampen capital flows. Conversely, increases in U.S. interest rates driven by positive real shocks have relatively benign effects on EMDE financial markets.

Third, increases in U.S. interest rates raise the likelihood that EMDEs could face financial crises—including currency, banking, and sovereign debt crises. Reaction shocks in particular boost the probability that an EMDE will experience a crisis (especially a currency crisis); by comparison, rising U.S. interest rates driven by real shocks lead to only small changes in the likelihood of a crisis.

Fourth, more vulnerable EMDEs face more adverse impacts from reaction shocks. Economies with weaker credit ratings, higher sovereign risk spreads, and "twin" fiscal and current account deficits tend to experience greater financial market spillovers, including larger increases in local-currency long-term bond yields and sovereign risk premiums, as well as larger declines in equity prices. In fact, for any given increase in U.S. interest rates driven by reaction shocks, more vulnerable economies tend to experience local-currency yield increases that are almost twice as large. Financial crises are also more likely in economies with weaker credit ratings and macroeconomic imbalances.

Fifth, these findings, based on historical responses of EMDEs to changes in U.S. interest rates, are consistent with developments in EMDE financial markets in the past year and a half. Financial conditions in EMDEs with strong fundamentals and adept macroeconomic management have generally remained stable. Conversely, EMDEs with weaker fundamentals and less prudent fiscal and monetary policies, including so-called "frontier markets" and non-investment-grade countries, have experienced more pronounced financial downdrafts (figure 3.1.C).

Finally, the emergence of banking strains in the United States and Europe since March has led to some downshifting of the expected path of interest rates in these economies. In the case of the United States, this can be partly interpreted as a negative real shock to interest rates amid expectations of weaker U.S. growth. As noted above, positive real shocks pose generally benign effects on EMDEs; therefore, negative real shocks are likely to be adverse. As a result, the recent developments in the U.S. banking sector and associated declines in U.S. interest rates are unlikely to be helpful to EMDEs since the lower rates reflect diminished growth prospects and heightened risk aversion, and therefore could lead to reduced exports, dampened capital inflows, and disrupted financial

markets for EMDEs. Indeed, when those banking strains materialized, EMDE credit spreads jumped—especially those in more vulnerable economies, such that those with non-investment-grade ratings (figure 3.1.D).

The analysis presented in this chapter makes several contributions to the literature on the determinants of U.S. interest rates and their spillovers to EMDEs:[1]

- It decomposes the evolution of U.S. interest rates since the onset of the COVID-19 pandemic into real, inflation, and reaction shocks in order to understand the evolving drivers of recent movements in U.S. interest rates.

- It extends the sample of EMDEs studied and employs a battery of econometric techniques to develop a full picture of the different channels through which U.S. interest rates affect EMDE financial markets.

- It examines how different types of U.S. interest rate shocks—real, inflation, and reaction—affect the likelihood of EMDE financial crises.

- It analyzes the influence of financial vulnerabilities and macroeconomic imbalances on the effects of U.S. interest rate movements on EMDEs.

- Finally, it discusses the practical implications of these results for policy makers.

Methodology and data

Each of the questions to investigate—the sources of shocks to U.S. interest rates, the effects of such shocks on EMDE financial markets, and their effects on the probability of crisis—requires analyzing different sets of data based on different modeling approaches. To that end, this chapter employs three distinct empirical methodologies (see the appendix for further details). First, to identify the mix of real, inflation, and reaction

---

[1] See Arteta, Kamin, and Ruch (2022) for a comprehensive literature review.

shocks that have been driving U.S. interest rates, the analysis applies a *sign-restricted Bayesian vector autoregression (VAR) model* to monthly U.S. data on bond yields, stock prices, and inflation expectations. It then estimates *panel local projection models* to assess the impact on EMDE financial variables at a quarterly frequency of the different types of U.S. interest rate shocks identified by the VAR model. Finally, a *logit model* is applied to annual data to determine how these different types of interest rate shocks affect the probability that an EMDE will experience a financial crisis.

Differentiating between real, inflation, and reaction shocks

A key factor behind the effects of rising U.S. interest rates is the differentiation between inflation, reaction, and real shocks. Inflation shocks are defined as changes in interest rates that reflect changing prospects for inflation—for example, a disruption to supply chains that boosts inflation expectations would likely also boost interest rates. Reaction shocks are defined as changes in interest rates due to changing market perceptions of the Fed's reaction function—for example, if comments from a Fed official were to indicate an especially pronounced distaste for ongoing inflation trends, and such comments led markets to believe that the Fed would tighten policy by more than expected, the resultant rise in interest rates would be considered a reaction shock. Finally, real shocks are defined as changes in interest rates that are caused by changing prospects for U.S. economic activity—an example would be a rise in rates triggered by a new fiscal support program.

In large part, the changes in market interest rates described above reflect markets' expectations of how the Fed will adjust monetary policy. However, the analysis focuses on these rates—in particular, U.S. Treasury bond yields—rather than directly on Fed policy rate actions for two reasons. First, more than the overnight Federal funds rate that the Fed directly controls, it is longer-term rates that most directly affect economic agents. Second, economic developments may prompt changes in expectations of Fed policy that trigger changes in interest rates, even in the absence of immediate Fed actions.

The shocks to interest rates described above are identified using sign restrictions in a Bayesian VAR model that includes four variables: 2-year and 10-year U.S. Treasury bond yields, the S&P 500 index, and inflation expectations as measured (primarily) by breakeven inflation rates derived from inflation-protected Treasury bonds. The identification strategy is as follows:

- Inflation shocks are identified as those that raise U.S. yields and inflation expectations but reduce equity prices.

- Reaction shocks are identified as those that, like inflation shocks, raise U.S. yields but reduce equity prices; however, unlike inflation shocks, reaction shocks are assumed to lower inflation expectations.

- Real shocks are identified as those that raise U.S. yields, inflation expectations, and U.S. equity prices.

Estimating the impact on EMDEs

Next, armed with the identification of the different types of U.S. interest rate shocks, the analysis then uses panel local projection models to assess the impact of these shocks on EMDE financial variables, including bond yields, sovereign spreads, equity prices, capital flows, and exchange rates. These models are estimated using data for up to 40 EMDEs from 1997Q1 to 2019Q4. The models also include control variables, which vary slightly depending on the dependent variable but generally include GDP, CPI, capital flows, government debt, the real exchange rate, and the policy interest rate in EMDEs.

Modeling financial crisis probability

The analysis then explores how different U.S. interest rate shocks shape the probability of financial crises in EMDEs. To that end, it uses a logit model to assess the impact of different underlying shocks on the probability of crisis in EMDEs. This is estimated using annual data from 1985 to 2018. Data on crisis events are based on Laeven and Valencia (2020) through 2017, and on Kose et al. (2021) for 2018, and encompass sovereign debt, banking, and currency crises.

Assessing the role of financial market vulnerabilities and macroeconomic imbalances

Finally, to further scrutinize the role of financial vulnerabilities and macroeconomic imbalances, the local projection and logit models are extended to take into account interactions between U.S. interest rate shocks and measures of EMDE vulnerability. First, EMDE responses are divided across creditworthiness, between investment grade and non-investment grade, using the average foreign-currency long-term sovereign debt rating by Fitch Ratings, Moody's, and Standard and Poor's (Kose et al. 2017). Second, EMDEs are divided into those with high (above median) and low sovereign risk spreads. Third, EMDEs are divided into those with both fiscal and current account deficits (twin deficits) and those without. Finally, frontier markets—those with less developed financial markets and more limited access to international capital markets—are compared with emerging markets.

Shocks to U.S. interest rates and impact on EMDE financial markets

Shock decomposition during major episodes of sharp U.S. interest rate movements

This section explores how different shocks drove changes in U.S. Treasury yields during major episodes of sharp U.S. interest rate movements in the past decade. These episodes include the 2013 "taper tantrum"; the onset of the COVID-19 pandemic; and the response of the Fed to rising inflation since early 2022. The discussion is informed by the decomposition of movements in Treasury yields into the respective contributions of real, inflation, and reaction shocks.

The 2013 taper tantrum. In 2013, Fed Chairman Bernanke unexpectedly signaled that the Fed would soon start tapering asset purchases, bringing an end to its QE III program of quantitative easing. In response, 10-year government bonds experienced a sharp selloff and their yield rose

significantly, by about 100 basis points—an event known as the taper tantrum. The 2-year bond yield rose little, likely indicating that the Fed was perceived as adjusting its unconventional policy but not expected to raise short-term rates for some time. Nearly all the initial increase in 10-year yields following Bernanke's remarks (through June 2013) was accounted for by reaction shocks (figure 3.2.A).

COVID-19. At the onset of COVID-19, economic activity collapsed, inflation declined, the Fed pushed the federal funds rate back to zero, and Treasury yields plummeted (figure 3.2.B). These developments are illustrated by the sizable negative real shocks that followed the emergence of the pandemic. Subsequently, by late 2020, 10-year yields rose, driven by the recovery in economic activity and inflation. The recovery, however, did not translate into higher 2-year yields, as in August 2020 the Fed announced a new monetary policy strategy that implied an extended period of low rates. Specifically, the Fed would seek to achieve inflation "that averages 2 percent over time" by aiming for inflation above its 2 percent target following periods of persistent inflation below 2 percent; it would also desist from tightening policy solely in response to tightening labor markets unless accompanied by evidence of inflationary pressures (Federal Reserve 2020). In part reflecting this dovish announcement, the analysis indicates mounting negative reaction shocks starting at about this time. However, in 2021, inflation started to rise above pre-pandemic levels, and, by September of the same year, 2-year yields began to increase in anticipation of Fed tightening (figure 3.2.B).

The Fed's response to rising inflation. By the start of 2022, it had become clear to the Fed that the surge in inflation was not transitory and would require a concerted response. The Russian Federation's invasion of Ukraine in late February 2022 triggered further increases in food and energy prices that added to inflationary pressures. Five-year breakeven inflation expectations breached 3 percent for the first time in the two-decade history of the series. Starting in March 2022, the Fed started raising policy rates briskly, and yields also rose precipitously, reflecting both rising inflation

FIGURE 3.2 Decomposition of U.S. interest rates

During the 2013 taper tantrum, a substantial part of the initial increase in 10-year U.S. yields was accounted for by perceptions of a more hawkish stance by the Fed. At the onset of the COVID-19 pandemic, 2-year U.S. yields fell, first reflecting a collapse in activity and, subsequently, expectations of more dovish Fed policy. The current hiking cycle has predominately been driven by a perceived hawkish shift by the Fed. This cycle differs from all cycles since the mid-1980s, as it is mainly driven by reaction shocks, and it is also one of the most uncertain.

A. 2013 taper tantrum, cumulative

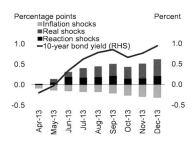

B. COVID-19 pandemic, cumulative

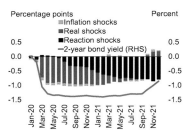

C. Current hiking cycle, cumulative

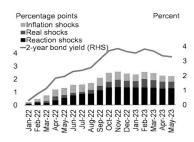

D. Current hiking cycle, change

E. Contributions of shocks during Fed hiking cycles, cumulative

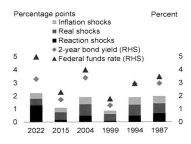

F. Uncertainty in 2-year U.S. Treasury yields

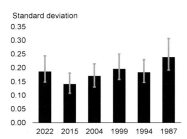

Sources: Federal Reserve Bank of St. Louis; World Bank.
Note: Based on a sign-restricted Bayesian VAR model with stochastic volatility. Inflation shocks are prompted by rising expectations of U.S. inflation. Reaction shocks are prompted by investors' assessments that the Federal Reserve has shifted toward a more hawkish stance. Real shocks are prompted by anticipation of improving U.S. economic activity.
A. Cumulative change in underlying shocks and yield.
B.C.D. Data for May reflects an average to the 15th of the month.
D. Figure reflects the 3-month change in the 2-year bond yield (for example, January to April) and underlying drivers.
F. Figure reflects average model-based volatility in 2-year yields during Fed hiking cycles. Orange whiskers reflect 95 percent confidence intervals.

expectations as well as a reassessment of the Fed's reaction function as being more hawkish than previously believed (figure 3.2.C). Since January 2022, and over the course of the current hiking cycle, reaction and inflation shocks have accounted for three-quarters of the explained cumulative increase in yields.

By early 2023, yields flattened out and estimated shocks to interest rates fell as markets anticipated the Fed's tightening cycle to end soon (figure 3.2.D). Then, in early March, yields declined as markets came to expect the Fed to soon reverse some of its tightening in response to U.S. bank stress. Subsequent declines appear to have reflected negative real and inflation shocks as expectations of U.S. growth slowed.

The current hiking cycle is different from most hiking cycles since the mid-1980s (figure 3.2.E). First, it is the steepest and fastest hiking cycle in nearly four decades, given inflation outcomes not seen since the early 1980s. Since early 2022, the Fed increased its policy rate by 500 basis points. In contrast, the hiking cycle that started in 2015 was about half the size but took almost four times as long, while the 2004 hiking cycle was about equal in size but twice as long. Second, the underlying drivers of the 2022 hiking cycle are different from all cycles since the mid-1980s. The 1987, 1994, 1999, 2004, and 2015 hiking cycles were prominently a response to expectations of firming economic activity. The current hiking cycle, however, has mainly been driven by reaction shocks as the Fed has pivoted toward more aggressive action.[2] Finally, the current hiking cycle is one of the most uncertain (as measured by the volatility of 2-year U.S. yields) since that of the late 1980s (figure 3.2.F).

Impact of U.S. interest rate shocks on EMDE financial markets

In the initial pandemic-related turmoil of March 2020, all gauges of EMDE financial markets—

---

[2] The large role of reaction shocks in the current tightening cycle in large part reflects the Fed's delay in responding to rising inflation. Had the Fed started tightening in the second half of 2021, 2-year bond yields would have risen sooner, and the methodology would likely have estimated a much larger role for inflation shocks and a smaller role for reaction shocks.

currencies, bond valuations, and equities—collapsed and then, following accommodative actions by the Fed and other major central banks, steadily improved through the first half of 2021 (figure 3.3.A). At that point, EMDE financial markets generally plateaued. After September 2021, they began to deteriorate to various degrees, when anticipations of Fed tightening mounted and shorter-term Treasury yields started moving up sharply. At the same time, portfolio and banking flows to EMDEs, having rebounded strongly from their pandemic "sudden stop" in late 2020 and early 2021, fell off sharply by the end of the year (figure 3.3.B). Bond issuance in the first quarter of 2022 across EMDEs was weaker than in any first quarter since 2016. The invasion of Ukraine in March 2022 saw equity and debt flows to EMDEs turn sharply negative, while EMDE financial conditions deteriorated further through much of the year, reaching their tightest level since the start of the pandemic.

Since late 2022, financial conditions in EMDEs have remained tight but have eased somewhat, aided by declines in U.S. inflation that signaled an eventual end to the Fed's tightening cycle and, as a related matter, a decline in the value of the U.S. dollar since its peak last year. Portfolio debt and equity flows to EMDEs picked up in 2023, albeit predominantly because of optimism regarding China's reopening. However, following the stress in the U.S. and European banking sectors that began in March, EMDE credit spreads ratcheted up but remain well below their early 2020 levels.

How well do developments in EMDEs since the pandemic conform to the historical experience of spillovers from U.S. reaction shocks? To address this question, this section compares the effects on financial variables in EMDEs, as estimated using local projections models, of the U.S. interest rates shocks identified by the VAR analysis described above. Figures 3.4A and 3.4B describe the impact of a 25-basis-point shock—real, inflation, or reaction—to U.S. 2-year bond yields on EMDE variables.[3] The size of the shock corresponds to

---

[3] The terms "25-basis-point increase in interest rates driven by an inflation shock," "25-basis-point inflation shock," and "inflation shock" are used interchangeably in this section. This is also true of real and reaction shocks. U.S. interest rates reflect changes in 2-year bond yields.

FIGURE 3.3 EMDE financial developments since the onset of the pandemic

At the onset of the pandemic, key gauges of financial markets in emerging market and developing economies (EMDEs) initially worsened markedly. Following accommodative actions by the Fed and other major central banks, EMDE financial markets steadily improved throughout the first half of 2021. However, as U.S. interest rates began to rise toward the end of that year, EMDE financial markets began to deteriorate. The onset of the invasion of Ukraine was accompanied by a further deterioration in EMDE capital flows.

A. Equity and exchange rates in EMDEs

B. Portfolio flows, EMDEs excluding China

Sources: Haver Analytics; IIF (database); J.P. Morgan.
Note: EMDEs = emerging market and developing economies.
A. "Equity prices" is the Morgan Stanley Capital International (MSCI) index for emerging markets. "Nominal effective exchange rate" is based on J. P. Morgan's nominal broad effective exchange rate for emerging markets. Last observation is April 2023.
B. 3mma = 3-month moving average. Figure shows debt and equity nonresident portfolio flows for 25 EMDEs excluding China. Last observation is March 2023.

---

roughly a one standard deviation monthly move in the 2-year yield as measured since the 1980s.

Increases in U.S. interest rates driven by reaction shocks are associated with adverse movements in EMDE financial markets. This includes significant increases in 10-year yields and sovereign spreads (EMBI), declines in capital flows, and depreciation of real exchange rates. In addition, short-term interest rates rise and equities decline, although those movements are not statistically significant. Inflation shocks are also followed by increases in 10-year yields, lower capital flows, depreciating real exchange rates, and depressed equity prices; however, with the exception of the last of these, the movements are not statistically significant.

In contrast, real shocks to U.S. interest rates tend to be followed by benign short-term movements in EMDE financial markets, including significant declines in sovereign spreads, an increase in capital flows, an increase in equity prices, and an appreciation of the real exchange rate. Ten-year government bond yields rise, but this is to be expected, since bond markets are integrated

FIGURE 3.4 Impact of U.S. interest rate shocks on EMDE financial markets

Increases in U.S. interest rates driven by real shocks are generally benign for emerging market and developing economies (EMDEs). In contrast, inflation and, particularly, reaction shocks are associated with adverse impacts on EMDEs, such as rising borrowing costs and risk spreads, capital outflows, depreciating currencies, and falling equity prices.

A. Impact of 25-basis-point shock on EMDE interest rates after one quarter

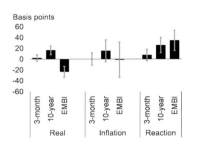

B. Impact of 25-basis-point shock on EMDE financial variables after one quarter

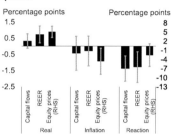

Sources: Haver Analytics; J.P. Morgan; World Bank.
Note: Panel local projection models with fixed effects and robust standard errors. See table 3.2 for details. Models estimated over periods as long as 1997Q2-2019Q4; they exclude observations during global financial crisis (2008Q4-2009Q4) and the COVID-19 pandemic. Blue bars reflect estimated impact in first quarter (y_{t+1}). Orange whiskers reflect 90 percent confidence intervals.
A. EMBI = emerging market bond index. Based on EMBI global spreads.
B. REER = real effective exchange rate. Positive "capital flows" values reflect an increase in net liabilities of portfolio and other investments as a percent of GDP for EMDEs. Positive "REER" values reflect an appreciation in the exchange rate. Figure excludes fixed exchange rate economies.

globally, and the bond yields of advanced economies tend to move together closely as well.

In summary, the dislocations in EMDE financial markets experienced during the Fed's most recent tightening cycle are consistent with the predictions of the estimated models.

Correlates of financial crises

This section describes the findings of a logit model used to assess the effects of real, inflation, and reaction shocks to U.S. interest rates on the likelihood of financial crisis in EMDEs. The model is estimated for three different types of financial crises as identified by Laeven and Valencia (2020): sovereign debt crises, banking crises, and currency crises (an "any crisis" model is also estimated).[4] The dependent variable is a dummy equal to one when there is a crisis and 0 otherwise.

The results suggest that reaction shocks exert large and significant effects on the likelihood of EMDE financial crises within one year, especially currency crises (figure 3.5.A; table 3.1).[5] By comparison, inflation shocks are associated with only small and insignificant effects. Real shocks reduce the likelihood of EMDE debt crises, consistent with their benign effects on financial markets, and perhaps reflecting their positive implications for EMDE exports and capital inflows; while they raise the likelihood of currency crises, they do so by much less than reaction shocks.

In the average EMDE, the probability of facing a crisis of any type in any one year (when the explanatory variables are at their sample mean) from 1985 to 2018 was 3.5 percent. If 2-year yields in the U.S. were to increase by 25 basis points driven by reaction shocks, then the estimated probability of crisis about doubles, to 6.6 percent (figure 3.5.B).

In the 12 months ending in mid-May 2023, reaction shocks accounted for a 72-basis-point increase in 2-year Treasury yields, which indicates a substantial increase in the probability of a financial crisis in EMDEs. Based on the model estimates, the probability of a financial crisis in the average EMDE increased 15 percentage points, to about 19 percent, assuming all other variables remain at their sample averages; in particular, the probability of a currency crisis jumped to 26 percent (figure 3.5.C). This large increase is explained by the non-linear relationship between the interest rate shock and the probability of financial crisis: a doubling of the interest rate shock leads to a more-than-doubling of the rise in the crisis probability.[6]

---

[4] Sovereign debt crises are defined as a default by the government to private creditors and/or restructuring of debt. Banking crises are defined as an event where there is significant distress in the banking system, accompanied by substantial banking policy intervention

measures in response to significant losses. Currency crises are defined as a "sharp" nominal depreciation (at least 30 percent) vis-a-vis the U.S. dollar. For additional details, see Laeven and Valencia (2020).

[5] The greater effect of reaction shocks on the likelihood of currency crises compared with debt or banking crises may reflect that currency crises are more common.

[6] This non-linearity flows from the use of the logistic function embedded in the model, but it is also a good description of reality. When borrowing costs are low, small increases are unlikely to lead to much distress, but when they are high, even small further increases may trigger widespread defaults.

To be sure, a very large confidence interval must be placed around the estimate, as no rise in yields as large and fast as what took place in 2022 occurred during the 1985-2018 estimation period. That said, there have indeed been various incidences of financial stress in 2022, with six EMDEs experiencing full-fledged currency crises (based on the definition in Laeven and Valencia 2020), several governments defaulting on their debts, and 21 EMDEs reaching agreements with the IMF for additional financing (figure 3.5.D).

Role of EMDE vulnerabilities and macroeconomic imbalances

Recent indications of EMDE financial distress have been somewhat less widespread and pronounced than might have been expected, given aggressive Fed tightening driven by reaction shocks. While the number of EMDE financial crises, and especially currency crises, has somewhat increased in recent years, it remains well below levels reached in earlier decades. Particularly in many middle-income EMDEs, credit spreads have remained contained. This likely reflects their stronger economic management, which has reduced susceptibility to external shocks; additionally, international investors may have become better at distinguishing between credit risks in different EMDEs. Some EMDEs have also benefitted from still-elevated commodity prices.

Conversely, many poorer and less structurally sound EMDEs have been harder hit by the combination of increased debt levels and higher interest rates, with almost 60 percent of low-income countries judged to be either in or at high risk of debt distress (Chelsky 2021; World Bank 2022). Indeed, sovereign risk spreads rose faster in EMDEs with weaker credit ratings (figure 3.6.A). And since the end of 2021, there has been a surge in the number of EMDEs with sovereign spreads exceeding 10 percentage points, a benchmark suggesting loss of market access and an elevated likelihood of default (figure 3.6.B). This is consistent with a widely held view that more vulnerable economies are more likely to exhibit adverse responses to higher U.S. interest rates and

FIGURE 3.5 Financial crises in EMDEs

Reaction shocks significantly raise the probability of financial crisis—in particular, currency crisis—in emerging market and developing economies (EMDEs). In particular, the reaction shocks seen in the past twelve months have substantially boosted the likelihood of a currency crisis. This follows a number of full-fledged EMDE currency crises seen in 2022.

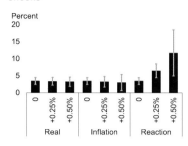

A. Likelihood of financial crises, by shocks

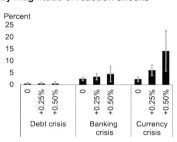

B. Likelihood of financial crises, by magnitude of reaction shocks

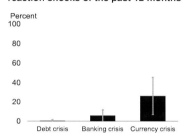

C. Likelihood of crisis in response to reaction shocks of the past 12 months

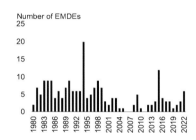

D. Currency crisis in EMDEs

Sources: Laeven and Valencia (2020); World Bank.
Note: Based on results from panel logit model with random effects.
A.B. "0" indicates the probability of a crisis in a given year when there is no change in the underlying shock and all other variables included in the regression are at their sample means. "+0.25%" and "+0.50%" indicate the crisis probabilities in the case of 25- and 50-basis-point increases in the 2-year U.S. Treasury yield driven by the underlying shock. Orange whiskers reflect 90 percent confidence intervals.
A. Probability of any crisis conditional on underlying shocks to U.S. interest rates.
C. Reflects a 0.72 percentage point increase in the 2-year U.S. Treasury yield driven by a reaction shock (the increase seen in the 12 months to mid-May 2023). Orange whiskers reflect 90 percent confidence intervals.
D. A currency crisis is defined as a "sharp" nominal depreciation (at least 30 percent) vis-a-vis the U.S. dollar. For additional details, see Laeven and Valencia (2020).

tighter global financing conditions than more resilient economies.[7]

More generally, the fact that credit spreads for non-investment-grade EMDEs rose more sharply

---

[7] That said, the role of vulnerabilities or inadequate policy frameworks is subject to some debate. Some researchers find that spillovers from U.S. monetary policy are smaller for countries with stronger fundamentals (for example, Ahmed, Coulibaly, and Zlate 2017; Bowman, Londono, and Sapriza 2015; and Chen, Mancini-Griffoli, and Sahay 2014) while others find a limited role for fundamentals (for example, Aizenman, Binici, and Hutchison 2016 and Eichengreen and Gupta 2015).

FIGURE 3.6 Sovereign spreads in EMDEs

More vulnerable emerging market and developing economies (EMDEs), particularly those with weak credit ratings, have experienced larger increases in sovereign risk spreads since the start of 2022. About one in four EMDEs currently have sovereign risk spreads exceeding 10 percentage points.

A. Sovereign spread changes in EMDEs, 2022-23

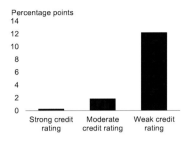

B. EMDEs with sovereign spreads above 10 percentage points

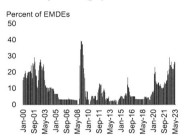

Sources: J.P. Morgan; Moody's; World Bank.

Note: EMDEs = emerging market and developing economies.

A. Change in emerging market bond index global (EMBIG) spreads from January 2022 across long-term foreign-currency sovereign debt ratings by Moody's. "Strong credit rating" includes "Aaa," "Aa," "A," and "Baa." "Moderate credit rating" includes "Ba" and "B." "Weak credit rating" includes "Caa," "Ca," and "C." Sample size includes 45 EMDEs. Sample excludes Belarus, Lebanon, the Russian Federation, Ukraine, and República Bolivariana de Venezuela. Last observation is May 24, 2023.

B. Figure shows the share of countries with J.P. Morgan emerging market bond index global (EMBIG) spread above 10 percentage points. Sample includes 50 EMDEs.

than those for investment-grade EMDEs following the emergence of U.S. and European banking problems in March 2023 suggests that economies with weak fundamentals are more vulnerable to many types of adverse shocks, not only rising U.S. interest rates. Some of these more vulnerable economies are so-called "frontier markets," which only recently gained access to international capital markets in an environment of low global interest rates, and which have been ill-prepared for the subsequent rise in those rates.

This section examines whether the effects of reaction shocks to U.S. interest rates are more detrimental in EMDEs with greater financial vulnerabilities or macroeconomic imbalances. First, EMDEs are classified by their degree of sovereign risk and ability to repay debts. To do so, the analysis explores the role of credit ratings and sovereign spreads. Second, EMDEs are classified by their fiscal and external positions. The analysis explores whether EMDEs that run both fiscal and current account deficits experience greater spillovers than other EMDEs.

Role of credit ratings and sovereign risk

To assess the role of sovereign risks and credit ratings, the analysis compares the response of investment-grade and non-investment-grade EMDEs to U.S. reaction shocks. Economies were categorized according to the average foreign-currency long-term sovereign debt rating of Fitch Ratings, Moody's, and Standard and Poor's.

Indeed, the effects of reaction shocks are more detrimental for non-investment-grade EMDEs than their investment-grade peers (figure 3.7.A). Non-investment-grade EMDEs showed greater increases in EMBI spreads and 10-year yields than did investment-grade EMDEs, and in the latter case, the difference was statistically significant. The increase in yields in non-investment-grade EMDEs is nearly twice as large as the increase in U.S. interest rates. Equity prices declines are also slightly more pronounced in non-investment-grade EMDEs.

There is limited evidence that the investment-grade rating of EMDEs also plays a role in the likelihood of a financial crisis (figure 3.7.B). EMDEs that have higher credit rating scores tend to see a lower probability of facing a crisis due to U.S. reaction shocks, though the differences are not statistically significant.

An alternative way to explore the role of sovereign risk is to compare EMDEs based on their sovereign risk spreads (figure 3.7.C). EMDEs with EMBI spreads below the median tend to see smaller impacts of reaction shocks on their 10-year local currency bond yields and their sovereign spreads. These economies also tend to see smaller equity price losses in response to reaction shocks.[8]

---

[8] The evidence for exchange rate movements and capital flows (not shown) are less intuitive. EMDEs with investment-grade ratings and with low sovereign spreads see more pronounced outflows of portfolio investments and larger currency depreciation in the face of rising U.S. interest rates. It is possible that investment-grade EMDEs have greater exposure to international capital markets through inclusion in global benchmark indexes, making these economies more sensitive to global financing conditions (Arslanalp and Tsuda 2015; Cerutti, Claessens, and Puy 2019; Miyajima and Shim 2014).

Role of twin deficits

Countries running fiscal and current account deficits often depend on foreign investors to finance such deficits, and therefore are especially exposed to U.S. interest rates. During the 2013 taper tantrum, for example, EMDEs that were running large current account and fiscal deficits suffered particularly adverse consequences (figure 3.7.D). To assess this measure of vulnerability, the analysis classifies EMDEs between twin-deficit countries—those running both primary fiscal and current account deficits—and others.

The results of the econometric analysis suggest that twin-deficit EMDEs experience more adverse impacts from reaction shocks than their non-twin-deficit peers (figure 3.7.E). Twin-deficit EMDEs tend to see an increase in 10-year local currency yields that is greater than the change in U.S. interest rates, and which is statistically different from the response in economies that do not have twin deficits. Twin deficits are also associated with larger increases in sovereign risk spreads and larger falls in equity prices. In addition, the increase in the probability of financial crisis—especially a currency crisis—due to reaction shocks is magnified in twin-deficit EMDEs (figure 3.7.F).

Role of frontier market status

There are notable differences across EMDEs in terms of their financial development (the number of companies listed on stock exchanges), depth (the size of their market capitalization and liquidity), and infrastructure (their regulatory structure and trading rules), which offer different levels of opportunity, access, and risk for international investors. They also differ in their macroeconomic and political stability and institutional quality. So-called "frontier market" economies are those with less developed financial markets and more limited access to international capital markets than "emerging markets," but which have more advanced markets and greater access to external private investment than the poorest and least developed EMDEs. Market participants usually invest in frontier markets to access higher returns, but at greater risk, and to diversify portfolios. In the years following the global financial crisis of

FIGURE 3.7 Impact of reaction shocks on EMDE financial variables, by vulnerabilities

Reaction shocks are more detrimental for emerging market and developing economies (EMDEs) that have non-investment-grade credit ratings, exhibit higher sovereign risk spreads, and run twin current account and fiscal deficits. The probability of crisis is also higher in EMDEs that have non-investment-grade ratings or run twin deficits.

A. Impact of 25-basis-point reaction shock on EMDE financial variables after one quarter, by credit rating

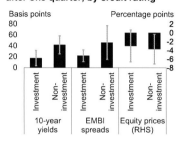

B. Likelihood of a financial crisis in response to reaction shocks of the past 12 months

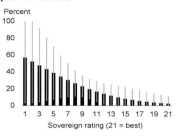

C. Impact of 25-basis-point reaction shock on EMDE financial variables after one quarter, by sovereign spreads

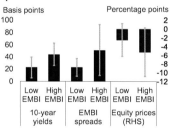

D. Change in sovereign risk spreads, 2013 taper tantrum

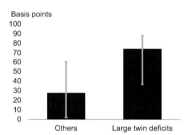

E. Impact of 25-basis-point reaction shock on EMDE financial variables after one quarter, by twin deficit status

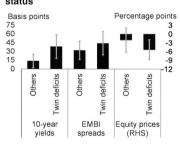

F. Likelihood of crisis in response to reaction shocks of the past 12 months

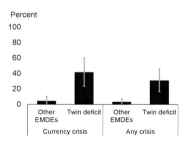

Sources: J.P. Morgan; World Bank.
Note: Panel non-linear local projection model with fixed effects and robust standard errors. Models exclude observations during global financial crisis (2008Q4-2009Q4) and the COVID-19 pandemic. EMBI = emerging market bond index.
A.C.E. Blue bars reflect estimated impact in first quarter (y_{t+1}). Orange whiskers reflect 90 percent confidence intervals.
B. Figure reflects the probability of any crisis across sovereign debt ratings of EMDEs where the credit score is translated to numerical ratings. Ratings below 12 are non-investment grade while those above are investment grade. Based on a logit model with random effects that includes an interaction term for sovereign credit rating. Reflects a 0.72 percentage point increase in the 2-year U.S. Treasury yield driven by a reaction shock (the increase seen in the 12 months to mid-May 2023). Orange whiskers reflect 68 percent confidence intervals.
D. Large twin deficit economies are those that had a current account deficit wider than 2.5 percent of GDP and a primary fiscal deficit wider than 1 percent of GDP. Based on data for 50 EMDEs. Change in EMBI from 2013Q1 to 2013Q4. Orange whiskers reflect interquartile range across economies.
F. Based on a logit model with random effects that includes an interaction term for economies that run twin current account and primary fiscal deficits. Reflects a 0.72 percentage point increase in the 2-year U.S. Treasury yield driven by a reaction shock (the increase seen in the 12 months to mid-May 2023). Orange whiskers reflect 68 percent confidence intervals.

FIGURE 3.8 Impact of reaction shocks on EMDE financial variables, by market status

Frontier markets—countries with less well-developed financial markets and more limited access to international capital markets—have seen a much larger increase in sovereign risk spreads since the start of 2022. Frontier markets tend to see much larger adverse impacts from reaction shocks.

A. Change in sovereign risk spreads over 2022-23, by market type

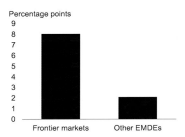

B. Impact of 25-basis-point reaction shock on EMDE financial variables after one quarter

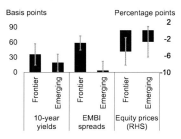

Sources: J.P. Morgan; MSCI; World Bank.
Note: Panel non-linear local projection model with fixed effects and robust standard errors. Models exclude observations during global financial crisis (2008Q4-2009Q4) and the COVID-19 pandemic. EMBI = emerging market bond index; MSCI = Morgan Stanley Capital International.
A. Based on data for 45 EMDEs, of which 11 are frontier markets, using the 2022 classification from MSCI. Average change in EMBI global spreads from January 2022 to May 2023.
B. Based on the MSCI country classification in 2022. Frontier markets include up to 9 economies while emerging markets include up to 19 economies. Frontier markets include Argentina, Bahrain, Croatia, Georgia, Jordan, Kazakhstan, Morocco, Nigeria, Romania, Serbia, Sri Lanka, and Vietnam. Emerging markets include Brazil, Chile, China, Arab Republic of Egypt, Hungary, Indonesia, India, Kuwait, Malaysia, Mexico, Peru, Philippines, Poland, Qatar, Saudi Arabia, South Africa, Thailand, and Türkiye. Orange whiskers reflect 90 percent confidence intervals. "EMBI spreads" based on EMBI global.

2008—a period of low global interest rates and limited risk aversion—frontier markets enjoyed substantial capital inflows and accumulated considerable external debt. However, in recent years, as sentiment shifted and rising interest rates offered better returns in developed markets, flows to frontier markets declined. This is exemplified by the outsized rise in sovereign risk spreads of these economies (figure 3.8.A).

To test the impact of reaction shocks on frontier markets, EMDEs are classified as "frontier markets" and "emerging markets" based on the MSCI country classification in 2022 (MSCI 2022).[9] Frontier markets tend to see much larger impacts from reaction shocks than those classified as emerging markets (figure 3.8.B). Ten-year local

---

[9] The classification of an EMDE into frontier market status differs across firms that provide classifications. Despite these differences, frontier markets generally show a higher tendency to be adversely affected by spillovers from rising U.S. interest rates. For example, using the frontier market classification in the S&P Extended Frontier 150 index yields similar results to the MSCI classifications.

currency bond yields tend to increase by 50 percent more in frontier markets than other EMDEs. Sovereign risk spreads in frontier markets tend to increase by more than three times the size of the increase seen in other EMDEs; this difference is statistically significant. Finally, equity prices decline by almost twice as much in frontier markets.

Conclusions and policy implications

The global context is particularly challenging for EMDEs. To rein in persistent inflation pressures, the U.S. Federal Reserve and other major central banks will likely need to maintain an aggressive policy stance for an extended period, leading to substantial financial spillovers to EMDEs. This is taking place in an environment of unprecedented high debt levels both in the public and private sectors in many EMDEs.

The ultimate impact of rising U.S. interest rates depends on the types of shocks that drive them. This chapter decomposes U.S. interest rate moves into those driven by better economic activity (real shocks), inflation expectations (inflation shocks), and changes in the central bank's policy stance (reaction shocks). The analysis finds that the rapid increase in U.S. interest rates over the past year and a half predominantly reflected both rising inflation expectations and, especially, a perceived shift in the Fed's reaction function toward a more hawkish stance. The recent moderation in U.S. yields since the onset of U.S. banking sector stress appears to reflect negative real shocks amid heightened risk aversion and expectations of slower U.S. growth. Even so, these yields remain quite elevated.

With the rise in U.S. interest rates being driven principally by inflation and reaction shocks, the outlook for EMDEs is worrisome. The analysis of the spillovers of U.S. interest rates indicates that inflation and, especially, reaction shocks are associated with tighter financial conditions and more adverse outcomes for EMDEs: a widening of sovereign spreads, declining capital flows, decreasing equity prices, and depreciating real exchange rates. They also suggest that increases in U.S.

interest rates driven by reaction shocks substantially boost the likelihood that EMDEs could face financial crisis, especially a currency crisis.

These findings also underscore the role of financial vulnerabilities and less robust macroeconomic management. More vulnerable EMDEs—as indicated by weaker credit ratings, wider risk spreads, and fiscal and current account deficits—face more adverse impacts from reaction shocks than do EMDEs with stronger fundamentals. They experience larger increases in risk spreads, larger declines in equity prices, and larger increases in long-term local currency bond yields; in fact, for the more vulnerable EMDEs, these increases in bond yields amount to nearly twice the size of the original increases in U.S. interest rates.

To date, developments in EMDEs since the start of the Fed's tightening cycle last year have been largely in line with the findings described above. Driven by the spillovers of increases in U.S. interest rates that predominantly reflected reaction shocks, EMDE yields have risen, currencies have depreciated, credit spreads have widened, and capital inflows have tailed off. This tightening of financial conditions has been greater for more vulnerable EMDEs, including so-called "frontier market" economies, than for economies with stronger fundamentals and more prudent macroeconomic management. Moreover, the recent decline in U.S. yields and downshift in expectations for further Fed tightening triggered by ongoing banking difficulties will do little to help EMDEs, since that downshift reflects worries about the U.S. economy and financial sector, which will in turn weigh on conditions in EMDEs.

The risks to EMDEs posed by the tightening of monetary policy in the United States, and across the world, call for concerted policy responses. To start, central banks in advanced economies can attenuate the risk of disruptive spillovers to global financial markets by communicating their intentions as clearly as possible and calibrating their strategies so as to avoid abrupt changes in the policy outlook. (For example, during the 2016-2018 period, the Fed pursued a path of monetary tightening that was both gradual and well-telegraphed through policy statements, press conferences, and economic projections.) Clear communication to the public will reduce the likelihood of shocks to markets' assessments of central bank reaction functions, which has been shown to be especially destabilizing for EMDEs. Enhanced communication among central banks aimed at mitigating financial stability risks and monitoring cross-border spillovers will also be helpful in this regard (Avdjiev et al. 2020; Obstfeld 2022a). Finally, coordination among authorities in advanced economies to improve financial regulations and strengthen the resilience of their financial systems will redound to the benefit of EMDEs.

Second, in response to tighter monetary policies in advanced economies, EMDE monetary authorities may need to tighten their own policies in order to moderate capital outflows, currency depreciation, and resultant increases in inflation, all of which could destabilize domestic financial markets and lead to further rounds of capital outflows and depreciation. Indeed, over the past couple of years, some EMDE monetary authorities have been able to limit the rise in inflation and avert disruptive exchange rate dynamics through early and swift increases in policy rates. In countries where inflation remains elevated, authorities may have to continue tightening monetary policy. Critically, communicating monetary policy decisions clearly, leveraging credible monetary frameworks, and safeguarding central bank independence will help EMDEs to keep inflation expectations from becoming de-anchored and avoid disruptive capital outflows. In some countries, monetary policy responses to high inflation may need to be complemented by fiscal consolidation. At the same time, monetary and financial authorities need to be mindful of contractionary "overkill" by taking into account the effects of both domestic tightening and cross-border spillovers from higher policy rates in advanced economies (Guénette, Kose, and Sugawara 2022; Obstfeld 2022b).

To smooth disruptive short-term volatility in currency markets and bolster investor sentiment, EMDEs with adequate reserves may also consider complementing monetary tightening with foreign exchange interventions. In 2022, about one-fifth of EMDEs liquidated more than 15 percent of gross official reserves to cushion the fall in domestic currencies, with larger losses among countries contending with higher inflation. However, while these actions may alleviate immediate pressures, policy makers will eventually need to rebuild foreign exchange reserve buffers and realign prudential policy to prepare for the possibility of financial stress.

Third, besides directly responding to rising advanced-economy interest rates through monetary and foreign exchange policies, authorities in EMDEs can mute the effects of disruptive spillovers by reducing the fundamental vulnerabilities of their economies and financial systems. As noted earlier, countries with lower credit ratings, higher risk spreads, and larger fiscal and current account deficits face more adverse impacts from such spillovers. The credible monetary policy frameworks and inflation containment referred to earlier not only address the direct effects of external shocks but also help to reduce the economy's vulnerabilities more generally. On top of that, reducing vulnerability will require strengthening financial and fiscal policies.

To build the resilience of the financial system, prudential (and macroprudential) policy efforts will need to prioritize, among other things, adequate bank capital and liquidity, better currency alignment of assets and liabilities, better management of currency and rollover risk, and appropriate levels of leverage in the household and corporate sectors. Such measures, while generally important, may be particularly crucial for frontier markets that are early in the process of opening up to international capital flows. Credit quality, non-performing loans, and currency mismatches need

to be reported transparently such that prompt corrective action can be taken. The buffers of both banks and non-bank financial institutions need to be sufficient to absorb the impact of dislocating adverse shocks and should be stress-tested where institutions pose potentially systemic risks. In addition, risks from highly indebted corporate sectors can be allayed through insolvency reform and rapid, transparent treatment of non-performing loans.

A key measure of vulnerability utilized in the analysis relates to the fiscal position. For many EMDEs, promoting and/or restoring fiscal sustainability will require concerted action on many fronts. Tax collection and administration must be improved to boost often-inadequate revenue levels. Fiscal spending may need to be reduced while ensuring that fiscal support is carefully targeted toward vulnerable populations and critical capital and infrastructure investments. In low-income EMDEs, special care must be taken to ensure that funding sources are low-cost (concessional) and debt maturities are carefully managed to reduce rollover risk.

Fourth and finally, the international community can take steps to address the spillovers of monetary tightening in the advanced economies by strengthening the global financial safety net. This involves ensuring that international financial institutions are adequately funded and focused on rapid support for EMDEs in distress. It also requires further efforts to facilitate the restructuring of external debts for EMDEs in debt distress. As noted above, the weaker and more vulnerable EMDEs have been especially hard-hit by the rise in interest rates, and helping them meet their challenges is a global priority.

ANNEX 3.1 Identifying U.S. interest rate shocks

The vector autoregression model employed to decompose U.S. monetary policy shocks is based on the frameworks used in Matheson and Stavrev (2014); Arteta et al. (2015); and Hoek, Kamin, and Yoldas (2021, 2022).[10] The model includes four variables: 2-year and 10-year bond yields, the S&P 500 index, and inflation expectations as measured by inflation compensation derived from Treasury inflation-protected bonds.[11] The data are monthly, from January 1982 to mid-May 2023. (Use of daily data did not appear to offer any advantages in terms of identification of shocks.) The inclusion of the 10-year yield in addition to the 2-year yield is used to capture the persistent part of expectations of inflation, as well as to identify the effects of unconventional monetary policy decisions that might not show up in 2-year yields. The model is specified as:

$$Y_t = BX_t + M_t,$$

where Y_t is an N × 1 vector of endogenous variables, X_t is an N × p + 1 vector of lagged dependent variables and an intercept term, and where p is the lag length, B is a matrix of coefficients, and M_t is a N × 1 vector of residuals. As part of the identification strategy, the following sign restrictions are imposed on a four-variable VAR model as:

$$\begin{bmatrix} \mu_t^{TB2} \\ \mu_t^{TB10} \\ \mu_t^{SPX} \\ \mu_t^{E\pi} \end{bmatrix} = \begin{bmatrix} + & + & + & * \\ + & + & + & * \\ - & + & - & * \\ - & + & + & * \end{bmatrix} \begin{bmatrix} \varepsilon_t^{reaction} \\ \varepsilon_t^{real} \\ \varepsilon_t^{inflation} \\ \varepsilon_t^{*} \end{bmatrix},$$

where μ_t^{TB2} and μ_t^{TB10} represent reduced-form residuals to 2-year and 10-year U.S. Treasury bond yields, μ_t^{SPX} represents a residual to the S&P 500 index, and $\mu_t^{E\pi}$ represents reduced-form residuals to inflation expectations. The real shock ε_t^{real} is identified as one that raises both 2-year and 10-year interest rates (TB), inflation expectations (Eπ), and equity prices (SPX). The inflation shock $\varepsilon_t^{inflation}$ raises interest rates and inflation expectations but lowers equity prices. The reaction shock $\varepsilon_t^{reaction}$ raises interest rates but lowers inflation expectations and equity prices. Sign restrictions on both the 2-year and 10-year yield ensure that the identified shocks reflect changes from both conventional and unconventional policy moves by the Fed.

Since the period under review includes the COVID-19 crisis (whose unprecedented nature and size presents possible modeling challenges) and focuses on financial data (where heteroskedastic errors are common), the model includes stochastic volatility. Stochastic volatility in the error structure is modelled as in Jacquier, Polson, and Rossi (1994) and a generic version of what is suggested in Lenza and Primiceri (2022).

The data included in the VAR model used to decompose U.S. interest rate shocks are provided in table 3.3. The table indicates the transformation used in the model and the data source. Because of the secular decline in U.S. interest rates over the past four decades, the data are transformed to be stationary using first differences, as the focus is on shocks over the business cycle. Equity prices are measured by the S&P 500 composite index and transformed to percent changes using log first differences. As a measure of inflation expectations, the 5-year breakeven inflation rate is used from 2003 onward.[12]

ANNEX 3.2 Estimating the impact of U.S. interest rate shocks on EMDEs

Panel local projection models are used to link the U.S. interest rate shocks identified earlier to EMDE variables. The methodology, following

---

[10] The model is estimated using Bayesian techniques and the Minnesota prior with hyperparameters on the first lag coefficients at 0.8, on overall tightness at 0.1, on lag decay at 1.5, on the exogenous variable tightness at 100, and cross-variable weighting at 0.9. A total of 30,000 iterations were run, with the first 5,000 discarded and only every 5th iteration kept. The model includes 12 lags. The prior mean on the residual variance (that is, stochastic volatility) is 0 and the prior's variance is 10,000.

[11] Inflation expectations are measured at a 5-year maturity based on data availability and as a compromise between capturing information in both the 2-year and 10-year yields.

[12] Prior to 2003, the inflation expectations series is based on model estimates by Haubrich, Pennacchi, and Ritchken (2012).

Jorda (2005), identifies impulse response functions through consecutive regression models at different horizons (h):

$$y_{i,t+h} = \alpha_{i,h} + x_{i,t}\,\delta_h + shock_{j,t}\,\beta_h + \mu_{i,t+h} ,$$

where $\alpha_{i,h}$ are cross-section (EMDE) fixed effects, $x_{i,t}$ are a vector of control variables, and $shock_{j,t}$ are the U.S. interest rate shocks with $j \in \{reaction;\ real;\ inflation\}$. The models are estimated recursively eight quarters ahead. They are estimated separately for each of the three U.S. interest rate shocks and each of the dependent variables, covering between 20 and 39 EMDEs, depending on the availability of data for the specific EMDE variable of focus. The dependent variables include 3-month and 10-year local-currency government bond yields, sovereign spreads, capital flows, and the real effective exchange rate (see table 3.4 for details).[13] The control variables differ slightly depending on the dependent variable, as shown in table 3.2, but generally include GDP, CPI, capital flows, government debt, the real exchange rate, and the policy interest rate (table 3.4 indicates the transformations of the control variables).

The data are mainly sourced from Haver Analytics, collected for as long a time period as possible at a quarterly frequency. Seasonally adjusted data are used when available or adjusted using X13-ARIMA-SEATS (U.S. Census Bureau 2017). The datasets used to measure the impacts of different U.S. interest rate shocks differ based on the dependent variable. The sample size for the short-term yields is the most limited, consisting of 20 economies from 1997Q4 to 2019Q4, resulting in an unbalanced panel of 750 total observations (table 3.2).[14] The largest country sample used, such as in the case of capital flows, includes 39 EMDEs from 1997Q2 to 2019Q4, resulting in an unbalanced panel of 1,537 observations. The EMDEs included across all regressions are provided in table 3.5.

To transform the monthly monetary policy shocks identified earlier into a quarterly frequency and to reflect a one-percentage-point change in the 2-year U.S. yield, the shocks are adjusted in two ways. First, given that monthly shocks are in first differences, shifting to a quarterly change is done by adding monthly changes within each quarter. Second, to ensure comparability of the interpretation across shocks, the contribution of all shocks from the historical decomposition of the 2-year yield is used.[15]

ANNEX 3.3 Modeling financial crisis probability

A logit model, as in Kose et al. (2021), is used to assess the impact of different underlying shocks on the probability of crisis in EMDEs over the past 50 years. This is estimated using annual data from 1985 to 2018. Crisis events are based on Laeven and Valencia (2020) codified to 2017, and extended in Kose et al. (2021), and encompass sovereign debt, banking, and currency crises. The model is estimated as:

$$y_{i,t} = \beta'X_{i,t\text{-}1} + \mu_i + \epsilon_{i,t} ,$$

where $y_{i,t}$ is a binary variable of banking, currency, or sovereign debt crises for country i in year t taking the value of 1 if a crisis occurred; $X_{i,t\text{-}1}$ is a vector of determinants of crisis, including the real, inflation, and reaction shocks as well as other control variables; μ_i captures unobserved country heterogeneity; and $\epsilon_{i,t}$ are the residuals. The baseline specification is a panel logit model with random effects, as the Hausmann test suggests that the random effects model is appropriate for debt and banking crises. For robustness tests, see Arteta, Kamin, and Ruch (2022).

The variables selected are based on empirical findings in the early warning indicators literature on crises (see Chamon and Crowe 2012; Frankel and Saravelos 2012; and Kaminsky, Lizondo, and Reinhart 1998 for an extensive review) and Kose et al. (2021). The panel includes data on debt (public and private), balance of payments, and real, banking, and financial sectors (table 3.6).

---

[13] The real effective exchange rate is used to better capture financial conditions in EMDEs and to account for situations of high inflation. In this chapter, references to "capital flows" are defined as increases in net portfolio and other investment liabilities of EMDEs, excluding foreign direct investment liabilities.

[14] To avoid the outsized impact of outliers, models exclude observations between 2008Q4-2009Q4 to account for the period of the global financial crisis.

[15] The historical decomposition divides the 2-year yield into the contribution of each of the shocks to its evolution over time.

ANNEX 3.4 Assessing the role of EMDE vulnerabilities

The models are also extended to consider potential variations in responses based on specific characteristics of EMDEs. Four characteristics are studied. First, in each quarter of the estimation range, EMDEs are divided into investment grade and non-investment grade. The rating of investment-grade and non-investment-grade EMDEs is based on Kose et al. (2017) and uses the average foreign-currency long-term sovereign debt rating by Fitch Ratings, Moody's, and Standard and Poor's. Second, in each quarter, EMDEs are divided into those with high sovereign risk spreads (EMBI above the sample median) and those with low sovereign risk. Third, in each quarter, EMDEs are classified as twin deficit economies—running both a current account and primary fiscal deficit—and those that are not. Finally, economies are divided into "frontier markets" or "emerging markets" based on the MSCI classification for 2022.

A dummy variable approach is used, where, in separate regressions for each vulnerability measure, I_t is set equal to one if an EMDE's average rating at time t is below investment grade, if it has sovereign risk spreads (EMBI) below the sample median, if it runs twin deficits, or if it is a frontier market; and 0 otherwise. Consequently, the state-dependent impulse response function becomes a function of the dummy variable and the endogenous variables:

$$y_{i,t+h} = I_t \left[\alpha_{A,i,h} + x_{A,i,t}\, \delta_{A,h} + shock_{j,t}\, \beta_{A,h} \right] +$$

$$(1 - I_t)[\alpha_{B,i,h} + x_{B,i,t}\, \delta_{B,h} + shock_{j,t}\, \beta_{B,h}] + \mu_{i,t+h} \ .$$

ANNEX 3.5 Robustness analysis

The results of the VAR-based decomposition of U.S. interest rates, including their estimated impact on EMDEs, are generally robust with respect to alternative specifications of that VAR. A wide range of alternative specifications were tested, including:

- the inclusion of measures of current economic conditions (including industrial production and PCE inflation, and assuming no contemporaneous impact on both variables);

- the specification of only two types of shocks, real and "monetary" (combining reaction and inflation shocks);

- the use of alternative measures of inflation expectations;

- the use of the Russell 2000 equity price index instead of the S&P 500 to verify the model's robustness to changes in the composition of the S&P 500 index and to different interest rate sensitivities between the two indexes;

- the removal of the 10-year bond yield from the VAR, leaving only the 2-year yield as a measure of U.S. interest rates; and

- the inclusion of two additional variables in the VAR, the World Bank's CPI-deflated energy price index and the Chicago Board Options Exchange's VIX, in order to assess the possibility that measured reaction shocks might instead reflect surges in financial uncertainty or commodity prices.[16]

In all cases, the results were not materially different from the benchmark estimates, and the narrative regarding the evolution of U.S. interest rates around notable tightening events remained broadly unchanged. Moreover, the results continued to suggest that the impacts of inflation and reaction shocks on EMDE financial variables and the likelihood of crisis are more adverse than those of real shocks.[17]

There were minor differences between the benchmark and alternative specifications. The model including the Russell 2000 index suggests that inflation shocks played a larger role in the current hiking cycle but indicates little change in the

---

[16] To do so, the following restrictions are imposed. In addition to existing sign restrictions, the reaction shock is identified as one that has no contemporaneous impact on the VIX (zero restriction) and decreases real energy prices; the inflation shock is identified as that which has no contemporaneous impact on real energy prices; and the real shock leads to an increase in real energy prices.

[17] The first three of these robustness checks are explained in greater detail in the accompanying background paper (see Arteta, Kamin, and Ruch 2022).

impacts of these shocks on EMDE financial variables. The model controlling for commodity prices and the VIX suggests that the reaction shocks played a smaller but still-dominant role in the current hiking cycle. Moreover, this model highlights an amplification of the impact of reaction and real shocks on EMDE financial markets, though the differences with the bench-mark model are not statistically significant.

The local projection models exclude the COVID-19 pandemic and the global financial crisis periods to avoid the impact of outliers and extreme events. An alternative approach would be to include these observations with a dummy variable. Robustness tests using this alternative approach amplified the adverse impact of reaction shocks on EMDEs financial variables as well as the benign impact of real shocks.

TABLE 3.1 Crisis probability: Panel logit model with random effects

Explanatory variables	Debt crisis	Banking crisis	Currency crisis	Any crisis
Inflation shock	-0.012	-1.159	0.344	-0.327
	[2.502]	[0.780]	[1.131]	[0.984]
Reaction shock	0.301	1.245	4.528***	3.012***
	[2.813]	[1.030]	[1.309]	[1.113]
Real shock	-2.386**	-0.146	0.893**	-0.164
	[1.006]	[0.316]	[0.447]	[0.367]
GDP growth (t-1)	-0.214**	-0.041	-0.140***	-0.0545
	[0.093]	[0.032]	[0.047]	[0.0436]
Short-term debt (t-1)	-0.016	0.006	0.017	-0.016
	[0.048]	[0.014]	[0.019]	[0.018]
Debt service (t-1)	-0.004	0.016**	0.001	0.001
	[0.027]	[0.007]	[0.011]	[0.010]
Reserves cover (t-1)	-0.700**	-0.087*	-0.151*	-0.064
	[0.314]	[0.052]	[0.086]	[0.057]
Change in government debt (t-1)	0.007		0.042**	0.011
	[0.021]		[0.017]	[0.014]
Change in private debt (t-1)		0.063**	0.011	0.083**
		[0.030]	[0.047]	[0.036]
Change in government debt (t-1) x change in private debt (t-1)			0.005*	-0.001
			[0.003]	[0.002]
Concessional debt (t-1)	-0.123**			-0.017*
	[0.061]			[0.009]
Funding ratio (t-1)		0.003**		0.002
		[0.001]		[0.002]
Currency overvaluation (t-1)			0.000	0.147***
			[0.001]	[0.026]
Currency mismatch (t-1)			-0.001	-0.000
			[0.001]	[0.001]
FDI (t-1)			0.001	-0.019
			[0.031]	[0.030]
Constant	-3.150**	-3.962***	-3.321***	-2.796***
	[1.532]	[0.362]	[0.643]	[0.625]
No. of observations	1,634	2,085	1,325	1,271
No. of countries	103	92	88	88

Source: World Bank.
Note: Estimated on annual data from 1985-2018 excluding 2009. FDI = foreign direct investment. Standard errors in brackets.
*** $p<0.01$, ** $p<0.05$, * $p<0.1$

TABLE 3.2 Samples by dependent variable in panel local projection models

Dependent variable	Total observations	Number of economies	Sample*	Control variables
Long-term yields	926	24	2000Q2-2019Q4	GDP, CPI, portfolio inflows, Debt, REER, policy interest rate
Short-term yields	750	20	1997Q4-2019Q4	GDP, CPI, portfolio inflows, Debt, REER, policy interest rate
EMBIG spread	1261	34	1999Q3-2019Q4	GDP, CPI, portfolio inflows, debt, REER, policy interest rate
Capital flows	1537	39	1997Q2-2019Q4	GDP, CPI, debt, REER, policy interest rate
Real effective exchange rate	1225	21	1996Q3-2019Q4	GDP, CPI, portfolio inflows, policy interest rate
Equity prices	1744	35	1994Q1-2019Q4	GDP, CPI, REER, portfolio inflows, policy interest rate

Source: World Bank.
Note: *Sample excludes 2008Q4-2009Q4. CPI = consumer price index; EMBIG = emerging market bond index global; REER = real effective exchange rate.

TABLE 3.3 Variables for sign-restricted VAR (monthly data)

Variable	Transformation	Source
2-year Treasury note yield at constant maturity	First difference	Haver Analytics
10-year Treasury bond yield at constant maturity	First difference	Haver Analytics
Standard & Poor's 500 Composite Index	Log first difference	Haver Analytics
5-year inflation expectations (Jan 1982-Dec 2002)	First difference	Haubrich, Pennacchi, and Ritchken (2012)
5-year breakeven inflation rate (5-year nominal Treasury yield less the 5-year inflation-protected TIPS yield)	First difference	Federal Reserve Bank of St. Louis

Source: World Bank.

TABLE 3.4 Variables for the panel local projection models (quarterly data)

Variable	Transformation	Source
Real GDP in local currency, seasonally adjusted	Log first difference	Haver Analytics
Real private consumption expenditure, seasonally adjusted	Log first difference	Haver Analytics
Real gross fixed capital formation, seasonally adjusted	Log first difference	Haver Analytics
Real exports, seasonally adjusted	Log first difference	Haver Analytics
Headline consumer price index, seasonally adjusted	Log first difference	Haver Analytics
Real effective exchange rate based on 120 trading partners deflated using consumer inflation, not seasonally adjusted	Log first difference	Darvas (2021); Haver Analytics
Portfolio (and other) investment liabilities to GDP	NA	International Monetary Fund
Stock market index	Log first difference	Haver Analytics
10-year local-currency government bond yield (or nearest maturity)	First difference	Haver Analytics
3-month interest rate (or nearest equivalent)	First difference	Haver Analytics
EMBIG* spread	First difference	J.P. Morgan
Gross debt (general government or central government) to GDP	First difference	Haver Analytics; Quarterly Public Sector Debt Database, World Bank

Source: World Bank.
Note: *EMBIG = emerging market bond index global.

TABLE 3.5 Sample for panel local projection models

Emerging market and developing economies				
Albania*	Croatia*	Jordan*	Paraguay*	Serbia*
Argentina*	Dominican Republic*	Kazakhstan	Peru	South Africa*
Bahrain*	Ecuador*	Malaysia	Philippines	Sri Lanka*
Belarus*	Egypt, Arab Republic*	Mexico	Poland	Thailand
Brazil*	Georgia*	Mongolia*	Qatar	Türkiye*
Chile	Hungary	Morocco*	Romania	Uganda*
China	India	Nigeria*	Russian Federation	Ukraine*
Colombia	Indonesia	North Macedonia*	Saudi Arabia	Vietnam*

Source: World Bank.
Note: *Indicates countries that are non-investment grade based on average ratings in 2019Q4.

TABLE 3.6 Variables for panel logit and probit models (annual data)

Variables	Definition	Source
Crisis dummy	Sovereign debt, banking, or currency crisis	Laeven and Valencia (2020)
GDP growth	Annual percentage growth rate of GDP at constant market prices based on local currency	WDI
Short-term debt	Share of short-term debt (with a maturity of 1 year or less) in external debt	WDI
Debt service	Ratio of debt service on external debt to exports	WDI
Reserve cover	International reserves in months of imports	IDS
Change in government debt	Percentage point change in public debt-to-GDP ratio	WEO
Change in private debt	Percentage point change in private debt-to-GDP ratio	GDD
Concessional debt	Share of concessional debt in external debt	IDS
Funding ratio	Ratio of credit provided to private sector to total deposits	GFDD
Currency overvaluation	Percentage deviation of real effective exchange rate from HP-filtered trend	Bruegel
Currency mismatch	Ratio of foreign liabilities to foreign assets	Lane and Milesi-Ferretti (2018)
Foreign direct investment	Net inflows of foreign direct investment as a share of GNI	WDI

Source: World Bank.
Note: GFDD = Global Financial Development Database; WDI = World Development Indicators; WEO = World Economic Outlook; IDS = International Debt Statistics.

References

Ahmed, S., B. Coulibaly, and A. Zlate. 2017. "International Financial Spillovers to Emerging Market Economies: How Important Are Economic Fundamentals?" *Journal of International Money and Finance* 76 (September): 133-52.

Aizenman, J., M. Binici, and M. M. Hutchison. 2016. "The Transmission of Federal Reserve Tapering News to Emerging Financial Markets." *International Journal of Central Banking* 12 (2): 317-56.

Arslanalp, M. S., and M.T. Tsuda. 2015. "Emerging Market Portfolio Flows: The Role of Benchmark-Driven Investors." International Monetary Fund Working Paper 15/263, Washington, DC: International Monetary Fund.

Arteta, C., M. A. Kose, F. Ohnsorge, and M. Stocker. 2015. "The Coming U.S. Interest Rate Tightening Cycle: Smooth Sailing or Stormy Waters?" Policy Research Note 15/02, World Bank, Washington, DC.

Arteta, C., S. Kamin, and F. Ruch. "How Do Rising U.S. Interest Rates Affect Emerging and Developing Economies? It Depends." Policy Research Working Paper 10258, Washington, DC: World Bank.

Avdjiev, S., L. Gambacorta, L.S. Goldberg, and S. Schiaffi. 2020. "The Shifting Drivers of Global Liquidity." *Journal of International Economics* 125 (July): 103324.

Bowman, D., J. M. Londono, and H. Sapriza. 2015. "U.S. Unconventional Monetary Policy and Transmission to Emerging Market Economies." *Journal of International Money and Finance* 55 (July): 27-59.

Cerutti, E., S. Claessens, and D. Puy. "Push Factors and Capital Flows to Emerging Markets: Why Knowing Your Lender Matters More than Fundamentals." *Journal of International Economics* 119 (2019): 133-49.

Chamon M., and C. Crowe. 2012. "Predictive Indicators of Crises." In *Handbook in Financial Globalization: The Evidence and Impact of Financial Globalization*, edited by G. Caprio, 499-505. London: Elsevier.

Chelsky, J. 2021. "Here We Go Again: Debt Sustainability in Low-Income Countries." World Bank (blog). October 20, 2023. https://ieg.worldbankgroup.org/blog/here-we-go-again-debt-sustainability-low-income-countries

Chen, J., T. Mancini-Griffoli, and R. Sahay. 2014. "Spillovers from United States Monetary Policy on Emerging Markets: Different This Time?" IMF Working Paper 14/240, International Monetary Fund, Washington, DC.

Darvas, Z. 2021. "Timely Measurement of Real Effective Exchange Rates." Working Paper 2021/15, Bruegel, Brussels.

Eichengreen, B., and P. Gupta. 2015. "Tapering Talk: The Impact of Expectations of Reduced Federal Reserve Security Purchases on Emerging Markets." *Emerging Market Review* 25 (September): 1-15.

Federal Reserve. 2020. "Statement on Longer-Run Goals and Monetary Policy Strategy." Federal Reserve, Washington, DC.

Frankel, J. A., and G. Saravelos. 2012. "Can Leading Indicators Assess Country Vulnerability? Evidence from the 2008-09 Global Financial Crisis." *Journal of International Economics* 87 (2): 216-31.

Guénette, J. D., M. A. Kose, and N. Sugawara. 2022. "Is a Global Recession Imminent?" EFI Policy Note 4, World Bank, Washington, DC.

Haubrich, J., G. Pennacchi, and P. Ritchken. 2012. "Inflation Expectations, Real Rates, and Risk Premia: Evidence from Inflation Swaps." *The Review of Financial Studies* 25 (5): 1588-629.

Hoek, J., S. Kamin, and E. Yoldas. 2021. "Are Rising U.S. Interest Rates Destabilizing for Emerging Market Economies?" FEDS Notes, Board of Governors of the Federal Reserve System, Washington, DC.

Hoek, J., S. Kamin, and E. Yoldas. 2022. "Are Higher U.S. Interest Rates Always Bad News for Emerging Markets?" *Journal of International Economics* 137 (July): 103585.

IIF (Institute of International Finance) database. Accessed on May 25, 2023. https://iif.com/Research/Download-Data.

Jacquier, E., N. Polson, and P. Rossi. 1994. "Bayesian Analysis of Stochastic Volatility Models." *Journal of Business and Economic Statistics* 12 (4): 371-89.

Jordà, O. 2005. "Estimation and Inference of Impulse Responses by Local Projections." *American Economic Review* 95 (1): 161-82.

Kaminsky, G. L., S. Lizondo, and C. M. Reinhart. 1998. "Leading Indicators of Currency Crises." *IMF Staff Papers* 45 (1): 1-48.

Kose, M. A., S. Kurlat, F. Ohnsorge, and N. Sugawara. 2017. "A Cross-Country Database of Fiscal Space." Policy Research Working Paper 8157, World Bank, Washington, DC.

Kose, M. A., P. Nagle, F. Ohnsorge, and N. Sugawara. 2021. *Global Waves of Debt: Causes and Consequences.* Washington, DC: World Bank.

Laeven, L., and F. Valencia. 2020. "Systemic Banking Crises Database: A Timely Update in COVID-19 Times." CEPR Discussion Paper 14569, Center for Economic and Policy Research, Washington, DC.

Lane, P. R., and G. M. Milesi-Ferretti. 2018. "The External Wealth of Nations Revisited: International Financial Integration in the Aftermath of the Global Financial Crisis." *IMF Economic Review* 66 (1): 189-222.

Lenza, M., and G. E. Primiceri. 2022. "How to Estimate a Vector Autoregression After March 2020." *Journal of Applied Econometrics* 37 (4): 688-99.

Matheson, T., and E. Stavrev. 2014. "News and Monetary Shocks at a High Frequency: A Simple Approach." *Economics Letters* 125 (2): 282-86.

Miyajima, K., and I. Shim. 2014. "Asset Managers in Emerging Market Economies." *BIS Quarterly Review.* September.

MSCI. 2022. *MSCI Global Market Accessibility Review.* June. New York: MSCI.

Obstfeld, M. 2022a. "Uncoordinated Monetary Policies Risk a Historic Global Slowdown." Peterson Institute for International Economics, Washington, DC.

Obstfeld, M. 2022b. "Emerging-Market and Developing Economies Need Support Amid Rising Interest Rates." *Peterson Institute for International Economics* (blog). October 6, 2022. https://www.piie.com/blogs/realtime-economics/emerging-market-and-developing-economies-need-support-amid-rising-interest.

U.S. Census Bureau. 2017. *X-13ARIMA-SEATS Reference Manual.* Washington, DC: U.S. Census Bureau.

World Bank. 2022. *Global Economic Prospects.* January. Washington, DC: World Bank.

CHAPTER 4

FISCAL POLICY CHALLENGES
IN LOW-INCOME COUNTRIES

The room for fiscal policy to maneuver has narrowed in low-income countries (LICs) over the past decade: LIC debt has grown rapidly as sizable and widening deficits have offset the debt-reducing effects of growth. Fiscal deficits have reflected growing spending pressures, including pressures on debt service, amid persistent revenue weakness, especially for grants and income tax revenues. As a result, 14 out of the 28 LICs were assessed as being in debt distress or at a high risk of debt distress as of end-April 2023. Creating room for fiscal policy requires generating higher revenues, making spending more efficient, and improving debt management practices. These measures need to be embedded in improvements to domestic institutional frameworks and need to be supported by well-coordinated global policies both to improve fiscal policy management and to address debt challenges.

Introduction

The pandemic and the severe global recession that accompanied it have triggered steep downturns in low-income countries (LICs). These, and the global repercussions of the Russian Federation's invasion of Ukraine, have significantly worsened LICs' fiscal positions and increased external and private-sector vulnerabilities. Nevertheless, LICs' policy challenges and economic vulnerabilities predate the pandemic. This chapter takes this longer view by examining long-standing fiscal policy challenges in LICs (table 4.1.A).

Even before the pandemic, LICs faced formidable development challenges. About 36 percent of LICs' population lived in extreme poverty in 2019 (figure 4.1). In 2000, LICs that have since turned middle-income countries (MICs) had better human development indicators and better access to infrastructure than today's LICs. Compared with LICs in 2000 that have since become MICs, public spending on healthcare in today's LICs was lower (relative to GDP) by one-fifth in 2019; measures of human capital development were lower by up to one-half, the share of their populations with access to electricity was half, and some measures of financial inclusion were lower by almost one-half (Steinbach 2019; World Bank 2019a). Even before the 2020 global recession raised global extreme poverty for the first year in decades, the goal of reducing global extreme poverty to 3 percent by 2030 would have been difficult to achieve on the basis of current growth prospects for LICs (World Bank 2022a).

The pandemic delayed progress toward the achievement of Sustainable Development Goals (SDGs) and widened gender disparities (United Nations 2021). In LICs with more than half of the population falling below the extreme poverty line, the pandemic reduced incomes per capita by 7-13 percentage points below their pre-pandemic trend between 2020 and 2024, adding to the development challenges. Food insecurity has intensified and is concentrated in fragile and conflict-affected countries and countries that have faced natural disasters. Adverse shocks such as extreme climate events and conflict are more likely to tip households into distress in LICs than elsewhere because of limited social safety nets.

Yet, fiscal resources to finance these development challenges are severely constrained, and were so already long before the pandemic. First, large informal sectors limit government revenues and rising interest payments in LICs are absorbing an increasing share of government revenues. On average, LIC government revenues amounted to 18 percent of GDP during 2011-19, about half of the advanced-economy average (39 percent of GDP) and 11 percentage points of GDP below the average of other emerging market and developing economies (EMDEs).[1] Second, during the same period, LIC primary government expenditure averaged about 20 percent of GDP, resulting in persistent fiscal deficits and a buildup of government debt. Government debt in LICs, on average, rose to 64 percent of GDP in 2019, from a low of 36 percent of GDP in 2011. In a few LICs, it climbed above to about 100 percent of GDP (Mozambique, Zambia) or even above 180 percent of GDP (Eritrea, Sudan). In others, such as those without international capital market access, government debt remained below 30

Note: This chapter was prepared by Joseph Mawejje, Franziska Ohnsorge, and Shu Yu.

[1] To ensure broad-based representation of LIC fiscal developments, averages in this chapter are unweighted unless otherwise specified.

FIGURE 4.1 Development challenges in LICs

About 4 out of 10 of the world's extreme poor reside in today's LICs. The income per capita in LICs is projected to remain below its pre-pandemic trend in the next few years, adding to the existing development challenges and the number of poor. In today's LICs, measures of human capital development and access to infrastructure are lower than in countries that were LICs in 2000 and became MICs later. Rising challenges from food insecurity, conflict, and debt distress further pose threats to development in LICs.

A. Number of extreme poor

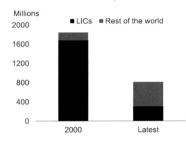

B. Income per capita in LICs

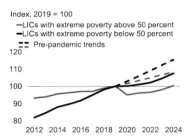

C. Human development indicators in LICs

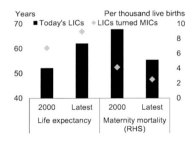

D. Electricity access in LICs

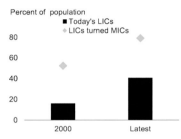

E. Food insecurity, by conflict

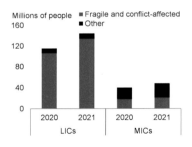

F. EMDEs in, or at risk of, debt distress

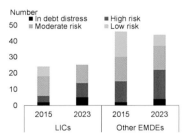

Sources: World Bank; World Bank (2022a); World Development Indicators; International Monetary Fund.
Note: LICs = low-income countries; MICs = middle-income countries.
A. The number of poor in the current 28 LICs and the rest of the world. "Pre-COVID" uses the latest available poverty headcount ratio in 2018 from WDI and population data from 2019. "Post-COVID" refers to the year 2021, which used the estimates from World Bank (2023).
B. Extreme poverty rate is measured as the share of people living on less than $2.15 per day. Per capita income is calculated as each group's GDP divided by each group's population. Dashed lines indicate per capita income assuming its growth rate equals to 2000-19 average after 2019. The sample excludes the Democratic Republic of Congo and Niger—both with over half of the population experiencing extreme poverty.
C. Simple average. "Latest" for life expectancy refers to 2020 (or the latest year available), while "Latest" for maternal mortality refers to 2017 (or the latest year available). The sample size includes 28 "Today's LICs," and 45 "LICs turned MICs" (countries that were classified as LICs in 2000 but are now classified as MICs).
D. Simple average. "Latest" refers to 2020 (or the latest year available). The sample size includes 60 "2000 LICs" for 2000 and 63 for the latest, 37 "LICs turned MICs" for 2000 and 45 for the latest, and 23 "Today's LICs" for 2000 and 28 for the latest.
E. Bars show the number of people in food crisis as classified by the Integrated Food Security Phase Classification (IPC/CH) Phase 3, that is, in acute food insecurity crisis or worse.
F. Number of LICs and other EMDEs in debt distress or at risk of debt distress, as of April 30, 2023.

percent of GDP (Afghanistan, Democratic Republic of Congo). Third, rising government debt increases debt-service burdens and makes LICs more vulnerable to increases in borrowing costs, especially while advanced economies are rapidly tightening monetary policy to rein in inflation.

Since the steep downturns of 2020 and the policy efforts to support economic activity, fiscal positions in LICs have weakened further. In 2021, 83 percent of LICs had government debt in excess of 50 percent of GDP, compared with less than one-half of other EMDEs. Despite the recovery in 2021-22, government debt in the average LIC is projected to reach 67 percent of GDP in 2022, up by about 2 percentage points of GDP from 2019, and the fiscal deficit is expected to reach 3 percent of GDP, about 2 percentage point of GDP wider than in 2019. Public gross financing needs in the average LIC rose by 3 percentage points of GDP to 11.4 percent of GDP in 2022 from 2019 (figure 4.2). Amid rising arrears, the need for debt restructuring, or unsustainably high debt levels or debt-service cost, debt vulnerabilities are elevated. Fourteen out of the 28 LICs were assessed as being in debt distress or at a high risk of debt distress as of end-April 2023 (IMF 2023).

In addition to a deterioration in fiscal positions, other macroeconomic indicators are weakening in LICs. Inflation has been edging up since the pandemic and further accelerated as a result of the global energy and food price surges triggered by Russia's invasion of Ukraine. Current account balances and terms of trade have deteriorated and, more broadly, external positions remained weaker in LICs than in other EMDEs. While growth is recovering, the short-run risks are tilted to the downside, further threatening fiscal positions in LICs. Against this backdrop, the chapter examines the following questions.

- How have fiscal positions in LICs evolved over the past decade?

- What have been the main sources of recent deterioration in fiscal positions?

- Which policies can help improve fiscal positions?

Contributions. The chapter contributes to the literature in three ways. First, while previous studies have examined the evolution of LIC debt and its composition, less analysis is available on other fiscal outcomes (such as the composition of spending and spending efficiency).[2] This chapter complements the debt discussion with a systematic assessment of the main drivers of debt, government revenues, and expenditures.

Second, domestic revenue mobilization and expenditure efficiency improvements are important elements in any strategy to improve fiscal outcomes, but not the only ones. Many countries have undertaken detailed public expenditure reviews, most recently in Burkina Faso, Guinea, and Mali (World Bank 2022b, 2022c, 2022d). In addition, several guidelines with best practices are available (see World Bank 2017 for education; and Manghee and van den Berg 2012 for water and sanitation). Ample policy work has been conducted on domestic resource mobilization (see Junquera et al. 2017 for an overview). What has been less explored is the relationship between the broader supporting environment and fiscal outcomes.

Third, to do justice to the special development challenges confronting the poorest countries in the world, the chapter focuses narrowly on the 28 lowest-income countries in documenting the evolution of fiscal positions since 2011. Previous studies have examined the fiscal positions of a larger group of lower-income EMDEs (for example, 76 EMDEs in IMF 2020). This study focuses on LICs because of their particular characteristics: they are heavily reliant on grant financing, lack international capital market access, include a large share of recipients of Highly Indebted Poor Country (HIPC) or Multilateral Debt Relief Initiative (MDRI) debt relief, and are more resource-reliant than other EMDEs. Despite these features, their debt buildup was faster and more broad-based than that in lower middle-income countries (LMICs; figure 4.2).

Main Findings. The chapter presents the following findings.

---

[2] See, for instance, Kose et al. (2020) on the evolution of LIC debt and its composition.

FIGURE 4.2 Government debt

Government debt rose in about 80 percent of LICs and EMDEs between 2011 and 2019, and on average by 28 and 13 percentage points of GDP, respectively. Between 2019 and 2022, government debt rose further in 14 out of 23 LICs, and on average by about 2 percentage points of GDP. The foreign currency and nonresident-held shares of LIC debt have risen since 2011, and the concessional debt share has fallen. As a result, interest spending has increased.

A. Government debt in LICs

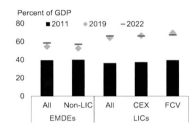

B. Share of EMDEs, by changes in government debt

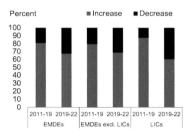

C. Composition of government debt

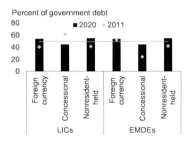

D. Government debt in LICs and LMICs

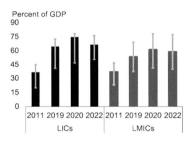

E. Share of EMDEs with high government debt

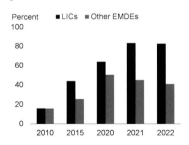

F. Public gross financing needs

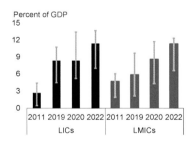

Sources: International Monetary Fund; World Bank.
Note: EMDEs = emerging market and developing economies, LICs = low-income countries, LMICs = lower-middle income countries; CEX = commodity-exporting countries; Other EMDEs = non-LIC EMDEs.
A.C.D.F. Unweighted averages.
B. Bars show the share of countries with increases (in red) or decreases (in blue) in government debt as a share of GDP over the corresponding time periods. Grey line indicates 50 percent.
C. Grey line indicates 50 percent. Latest available data are for 2020.
D.F. Bars show the unweighted averages. Orange whiskers show the interquartile ranges.
E. Percent of countries with government debt exceeding 50 percent of GDP (for LICs) or 60 percent of GDP (for other EMDEs excluding LICs).

First, between 2011 and 2022, government debt in the average LIC rose by 30 percentage points of GDP to 67 percent of GDP in 2022—much more than the 17 percentage points of GDP buildup in the average non-LIC EMDEs to 57 percent of GDP during 2011-22.[3] About four-fifths of it occurred already before the pandemic. The buildup was widespread among LICs: government debt rose in 91 percent of LICs.

Second, over the past decade, widening fiscal deficits offset the debt-reducing effects of growth and raised debt in LICs. The increase in government debt was largely due to sizable primary deficits that more than offset the debt-reducing effects of growth. In four-fifths of LICs, primary balances deteriorated between 2011 and 2022.

Third, the sizable primary deficits that drove the debt buildup in LICs mostly reflected rapid expenditure growth amid persistent revenue weakness. Total revenues in LICs were 11 percentage points of GDP below those in other EMDEs, on average, over 2011-22. A 3.8 percentage point of GDP decline in grant financing was only partially offset by rising income (and goods and services) taxes over the decade. The gap in revenue collection between LICs and other EMDEs mostly reflected weakness in indirect tax revenues. Meanwhile, in the decade before 2020, the composition of expenditures in LICs shifted away from health and education. Separately, government wage bills grew more rapidly (as a share of spending) than in other EMDEs.

Faced with large development needs, deteriorating fiscal positions, and shrinking grant finance, domestic revenue mobilization, improved spending efficiency, and broad-based policies to generate growth need to be policy priorities. High debt levels require strengthened debt management and, in some cases, may warrant debt relief. These measures need to be embedded in domestic reforms to strengthen institutional frameworks, ease structural constraints, and address informality, and need to be supported by well-coordinated

global policies to improve fiscal management, especially in tax policy design and implementation, deal with illicit financial flows, and address emerging debt challenges.

The rest of the chapter is organized as follows. The chapter describes how fiscal positions have evolved in LICs since 2000 and around the pandemic. It then summarizes the main sources of recent deterioration in fiscal positions. The final section concludes with a detailed account of the policy options to deal with these challenges.

Evolution of fiscal positions in LICs

Even before the pandemic and global recession of 2020, LIC debt rose sharply during 2011-19, largely because persistent fiscal deficits offset the debt-reducing benefits of robust growth. Considerably larger fiscal deficits in LICs than in other EMDEs have mainly reflected revenue weakness, especially income tax revenue weakness. Spending pressures during the pandemic and in its runup further widened fiscal deficits in LICs. Conflict and fragility have compounded these fiscal challenges by tilting revenue collection away from income taxes toward trade taxes and tilted spending away from health and education toward military spending.

Conceptual framework

An accounting decomposition offers a framework for identifying the most pressing sources of fiscal weaknesses (World Bank 2005). Specifically, changes in the debt-to-GDP ratio over time can be decomposed into primary fiscal balances (the difference between revenues and non-interest expenditures), output growth, foreign and domestic interest rates, inflation, and other factors (annex 4.1).[4] These other factors include exchange

---

[3] Throughout this chapter, the period under consideration starts in 2011 to exclude both the global recession of 2009 and the robust economic rebound of 2010. This is consistent with the fourth global wave of debt identified in Kose et al. (2020), which marks the starting point of that wave as end-2010.

[4] The detailed framework for this decomposition exercise is presented in annex 4.1. The detailed decomposition requires data on the foreign-currency-denominated share of government debt. This is only available for 2020 and unavailable for all but two LICs (Democratic Republic of Congo, Uganda) and for 89 EMDEs. The foreign-currency-denominated share of government debt in 2021-22 is assumed to be constant at 2020 values and, for LICs and non-LIC EMDEs with missing data, is assumed to be the same as the average for LICs or non-LIC EMDEs, respectively.

rate depreciation, privatization proceeds, the materialization of contingent liabilities, or other ad-hoc changes to debt stocks such as the emergence of hidden debt. The primary balance, in turn, can be decomposed into revenues and primary expenditures.

The decomposition is applied to the whole period 2011-22, to 2011-19 to capture changes over the decade leading up to the pandemic, and to 2019-22 to capture changes during the pandemic. The exercise is conducted for up to 151 EMDEs, including 23 LICs (table 4.1.B). In addition, the exercise is conducted for a counterfactual scenario using five-year-ahead forecasts for real GDP growth, inflation, revenues, and non-interest expenditures from the October 2018 *World Economic Outlook*. These five-year-ahead forecasts represent expectations formed in October 2018 for fiscal and macroeconomic conditions up to 2022. By comparing these with actual debt-to-GDP ratios in 2022, the exercise can identify the main reasons for higher-than-anticipated debt in 2022.

Evolution of debt

Government debt in the average LIC has risen rapidly since 2011, with most of the buildup occurring well before the global economic collapse in the 2020 pandemic (Chuku et al. 2023). The debt buildup predominantly reflected persistent and widening fiscal deficits that offset the debt-reducing effect of growth.

Widespread rise in government debt

Between 2011 and 2022, government debt in the average LIC rose by 30 percentage points of GDP—almost twice as much as in other EMDE—to 67 percent of GDP in 2022, well above the level in other EMDEs (figure 4.2). The buildup was widespread among LICs: government debt rose in 91 percent of LICs. It was also unexpectedly large. Five years ago, when forecasts for 2022 began to be available, government debt in the average LIC was only expected to rise to 60 percent of GDP in 2022. While the magnitude of this debt buildup was unexpectedly large, the debt buildup itself was not unanticipated: five years

ago, government debt was already expected to rise in almost three-quarters of the LICs in which it did eventually rise between 2017 and 2022.

More than four-fifths of the government debt buildup between 2011 and 2022 occurred long before the pandemic tipped the global economy into collapse (figure 4.2). Countries with the fastest rise in debt were often fragile and affected by a combination of conflict, weak governance, or commodity dependence (World Bank 2019a). Only in three LICs (Afghanistan, Democratic Republic of Congo, Guinea) did government debt decline over this period, largely because of debt relief. In the 90 percent of LICs where government debt increased between 2011 and 2019, it rose much more than in other EMDEs with rising government debt.

In the pandemic recession of 2020, government debt in the average LIC rose by another 10 percentage points of GDP before contracting by 6 percentage points between 2021 and 2022. If macroeconomic and fiscal projections for 2023-24 materialize, government debt in an average LIC will fall to 62 percent of GDP in 2025. However, past forecasts have typically turned out too optimistic (Ho and Mauro 2016).

Deficit-driven government debt buildup

The 30 percentage point of GDP rise in government debt in the average LIC between 2011 and 2022 reflected persistent and widening primary fiscal deficits that more than offset the debt-reducing effects of growth (figure 4.3). In contrast, in the average non-LIC EMDE, the primary fiscal deficits were sufficiently small to not entirely offset the debt-reducing effect of growth—at least until the pandemic. The government debt buildup in non-LIC EMDEs since 2011 has been larger than anticipated just five years ago for many reasons: growth disappointed, primary deficits were larger than expected, interest cost were higher than expected and other factors raised debt more than twice as much as anticipated.

In the 91 percent of LICs where government debt rose between 2011 and 2022, the increase was almost entirely due to sizable primary deficits that

FIGURE 4.3 Decomposing increases in government debt

The debt buildup between 2011 and 2022, to a large extent, resulted from sizable fiscal deficits that more than offset the debt-reducing effect of robust growth in LICs, even before the pandemic. The larger-than-anticipated debt buildup over 2019-22 mainly reflected disappointing growth outcomes and higher-than-expected interest cost, whereas primary deficits materialized broadly as expected.

A. Contributions to government debt increase in the average LIC, 2011-19

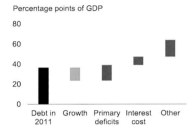

B. Contributions to government debt increase in the average LIC, 2019-22

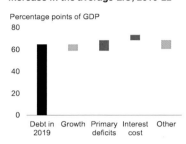

C. Contribution to government debt increase in the average LIC, 2011-22: Actual

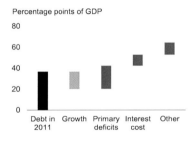

D. Contribution to government debt increase in the average LIC, 2011-22: Expected in October 2018

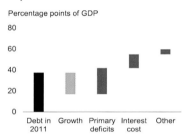

Sources: International Monetary Fund; World Bank.
Note: LICs = low-income countries. Debt in 2011 (2019 in B) is in percent of GDP. Red bars indicate debt-increasing contribution and orange bars indicate debt-decreasing contribution. Please note that the group of LICs with rising government debt differs by sample periods (i.e., 2011-19 in A; 2019-22 in B; and 2011-22 in C-D). "Other" factors include exchange rate depreciation, privatization proceeds, the materialization of contingent liabilities or other ad-hoc changes to debt stocks.
D. The decomposition is based on the 2022 forecasts from the October 2018 *World Economic Outlook.*

Yemen did output contractions raise debt. In all other LICs, growth helped lower government debt. Interest costs accounted for almost one-third to the debt buildup in LICs with rising debt—less than in other EMDEs because almost one-third of LIC external debt was on concessional terms.[6]

Riskier sources of financing government debt

In addition to a buildup, LIC debt has also shifted in composition toward riskier sources of financing. By 2021, the average LIC carried external debt equivalent to 51 percent of GDP—almost three-quarters of total government debt and more than twice as much as in 2012. A significant share of external debt in LICs was denominated in foreign currencies. Since 2011, the non-concessional share of government debt has risen in the average LIC by almost half, to 55 percent in 2020 (figure 4.2).

Before the pandemic, non-Paris Club creditors, notably China, have become a more important source of financing over the past decade, especially in Sub-Saharan Africa (Essl et al. 2019). In 2018, non-Paris Club debt accounted for more than one-fifth of the median LIC's external debt, and about 13 percent of their government debt. Lending arrangements for commercial and non-Paris Club debt are often not public, and they can be complex and varied (Horn, Reinhart, and Trebesch 2019). Moreover, while non-Paris Club creditors have agreed on temporary debt-service relief (especially under the Debt Service Suspension Initiative [DSSI]) in the G20 frameworks, increased exposure to commercial creditors may pose coordination challenges for debt resolutions in the future (World Bank and IMF 2018).

Higher levels of public debt and an increased reliance on riskier sources of financing make many

offset the debt-reducing effects of growth, although with wide variation (figure 4.4).[5] Of the 30 percentage points of GDP increase in government debt in these LICs over this period, primary deficits accounted for three-quarters and more than offset the debt-reducing effects of growth. Only in the Central African Republic, Sudan, and

---

[5] Three LICs saw a decline in debt during 2011-2022 (Afghanistan, Democratic Republic of Congo, Guinea) and this decline was largely due to solid growth and other factors, accompanied by near-balanced primary deficits. Interest costs also contributed less to the debt build up than in LICs with rising debt over this period.

---

[6] In some countries, the residual ("other factors" in the first accounting identity) was sizable. It includes the recognition (or realization) of contingent liabilities net of the privatization process, debt restructuring, and measurement error (World Bank 2005; figure 4.4). In Mozambique and Ethiopia, where state-owned enterprises created large contingent (or explicit) government liabilities, it accounted for 9 and 6 percentage points of GDP per year on average (IMF 2018a). In The Gambia, it accounted for about 3 percentage points of GDP per year, as a result of government bailouts of state-owned enterprises and widespread mismanagement of debt (World Bank 2018a).

LICs vulnerable to currency, interest rate, and refinancing risks (Essl et al. 2019). Because of rising arrears, the need for debt restructuring, or unsustainable debt levels, debt vulnerabilities are elevated. Fourteen LICs were assessed as being in debt distress or at a high risk of debt distress as of end-April 2023, compared with only six in 2015. For LICs assessed at low or moderate risk of debt distress, safety margins have eroded. Their government debt has risen by 14 percentage points of GDP and their primary deficits has widened by 0.5 percentage point of GDP since 2015.

Evolution of primary deficits

Persistent primary deficits

Persistent and sizable primary deficits have been the main source of debt accumulation in the average LIC since 2011. On average during 2011-22, the average LICs' primary deficit amounted to 2.2 percent of GDP, about 0.8 percentage point of GDP above the average for other EMDEs. During the pandemic, LICs' primary deficits averaged 3.1 percent of GDP, 0.5 percentage point of GDP above the average for other EMDEs. About 60 percent of LICs ran primary deficits in every single year during 2011-22.

The pandemic, which sharply increased spending needs, resulted in a jump in primary deficits, from 1.3 percent of GDP in 2019 to 3.4 percent of GDP in 2020. Despite a post-pandemic growth rebound, only about one-tenth of this widening of primary deficits was unwound during 2021-22 (figure 4.5). As a result, the primary deficit widened by 2.0 percentage points of GDP between 2011 and 2022 in the average LIC, to 3.1 percent of GDP in 2022—higher than what was expected five years ago when forecasts for 2022 first became available. Primary balances deteriorated in more than three-quarters of LICs between 2011 and 2022, considerably more than the three-fifths of non-LIC EMDEs (figure 4.6).

Sources of widening primary deficits

LICs have long had considerably lower revenue and expenditure ratios than non-LIC EMDEs (Akitoby et al. 2018). Slight revenue losses before the pandemic, during 2011-19, were compounded

FIGURE 4.4 Decomposing changes in government debt

In LICs with rising debt, primary deficits more than offset the debt-reducing benefits of growth, whereas in LICs with falling debt, primary deficits were nearly nil. In LICs where government debt rose between 2011 and 2022, the increase was almost entirely due to sizable primary deficits that offset the debt-reducing effects of solid growth, although with wide variation. In LICs where debt declined, primary deficits were nearly nil and growth was robust.

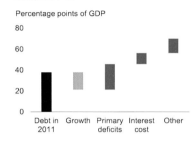

A. Contribution to changes in government debt in LICs with rising debt, 2011-22

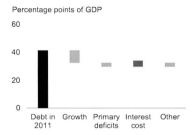

B. Contribution to changes in government debt in LICs with falling debt, 2011-22

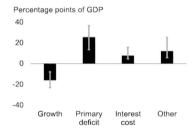

C. Range of contributions to changes in government debt in LICs with rising debt, 2011-22

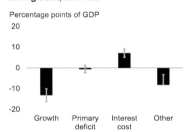

D. Range of contributions to changes in government debt in LICs with falling debt, 2011-22

Sources: International Monetary Fund; World Bank.
Note: LICs = low-income countries. "Other" factors include exchange rate depreciation, privatization proceeds, the materialization of contingent liabilities, or other ad-hoc changes to debt stocks. The sample covers LICs with rising (A, C) or falling (B, D) government debt-to-GDP ratios between 2011 and 2022.
A.-B. Debt in 2011 is in percent of GDP. Red bars indicate debt-increasing contribution and orange bars indicate debt-reducing contribution.
C.-D. Blue bars indicate median contributions to the decline in government debt-to-GDP ratios during 2011-22, and orange whiskers indicate interquartile ranges.

by sizable spending increases after the pandemic, which more than offset a post-pandemic improvement in revenue collection after 2019. As a result, the increase in primary expenditure between 2011 and 2022 accounted for the widening of the average LIC primary fiscal deficit.

While there was wide heterogeneity in the spending and revenue pressures underlying the changes in primary balance between 2011 and 2022, none of the LICs with improving primary balance suffered the magnitude of revenue losses

FIGURE 4.5 **Primary deficits**

While primary deficits were wider in non-LIC EMDEs than in LICs during the pandemic, primary deficits after the pandemic were similar. In the average LIC, the post-pandemic deterioration in primary balances compared with most of the pre-pandemic period largely reflected rising primary expenditures.

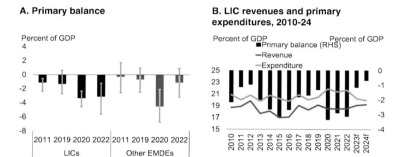

A. Primary balance

B. LIC revenues and primary expenditures, 2010-24

Sources: International Monetary Fund; World Bank.
Note: Unweighted averages, unless otherwise specified. LICs = low-income countries. Other EMDEs = non-LIC emerging market and developing economies.
A. Bars show unweighted averages, with whiskers showing interquartile ranges. Data for 2022 are estimated.
B. Data for 2022-24 are estimated or projected. f indicates forecasts.

of the quarter of LICs with deteriorating primary balances and the largest revenue losses (figure 4.6). They also experienced much smaller spending increases than the majority of LICs with worsening primary balances.

Evolution of revenues

Revenue weakness

In the average LIC, revenues accounted for 18 percent of GDP during 2011-22—11 percentage points of GDP lower than in the average non-LIC EMDE (figure 4.7).[7] While average revenue ratios were broadly stable during the past decade in LICs, there was some heterogeneity, with somewhat more volatile revenue ratios in LICs that are also FCVs.

Revenue composition

LICs' weak *overall* revenue collection largely reflected challenges in collecting *tax* revenues

---

[7] In part this may reflect tax expenditures, which include exemptions, reduced rates, special deductions, and tax credits (Mullins, Gupta, and Liu 2020). In the average LIC (among 10 LICs with available data), tax expenditures reduced revenues by 2.9 percent of GDP in 2019 (Global Tax Expenditures Database 2022).

(figure 4.7). While the differences in total revenues between LICs and other EMDEs amounted to 11 percentage points of GDP on average over the period 2011-21, tax revenues alone accounted for 7 percentage points of GDP of this gap and the difference was statistically significant.

Both direct and indirect tax revenues were statistically significantly weaker in LICs than in other EMDEs, by 2-3 percentage points of GDP. That said, the largest shortfalls in LICs were in goods and services taxes (3 percentage points of GDP) and in corporate income taxes (1 percentage point of GDP) whereas trade taxes were broadly similar in LICs and other EMDEs. Among goods and services taxes, revenues from value-added tax (VAT) were 2 percentage points of GDP (and significantly) lower in LICs than in other EMDEs. VAT is an intrinsically complex tax that imposes considerable administrative burdens on both the authorities and taxpayers, especially in institutionally weak environments (Ebrill, Keen, and Perry 2001). However, in countries, such as LICs, with low initial VAT rates, poor provision of public services, and commodity exporters, VAT rate increases have shown the potential to generate sizable revenue gains (Gunter et al. 2018, 2019).

The four-fifths of LICs that are commodity exporters struggled more than other LICs to collect tax revenues. Among commodity-exporting LICs, three-fifths are predominantly agricultural commodity exporters whereas the remainder relies on energy or industrial metal exports. Stronger dependence on commodities could weaken fiscal capacity (Cardenas, Ramirez, and Tuzemen 2011), worsen governance (Sinnot, Nash, and de la Torre 2010), or both (Cassidy 2019).

Since 2011, the composition of government revenues in LICs has been broadly stable, at least for the nine LICs for which a revenue breakdown is available. In these LICs, both indirect and direct taxes rose by almost 2 percentage points of GDP between 2011 and 2019 (figure 4.8). Indirect tax revenues in LICs rose by almost 2 percentage points of GDP to just over 8 percent of GDP in 2019, largely on account of an increase in goods and service tax. Personal income tax revenues also increased somewhat, although only about one-third as much as goods and services tax revenues.

Aid has traditionally played an important role in LICs. The association of higher grant funding with lower overall revenues, in particular tax revenues, is well-established although stronger institutions and a more equal income distribution may mitigate this negative association (Thornton 2014). In the period during 2011-15, grants accounted for about one-third of total government revenue in LICs (6.5 percent of GDP)—well above levels for the average non-LIC EMDE (0.3 percent of GDP). Since then, grants have declined steeply for LICs, such that they averaged 2.7 percent of GDP during 2016-21 (figure 4.7). At the same time, aid coordination has been hindered by increased donor fragmentation (World Bank 2022e). The decline in grant financing may reflect rising financing cost and other funding constraints in donor countries, but also limited absorptive capacity that constraint aid effectiveness (Feeny and McGillivray 2009).

Evolution of expenditures

Spending pressures

Revenue weakness constrained government spending in LICs (World Bank 2019b). During 2011-22, primary expenditures in the average LIC were about 10 percentage points of GDP lower than in the average non-LIC EMDE,—broadly in line with the revenue gap between LICs and non-LIC EMDEs (figure 4.9). In more than two-thirds of LICs, primary spending (relative to GDP) increased between 2011 and 2021.

Spending composition

In the average LIC, primary expenditures rose by 1.4 percentage points of GDP between 2011 and 2021, and interest expenditure by just under 1 percentage point of GDP to an average of 1.7 percent of GDP in 2021 (figure 4.9). However, there was wide heterogeneity, with some LICs spending as much as 6 percent of GDP on interest in 2021. In extreme cases (i.e., Malawi and Zambia), interest payments exceeded 20 percent of government revenues.

FIGURE 4.6 Decomposing changes in primary balances

A sharp increase in spending compounding revenue losses in LICs between 2011 and 2022, resulting in widening primary deficits—but with wide heterogeneity. The LICs with improving fiscal balances avoided the worst revenue losses over this period. Primary balances deteriorated in a larger share of LICs than of other EMDEs.

A. Contributions to changes in primary balance, 2011-22

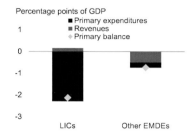

B. Share of economies with deterioration in primary balances between 2011 and 2022

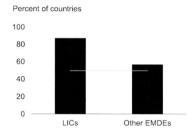

C. Range of changes in primary balances, revenues, and expenditures, 2011-22

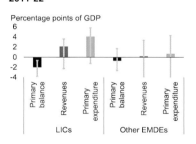

D. Range of contributions to changes in LICs with deteriorating or improving primary balances, 2011-22

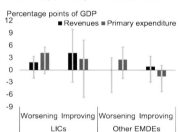

Sources: International Monetary Fund; World Bank.
Note: LICs = low-income countries. Other EMDEs = non-LIC emerging market and developing economies.
A. Bars show unweighted average changes between 2011 and 2022 in revenue-to-GDP ratio and primary-fiscal-balance-to-GDP ratio as well as negative of primary-expenditure-to-GDP ratio. Data includes 24 LICs and 122 other EMDEs for which data is available for both 2011 and 2022.
B. The grey line denotes 50 percent.
C. Bars indicate median contributions to change in primary balance (in blue), revenues (in red), and primary expenditures (in orange; all in percent of GDP) during 2011-22 with whiskers indicating the interquartile range.
D. "Worsening" ("Improving") primary balance refers to the 19 (5) LICs and 72 (44) other EMDEs where the primary balance in 2022 was below (above) the primary balance in 2011. Bars indicate median contributions to change in revenues (in blue), and primary expenditures (in red; all in percent of GDP) during 2011-22 with whiskers indicating the interquartile range.

Primary expenditures increased especially sharply between 2019-21—the pandemic recession and its aftermath. The increase between 2019 and 2021 was due to higher spending on health and social protection. Until 2019, primary spending had risen only marginally (less than 1 percentage point of GDP), with the largest increases in the average government wage bill, modest increases in health and education spending, and broadly stable defense spending in LICs.

FIGURE 4.7 Revenues

Overall revenues in LICs were below those in other EMDEs mainly because of gaps in collection of tax revenue, especially that from taxes on goods and services, but also from corporate income taxes. Commodity-exporting LICs have somewhat higher goods and services tax collections. Over the past decade, the composition of revenues has shifted somewhat toward goods and services taxes. Grants have declined steeply among LICs.

A. Revenues

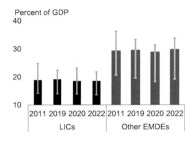

B. Revenues in LICs, by country groups

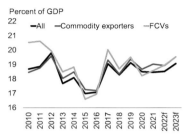

C. Differences in revenues between LICs and other EMDEs

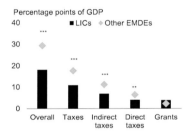

D. Differences in direct and indirect tax revenues between LICs and other EMDEs

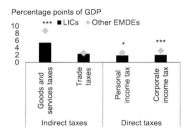

E. Differences in revenues between commodity-exporting LICs and other LICs

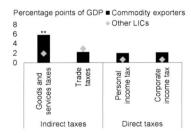

F. Composition of total revenues

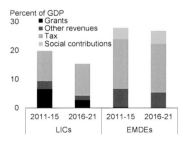

Sources: International Monetary Fund; World Bank.
Note: LICs = low-income countries. Other EMDEs = non-LIC emerging market and developing economies. FCVs = Fragile, conflict, and violence-affected areas. *** shows the significance level at 10 percent.
A.B. Bars (lines) show the unweighted average, with whiskers showing interquartile ranges. Based on up to 26 LICs. f indicates forecasts.
C.D. Unweighted average revenues (in percent of GDP) during 2011-2021 in LICs and other EMDEs.
E. Unweighted average revenues (in percent of GDP) during 2011-2021 in commodity-exporting LICs and other LICs.
F. Bars show the unweighted average. Based on 121 EMDEs and 18 LICs.

Between 2019 and 2020, LICs' combined spending on employee wages and interest payments averaged 47 percent of government expense, 12 percentage points of GDP higher than in the average non-LIC EMDE (figure 4.9). With a high proportion of rigid expenditures, the ability of LICs to reallocate resources toward growth-enhancing investments and social programs is limited. As a result, infrastructure spending in LICs, for example, has been shown to be highly procyclical (Foster, Rand, and Gorgulu 2022). At the same time, the high prevalence of conflict events and natural disasters among LICs and the fact that 80 percent of LICs are heavily commodity reliant generate macroeconomic volatility and constrain growth and tax revenue mobilization since countries with higher tax base variability tend to exhibit more procyclical fiscal policy (figure 4.10; Talvi and Vegh 2005). In addition, persistent conflict and violence increases pressures for defense spending at the expense other types of spending, including in the education, health, and infrastructure sectors.

Spending efficiency

Government spending efficiency was statistically significantly weaker in LICs than in other EMDEs in almost all major spending categories (figure 4.11; annex 4.2). Processes for project appraisal and evaluation were less rigorous, on account of a lack of capacity or the presence of corruption. Inefficient spending on health and education, combined with limited reallocation of spending toward these items over the past decade, can intensify the challenges facing LICs on these fronts.

In part, weak spending efficiency reflected broader underdevelopment and weak institutions that create capacity constraints. As an example of capacity constraints in LICs, in 2014, the Guinean government planned to build a $20 billion infrastructure project, which consisted of both heavy-duty railways and a new port, to help export some of the world's highest-grade iron ore from Simandou but the project stalled in 2017 (Sobják 2018; World Bank 2018b).

Fiscal policy options in LICs

Revenue weakness constrains LIC governments' ability to provide public services, conduct counter-cyclical policies, serve debt, and implement redistributive measures. It is particularly challenging for LICs now, as the rise of fragile and conflict-affected events (such as Russia's invasion of Ukraine) and natural disasters raise food inflation and threaten to increase hunger and poverty in LICs. The revenue weakness in LICs—and the resulting spending constraints and rising debt—highlight three policy priorities: domestic resource mobilization, spending efficiency, and sound debt management. Measures to strengthen institutions more broadly can support these efforts. These policies need to be embedded in broader reform efforts to ease structural constraints, address informality, and other market failures, strengthen institutions, and generate broad-based growth (Newbery and Stern 1987; Stiglitz and Rosengard 2015). Finally, aid in the form of grants or greater lending concessionality can be geared toward addressing critical emerging challenges, including the effects of climate change, fragility, and pandemics (Fardoust et al. 2023).

Domestic resource mobilization

There is wide scope to scale up revenue mobilization efforts among LICs, their low levels of development notwithstanding. Recent estimates show that LICs have been able to collect about two-thirds of their potential tax revenue over the past decade (Pessino and Fenochietto 2013; Mawejje and Sebudde 2019). Thus, substantial revenue gains could be generated in LICs by measures such as broadening tax bases, strengthening tax administration, and enhancing tax efficiencies. If implemented in a progressive manner, disproportionately raising taxes on higher-income brackets, tax reforms could also help achieve redistribution goals. Income and consumption tax efficiencies are lower in LICs than in other EMDEs—possibly reflecting widespread informality—while trade tax efficiency is higher (figure 4.12).

The effectiveness and efficiency of tax expenditures can be evaluated against country-specific

FIGURE 4.8 **Revenue composition**

Overall revenues in LICs were below those in other EMDEs mainly because of gaps in collection of tax revenue, especially that from taxes on goods and services taxes, but also that from corporate income taxes. Over the past decade, the composition of tax revenues in LICs has shifted somewhat toward indirect taxes (such as goods and services taxes).

A. Differences in revenues between LICs and other EMDEs

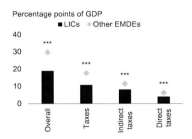

B. Differences in direct and indirect tax revenues between LICs and other EMDEs

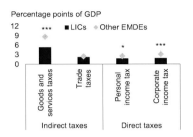

C. Differences in revenues between commodity-exporting LICs and other LICs

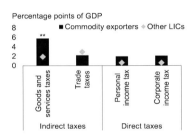

D. Tax revenues and overall revenues

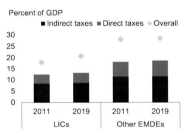

Sources: International Monetary Fund; World Bank.
Note: LICs = low-income countries. Other EMDEs = non-LIC emerging market and developing economies. *** shows the significance level at 10 percent.
A.B. Unweighted average revenues (in percent of GDP) during 2011-21 in LICs and other EMDEs.
C. Unweighted average revenues (in percent of GDP) during 2011-21 in commodity-exporting and other LICs.
D. Unweighted averages for 9 LICs and 85 other EMDEs. Data beyond 2019 is only available for one LIC, hence chart shows data for 2011 and 2019.

development policy objectives (World Bank 2023). Past episodes of successful tax revenue mobilization in LICs and EMDEs were usually accompanied by comprehensive tax policy and revenue administration reforms (Akitoby et al. 2018). In addition, unexpected revenue windfalls from improvements in a country's terms of trade can be set aside to reduce fiscal deficits and debt. These measures need to be supported by global mechanisms to coordinate tax policy design and implementation, and to limit illicit financial flows.

Tax policy. The most frequent tax policy measures were to increase indirect tax rates and broaden the tax base for both direct and indirect taxation. Tax

FIGURE 4.9 Expenditures

Primary spending was lower in LICs than in other EMDEs, in part reflecting weaker institutions. In some LICs, interest spending rose steeply between 2011 and 2022. Rising spending needs during the pandemic contributed to a steep rise in primary spending in the average LIC between 2019 and 2020.

A. Primary expenditures

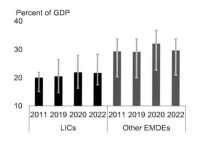

B. Primary expenditures in LICs, by country groups

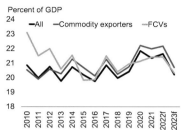

C. Net interest spending

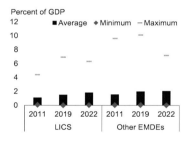

D. Composition of government spending

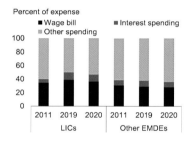

Sources: International Monetary Fund; World Bank.
Note: LICs = low-income countries. Other EMDEs = non-LIC emerging market and developing economies. FCVs = Fragile, conflict, and violence-affected areas. Based on 140 EMDEs, including 27 LICs and 13 FCVs. Data for 2022 (and onwards) are estimated or projected.
A. Bars show unweighted averages, and whiskers show interquartile ranges.
B. Lines show unweighted averages. Data for 2022-23 is estimated or projected. f indicates forecasts.
C. Net interest spending is defined as the difference between the primary balance and the overall balance. The solid blue bars show the unweighted average, the red diamonds and orange lines show the minimum- maximum range. Countries with negative net interest payments and those with incomplete data are not included in the sample.
D. Expense excludes net investment in government non-financial assets.

bases can be broadened by removing exemptions, especially for higher-income entities, in a way that minimizes economic distortions and strikes the right balance between efficiency and equity (Akitoby et al. 2019). Excise taxes, typically on petroleum, cigarettes, alcohol, and motor vehicles, are less frequently used in LICs than in advanced economies, yet can be administratively simple if designed in a way that reduces circumvention (IMF 2011). For example, The Gambia found that a switch from weight-based to pack-based taxation of cigarettes and weight-based taxation of

non-cigarette tobacco products reduced smokers' incentive to switch to less-taxed products (Akitoby et al. 2019).

Tax administration. Strengthening tax collection capacity is a crucial component of state-building and institutional development. Capacity-enhancing measures included risk-based audits, especially with a greater focus on large taxpayers; strengthened legislation to empower tax collectors; a shift in human resource management toward training and monitoring; as well as upgrades in information technology to facilitate registration, filing and payment enforcement (Akitoby et al. 2018).

Supporting structural policies. Widespread informality in LICs erodes government revenue collection (World Bank 2019b; Ohnsorge and Yu 2021). Since widespread informality is symptomatic of broader institutional weaknesses, lowering it requires a multi-pronged approach of which more efficient tax administration is only one aspect. For example, underdeveloped financial sectors in LICs also encouraged cash transactions that facilitated tax evasion or avoidance (World Bank 2015). Other priorities include streamlined and well-enforced regulatory frameworks; better access to finance, markets and inputs; stronger social safety nets; leveling the playing field between formal and informal firms; better public service delivery; better education; and less corruption (Ohnsorge and Yu 2021). Successful strategies have featured strong political commitment and early reform measures to build momentum (Akitoby et al. 2019).

Opportunities from information technology. Recent technological advances could empower tax policy makers to deepen the tax base and improve tax administration (World Bank 2019b). Digital technologies have helped some SSA countries to reduce compliance costs and to simplify taxpayer registration, filing and payment, audit, collection enforcement, and appeals. For example, after Rwanda rolled out its e-tax platform, it introduced mobile payments, integrated social contributions into the e-tax system, and rolled out electronic billing machines to raise VAT revenues (Akitoby et al. 2019).

Expenditure efficiency

LICs have significant spending needs to cope with the pressing policy challenges now (such as to support the poor and vulnerable against rising food inflation) and to achieve development goals in the long run (Clements, Gupta, and Jalles 2022). Greater expenditure efficiency and a reallocation toward more growth-enhancing spending can help meet these. The public sector wage bill rose significantly between 2011 and 2019 and accounted for about one-third of government primary spending in 2019 in the average LIC. Expenditure on defense in fragile and conflict-affected LICs averaged about 19 percent of government primary spending between 2011 and 2021 (figure 4.11).

Expenditure reallocation. There may be room to cut less productive spending to allow for more growth-enhancing or better-targeted programs. Subsidies on food and energy are pervasive in EMDEs but tend to be poorly targeted and fiscally costly (Coady, Falamini, and Sears 2015). Military spending may crowd out more growth-enhancing spending. During 2011-20, public sector employment absorbed almost half of formal employment in LICs (although only 7 percent of total employment) and employed more educated and older workers, and the wage bill accounted, on average, for almost 40 percent of government expenses (figure 4.13). In addition, changes in public wage bills move hand in hand with changes in revenues, suggesting that increased revenue collection could be allocated to more growth-enhancing spending line items. Higher wages in the public sector may attract better-qualified civil servants but have often not resulted in improved government effectiveness and control of corruption in LICs (Van Rijcke-ghem and Weber 2001). Governments can evaluate the composition of spending to examine if wages are squeezing out other productive spending and whether there is excessive employ-ment or too high a wage premium for public sector workers; based on such an analysis, an action plan can be formed.

Conversely, investments into resilience to climate change are cost-effective: each dollar invested in early warning systems is estimated to avoid more

FIGURE 4.10 Conflict, natural disasters, and volatility

Conflict and violence events are higher in LICs than in other EMDEs. The average LIC experiences more natural disasters in a year than the average EMDE. These factors combined to generate considerably higher growth volatility in LICs before the pandemic than in the average non-LIC EMDE.

A. Average number of conflict and violence events

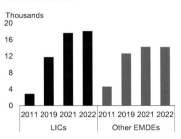

B. Average number of natural disasters

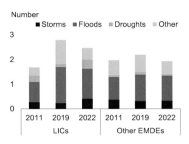

C. Real GDP growth volatility

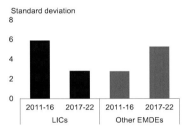

D. Share of commodity exporters

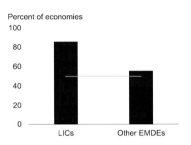

Sources: International Monetary Fund; The Armed Conflict Location & Event Data Project (ACLED); World Bank.
Note: LICs = low-income countries. Other EMDEs = non-LIC emerging market and developing economies.
A. Bars show the average number of reported conflict and violence events per country between 2011 and 2022 both for LICs and other EMDEs.
B. Bars show the average number of natural disasters recorded in a specific year for each country grouping. Other includes: wildfires, volcanic activity, mass movement, land slides, insect infestation, glacial lake outburst, food, epidemics, earthquakes, animal accident.
C. Bars show the standard deviation of real GDP growth over six year-periods (2011-16, 2017-22) and for the entire period (2011-22).
D. Share of commodity exporters among LICs and EMDEs, as classified in table 4.1.B.

than $4 in losses (Hallegatte, Rentschler, and Rozenberg 2019). Spending that improves education and health outcomes has been associat-ed with greater long-term growth and productivity growth (World Bank 2018c). Separately, well-targeted social benefit systems can reduce the permanent damage done by adverse shocks. The coverage of social protection programs remains limited in LICs. On average, only 1 percent of population in LICs is covered by unemployment benefits, while about 15 percent of population has access to social protection and social safety net programs. The coverage of such programs is significantly lower than in other EMDEs over the

FIGURE 4.11 Composition and efficiency of primary expenditures

LICs have significantly lower spending than other EMDEs on education and health. The wage bill rose significantly between 2011 and 2019. Spending efficiency is weaker in LICs, especially in infrastructure and health. In part, this reflects weaker institutions: corruption and disregard for law and order are associated with less efficient spending.

A. Expenditures on major spending categories, 2011-21 average

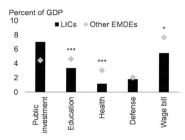

B. Expenditures on major spending categories

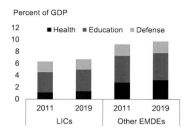

C. Spending efficiency

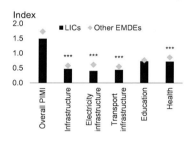

D. Difference in infrastructure spending efficiency between top and bottom quartile of EMDEs, 2011-19

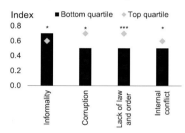

Sources: Dabla-Norris et al. (2011); International Monetary Fund; World Bank; World Economic Forum.
Note: LICs = low-income countries. Other EMDEs = non-LIC emerging market and developing economies. *** shows the significance level at 1 percent, ** at 5 percent, and * at 10 percent. Unweighted averages for LICs and other EMDEs for each spending category in percent of GDP.
A. Data for up to 26 LICs.
B. Data for up to 20 LICs.
C. D. Spending efficiency overall and for infrastructure is the Public Investment Management Index by Dabla-Norris et al. (2012); Spending efficiency for education and health is the output efficiency calculated by Herrero and Ouedraogo (2018).
C. Data for up to 120 EMDEs, including up to 21 LICs, for the latest year available.
D. Data for up to 95 EMDEs.

past decade. Strengthening these systems begins with developing the administrative capacity to target and distribute benefits effectively. Conditional cash transfers have been found to be effective means of delivering social benefits in some circumstances (Garcia and Saavedra 2017; Rawlings and Rubio 2005).

Expenditure efficiency by sector. There is room to use existing spending envelopes at the sectoral level for purposes that are more effective at achieving policy goals. For example, access to

education is not the same as improved learning outcomes; education systems in many developing economies do not deliver the learning that builds human capital (World Bank 2018c). This may involve measures such as improving measurement and monitoring of learning outcomes; incentives for teacher performance; community involvement in monitoring school performance; and providing health care and nutrition in early childhood. Better public spending on agriculture in Sub-Saharan Africa is also crucial for improving agricultural productivity (Goyal and Nash 2017). Government investment in local agricultural research and development; removal of urban subsidies; improvements in rural infrastructure and efforts to facilitate access to financial services can lay the foundation for important agricultural productivity gains. In infrastructure spending, there is scope to improve institutions and procedures governing project appraisal, procurement, and monitoring spending, and more systematic investment in maintenance can significantly outweigh the costs of repairs or reconstruction (Hallegatte, Rentschler, and Rozenberg 2019; World Bank 2019b).[8]

Overall expenditure efficiency. Increasing fiscal transparency and accountability has been linked with improving public spending efficiency. In one cross-country study, it was found that a country moving from the bottom one-fifth to the top one-fifth of fiscal transparency, measured by the "open budget index," is associated with an improvement in government spending efficiency by one standard deviation (Montes, Bastos, and de Oliveira 2019). This association has been attributed to a reduction in information asymmetry on public resource allocation between politicians and the general public, the adoption of better policies, and better information as a prerequisite for accurately assessing input cost and achieved outputs. In particular, enhancing transparency in state contracting leads to better government procurement and more efficient utilization

---

[8] By one estimate, a country moving from the lowest quartile to the highest quartile in the efficiency of public investment could double the impact of that investment on growth (IMF 2015). Especially among lower-income countries, better project selection and implementation has been statistically significantly associated with higher growth (Gupta et al. 2014).

of public resources (Evenett and Hoekman 2004). More broadly, improving the quality of public investment management across the entire expenditure cycle is associated with better development outcomes (Dabla-Norris et al. 2012).

Supporting structural policies. Most spending initiatives require ancillary reforms to be effective. More efficient infrastructure spending typically requires addressing land acquisition restrictions, streamlining licensing and permitting requirements, coordinating effectively between various agencies, and accessing private finance. More efficient education spending often requires addressing teacher absenteeism (Muralidharan et al. 2016).

Robust fiscal frameworks

Government spending in LICs tends to be procyclical, rising and falling in tandem with revenues (figure 4.14). Thus, fiscal policy amplifies economic volatility in LICs.

Credible, well-designed, and politically supported institutional arrangements—such as fiscal rules, stabilization funds, medium-term expenditure frameworks, and independent central banks—can help build fiscal space, improve the management of revenue windfalls, and strengthen policy outcomes (Huidrom, Kose, and Ohnsorge 2016; Strong and Yayi 2021). Until the early 1990s, fiscal rules were only present in only a few EMDEs and virtually no LICs. In the early 2000s, LICs started adopting fiscal rules and, by 2021, 12 LICs had adopted fiscal rules. 11 of these countries have budget balance rules, 5 have revenue rules, none have expenditure rules, and all 12 have debt rules. Few LICs have independent fiscal councils.

The use of fiscal rules, in particular, has been associated with improved fiscal performance and more successful fiscal consolidations (IMF 2009). While fiscal rules are associated with improved fiscal policy management, their success crucially depends on effective institutions and governance underpinned by the rule of law and strong accountability mechanisms (Bergman and Hutchison 2015). Fiscal frameworks not involving formal rules but focused on transparent and credible strategies backed by proper fiscal institu-

FIGURE 4.12 Domestic resource mobilization

Income and consumption tax efficiencies are lower in LICs than in other EMDEs—possibly reflecting widespread informality—while trade tax efficiency is higher.

A. Personal income tax efficiency

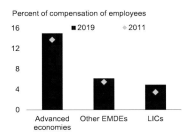

B. Consumption tax efficiency

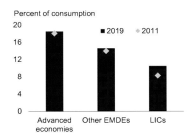

C. Trade tax revenue efficiency

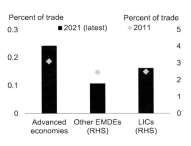

D. Differences in fiscal indicators between EMDEs with above-median and below-median informality

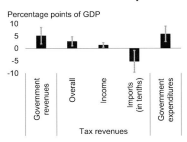

Sources: Dabla-Norris et al. (2011); International Monetary Fund; Ohnsorge and Yu (2021); Penn World Table 9.1; World Bank; World Economic Forum.

Note: Unweighted averages in A-C. LICs = low-income countries; Other EMDEs = emerging markets and developing economies excluding LICs. AE= advanced economies

A. The ratio of personal income tax over total labor compensation. Share of labor compensation in GDP and real GDP (2011 USD) are from Penn World Table. Based on 35 AEs, 66 EMDEs (excl. LICs), and 12 LICs.

B. The ratio of consumption tax revenue over real consumption. Consumption tax is the sum of goods and services tax, value-added tax and excise tax. Real consumption and real GDP (2011 U.S. dollars) are from Penn World Table 9.1. Based on 34 AEs, 81 EMDEs (excl. LICs), and 18 LICs.

C. The ratio of trade tax revenue over total trade, which equals the sum of imports and exports of goods and services (local currency, International Financial Statistics). Based on advanced economies (AEs), 103 EMDEs (excl. LICs), and 24 LICs.

D. Difference (in percentage points of GDP) between the average fiscal indicators among the third of EMDEs with above-median and below-median informality by the share of informal output in percent of official GDP (DGE-based estimates from Ohnsorge and Yu 2021). Vertical bars indicate 90 percent confidence intervals of the differences. Fiscal indicators and informality measures are
2000-18 averages. The sample includes 70 non-energy-exporting EMDEs with populations above 3 million people. Blue bars show the unweighted averages, whiskers interquartile range. unless otherwise specified. Based on 117 EMDEs, including 24 LICs.

tions could also provide a viable approach to support fiscal discipline (tables 4.2 and 4.3).

Debt and fiscal management and debt treatment

While there is scope for raising revenues and strengthening expenditure efficiency in LICs, LICs will in all likelihood continue to rely on external financing, including government borrowing to

FIGURE 4.13 Expenditure efficiency

Government expenditure efficiency can be improved by reallocating spending, including from public wage bills to more growth-enhancing spending. Spending on education could be redirected or augmented to increase monitoring capacity (including information gathering), which encourages learning.

A. Share of public sector employment

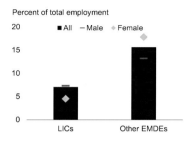

B. Characteristics of public sector employees

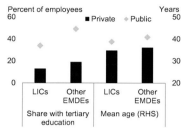

C. Changes in public wage bill and revenues

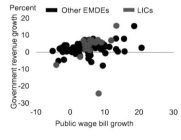

D. Learning outcomes and years of schooling

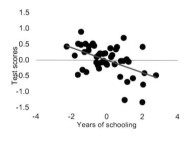

Sources: Dabla-Norris et al. (2011); International Monetary Fund; UNESCO Institute for Statistics; World Bank; World Economic Forum.

Note: LICs = low-income countries. Other EMDEs = emerging markets and developing economies excluding LICs. EMDEs excl. LICs = emerging markets and developing economies (excluding LICs). LICs = low-income countries.

A.B. Unweighted averages over the period 2011-20 (i.e., latest year available). Based on 18 LICs and 73 Other EMDEs.

A.B. Unweighted averages over the period 2011-20 (i.e., latest year available). Based on 73 EMDEs (excl. LICs), 18 LICs.

C. Based on 15 LICs and 95 Other EMDEs. Based on 95 EMDEs (excl. LICs) and 15 LICs. Public wage bill is calculated using share of public sector employee compensation in percent of GDP from the IMF's *Government Finance Statistics* and World Bank's Worldwide Bureaucracy Indicators. Government revenue is obtained from the IMF's *World Economic Outlook*. Growth is calculated as the average growth over the period 2011-21 (i.e., latest year available).

D. Test scores are conditional on initial GDP per capita and years of schooling while years of schooling are conditional on the initial GDP per capita and test scores. See World Development Report (2018) for details. Based on 46 countries.

address their large development needs. Hence, prudent debt management becomes a priority. Effective debt management aims to fund the government's financing needs in a timely fashion, help ensure low debt-servicing costs at an acceptable degree of risk, and support the development of domestic securities markets (World Bank 2019b). In addition, debt management can help minimize fiscal risks stemming from contingent liabilities, such as guarantees or on-lending to state-owned enterprises or through public-private partnerships,

through effective monitoring and reporting. If supported by political will, fiscal rules can help in ensuring sustainable fiscal positions.

Debt and fiscal transparency. Weaknesses in debt and broader fiscal transparency, notably in monitoring and reporting, are pervasive in LICs. Better compilation and monitoring of public debt and guarantees can help ensure that risks are detected before they materialize (World Bank 2007). Recent examples of hidden debt and discrepancies among debt statistics point to continued low debt recording capacity, weak legal frameworks, and governance challenges.[9] They are a reminder of the need to monitor and mitigate contingent liabilities. In a recent survey, most public debt managers reported monitoring risks of contingent liabilities but only a minority reported using risk mitigation tools, such as reserve accounts (40 percent of respondents) or risk exposure limits on contingent liabilities (30 percent of respondents; Lee and Bachmair 2019).

More broadly, greater fiscal transparency has been associated with lower borrowing costs, improvements in government effectiveness, and lower government debt (Montes, Bastos, and de Oliveira 2019). Improvements in data collection practices for LIC debt have been associated with lower borrowing costs (Cady and Pellechio 2006). More importantly, the returns from transparency (in terms of lower borrowing costs) are greater in countries with better institutional quality and lower external debts (Kubota and Zeufack 2020).

Debt management. Debt Management Performance Assessments (DeMPA), diagnostic tools used to evaluate a country's debt management processes and institutions, suggest that of the seventeen LICs with available data in 2018, minimum requirements in debt recording were met by only eight, and monitoring guarantees are met by only four (World Bank 2019b). Because of shortcomings in accuracy, timeliness, coverage, and completeness of debt records, only four of these seventeen countries met the minimum

---

[9] The examples include the discovery of unreported loans by major state-owned enterprises' (SOE) borrowing in Mozambique (IMF 2018b); and the rise in contingent liability in 2016 due to the distressed major SOEs in The Gambia (IMF 2018c).

requirements for debt reporting and evaluation (figure 4.15). Only one-third of the 59 countries eligible for International Development Association borrowing reported private sector external debt statistics in 2018 (World Bank and IMF 2018b). Medium-term debt strategies are becoming more common but have shortcomings in quality and implementation. A growing number of countries are producing medium-term debt management strategies. However, their quality varies significantly, and implementation often lags (World Bank 2019b). Few countries align the processes for managing medium-term debt with their budget process. Weak capacity, insufficient legal frameworks, lack of coordination between fiscal and monetary policy, inefficient management of cash and fiscal risks, and poor audit and risk control procedures often present weaknesses in debt management.

Conclusion

LICs are faced with formidable development challenges, which have been compounded by the pandemic, growing climatic vulnerabilities, and the effects of Russia's invasion of Ukraine. Yet, fiscal resources to finance the development needs in LICs are increasingly constrained. Between 2011 and 2022, government debt in the average LIC rose by 30 percentage points of GDP— almost twice as much as in other EMDE—to 67 percent of GDP in 2022, well above the level in other EMDEs. More than four-fifths of this LIC government debt buildup between 2011 and 2022 occurred long before the pandemic tipped the global economy into collapse. It reflected persistent and widening primary fiscal deficits that more than offset the debt-reducing effects of growth. The 1.7 percentage point of GDP increase in primary expenditure between 2011 and 2022 was double the increase in revenues over the same period. In the average LIC, revenues accounted for about 18 percent of GDP during 2011-22—11 percentage points of GDP lower than in the average non-LIC EMDE.

Deteriorating fiscal positions, rising borrowing costs, declining aid flows, and elevated public gross financing needs warrant a renewed effort to mobilize domestic revenues and to strengthen

FIGURE 4.14 Fiscal frameworks

Spending growth in LICs moves in tandem with revenue growth. A growing number of LICs have implemented fiscal rules, in part to stabilize spending growth.

A. Revenue and expenditure growth

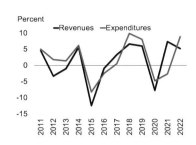

B. Fiscal rules in LICs and other EMDEs

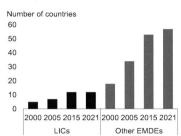

Sources: International Monetary Fund; World Bank.
Note: LICs = low-income countries. Other EMDEs = non-LIC emerging market and developing economies.
A. Based on 26 LICs (excl. Democratic People's Republic of Korea and the Syrian Arab Republic). Computed as the annual percentage growth of real revenue and expenditure (constant 2015 dollars).
B. Bars show the number of EMDEs (LICs) with fiscal rules. There are 59 EMDEs (excluding LICs) and 12 LICs in the IMF Fiscal Rules Dataset. The dataset covers four types of rules: budget balance rules (BBR), debt rules (DR), expenditure rules (ER), and revenue rules (RR), applying to the central or general government or the public sector.

FIGURE 4.15 Debt management and institutional quality

Weaknesses in debt transparency, notably in monitoring and reporting, remain pervasive in LICs. Participants in the Debt Service Suspension Initiative have provided greater transparency on debt obligations.

A. Countries meeting DeMPA minimum requirements, select categories

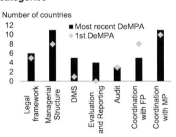

B. Countries meeting DeMPA minimum requirements, select categories

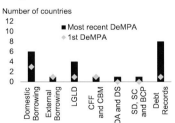

Sources: Debt Management Performance Assessments (DeMPA); International Monetary Fund; World Development Indicators.
Note: BCP = Business Continuity Planning; CBM = Cash Balance Management; CFF = Cash Flow Forecasting; DA = Debt Administration; DMS = Debt Management Strategy; DS = Data Security; FP = Fiscal Policy; GLD = Loan Guarantees, On lending Derivatives; MP = Monetary Policy; SD = Segregation of Duties; SC = Staff Capacity. Sample covers 17 low-income countries.

spending efficiencies. Better debt management can help reduce some of the vulnerabilities associated with high debt. Meanwhile, robust fiscal frameworks need to be established and maintained to reduce and manage fiscal risks over the longer term.

These national policy initiatives need to be complemented with global support, both to address debt challenges—including through debt relief, grants, or greater concessionality in lending—and to improve fiscal management, especially in tax policy design, implementation, and curbing illicit financial flows. The international community has taken several initiatives to further these goals. In November 2020, following on the DSSI, the *Common Framework,* a G20 initiative, was announced as a framework for offering debt treatment to DSSI-eligible countries with unsustainable debt beyond the DSSI (IMF 2021). This Framework has been hampered by implementation delays such that, by May 2023, only four countries had requested debt relief under the Framework and negotiations had stalled for several of them. One reason may be the absence of private sector participation. In addition, potential applicants fear their access to commercial financing will be cut off if they apply, while the slow pace and uncertainty of restructuring also deter countries from applying (Gill 2022). To improve the Common Framework, it is crucial to bring commercial creditors into the restructuring negotiations and establish a standard mathematical formula for determining the size of debt relief that all creditors will provide (Rivetti 2022).

In an effort to prevent the emergence of new fiscal risks, the *Sustainable Development Finance Policy (SDFP)* replaced the *Non-Concessional Borrowing Policy (NCBP)* in July 2020. The SDFP, which applies to client countries of the international development association (IDA), aims to incentivize countries to move toward transparent and sustainable financing. The policy also aims to further enhance coordination between IDA and other creditors in support of the countries' reform efforts toward sustainable development finance (World Bank 2020). While it is too early to assess the effectiveness of the SDFP, the increased debt vulnerabilities arising from the pandemic encouraged most countries to look for ways to strengthen debt management, enhance debt transparency, and improve fiscal sustainability, supported by the SDFP (World Bank 2021, 2022f).

ANNEX 4.1 Debt decomposition

Following World Bank (2005), changes in public debt-to-GDP ratios (denoted by d in the equations in this annex) is decomposed into a number of explanatory factors. Specifically, changes in debt over time can be decomposed into primary fiscal balances (the difference between revenues and non-interest expenditures), output growth, interest rates, inflation, and other factors.[10] In a highly stylized version, this accounting decomposition is the following:

$$d_t - d_{t-1} = pb_t + \frac{i_t - \pi_t - g_t(1 + \pi_t)}{(1 + g_t)(1 + \pi_t)} d_{t-1} \quad (4.1.1)$$
$$+ \textit{other factors},$$

where government debt d_t and the primary balance pb_t are scaled by GDP. Real output growth is g_t, inflation (defined as GDP deflator growth) is π_t, and the weighted average of foreign and domestic nominal interest rates is i_t. Other factors include exchange rate depreciation, privatization proceeds, the materialization of contingent liabilities or other ad-hoc changes to debt stocks.

Equation (4.1.1) is originated from the following decomposition equation:

$$\Delta d_t = pd_t - \frac{g_t}{1 + g_t} d_{t-1}$$
$$+ \frac{d_{t-1}}{1 + g_t} \left[\frac{i_t}{1 + \pi_t} - \frac{\pi_t}{1 + \pi_t} - \frac{\alpha(\pi_t^* - \pi_t)}{(1 + \pi_t)(1 + \pi_t^*)} \right] \quad (4.1.2)$$
$$- \alpha \frac{RXR_t}{(1 + \pi_t^*)(1 + RXR_t)} d_{t-1} + \textit{other factors},$$

where foreign inflation is π_t^*. RXR_t is the change in the bilateral real exchange rate against the U.S.

---

[10] The detailed decomposition requires data on the foreign currency-denominated share of government debt. This is only available for 2018 and unavailable for all but two LICs (Democratic Republic of Congo, Uganda) and for 89 EMDEs. The foreign currency-denominated share of government debt in 2019 is assumed to be constant at 2018 values and, for LICs and non-LIC EMDEs with missing data, is assumed to be the same as the average for LICs or non-LIC EMDEs, respectively.

dollar (U.S. dollar per local currency unit) and RXR_t is defined by:

$$\frac{1}{(1+RXR_t)} = \frac{(1+s_t)(1+\pi_t^*)}{1+\pi_t},$$

with $RXR_t > 0$ denoting a real exchange rate appreciation and s_t denoting nominal exchange rate appreciation. The original decomposition equation is reorganized into equation (4.1.1) to form the basis for decomposing the change in public debt-to-GDP ratio into the following attributable components: (1) the primary fiscal balance net of seigniorage; (2) real GDP growth; (3) the implicit nominal interest rate; and (4) other factors.[11]

The last term, "other factors," is the actual change in the debt-to-GDP ratio minus the sum of components (1) to (3). It includes privatization receipts, the real exchange rate, government support to banks and corporates or other ad hoc sources of debt. Since this accounting identity is highly nonlinear, decompositions of cumulative changes are conducted recursively comparing actual debt changes with these in counterfactuals of zero output growth, constant primary balances, zero inflation, or nominal interest rates that equal nominal GDP growth.

Implicitly, this approach generates a lower bound for the contribution of inflation and growth to debt dynamics. Growth and inflation drive up revenues and, thus, narrow deficits. Narrower deficits, in turn, can lower pressures for rising government debt. This indirect effect is not accounted for in the accounting decomposition used here.

ANNEX 4.2 Measuring spending efficiency

Indicators on public spending efficiency include two aggregate spending efficiency measures and five specific spending efficiency measures.

The first aggregate spending efficiency measure is the efficiency of government spending indicator provided by the World Economic Forum (WEF). It based on a survey question "In your country, how efficient is the government in spending public revenue? (1 = extremely inefficient; 7 = extremely efficient)" and is available for 149 countries (114 EMDEs and 35 advanced economies) for 2008-2018. The second aggregate spending efficiency measure is the Public Investment Management Index (PIMI) provided by Dabla-Norris et al. (2012). The overall index consists of four sub-indices, which measure the efficiency of four stages of the public investment management cycle: strategic guidance and project appraisal; project selection; project implementation; and project evaluation and audit. The four sub-indices are scored based on 17 indicators on a scale from 0-4. A higher score suggests better public investment management performance. The overall index is the average of four sub-indices. The index is available for 71 EMDEs (including 28 LICs) for 2011.

Specific spending efficiency measures relate to human development outcomes and access to infrastructure and are sourced from Herrera and Ouedraogo (2018).[12] The human-development related measures cover primary school enrollment and life expectancy at birth. The infrastructure-related measures include quality of overall infrastructure, quality of electric supply and quality of transport infrastructure. All these indicators are cross-sectional estimates using data from 2006-16 and available for 175 economies (139 EMDEs and 36 advanced economies). Although magnitudes differ across indicators, for all indicators higher values indicate higher spending efficiency.

---

[11] Because of the lack of data on real exchange rate in LICs, the framework here uses "other factors" to cover the contribution from changes in real exchange rates rather than showing it as a separate component.

[12] Output efficiency measures estimated using Data Envelopment Analysis (DEA) approach are used here.

TABLE 4.1 List of Low-Income Countries

A. List of all LICs (28)				
Afghanistan	Ethiopia	Mali	Sudan	Togo
Burundi	Guinea	Mozambique	Sierra Leone	Uganda
Burkina Faso	Gambia, The	Malawi	Somalia	Yemen, Rep.
Central African Republic	Guinea-Bissau	Niger	South Sudan	Zambia
Congo, Dem. Rep.	Liberia	Korea, Dem. People's Rep.	Syrian Arab Republic	
Eritrea	Madagascar	Rwanda	Chad	

B. List of LICs included in the debt decomposition analysis (23)				
Afghanistan	Eritrea	Liberia	Niger	Togo
Burundi	Ethiopia	Madagascar	Rwanda	Uganda
Burkina Faso	Guinea	Mali	Sudan	Yemen, Rep.
Central African Republic	Gambia, The	Mozambique	Sierra Leone	
Congo, Dem. Rep.	Guinea-Bissau	Malawi	Chad	

Source: World Bank.

TABLE 4.2 Difference in revenues, with per capita GDP and commodity exporter status controlled for, between the means for the bottom and top quartiles among EMDEs, by indicator of institutional environment

(percentage points of GDP)

	Overall revenues									
		Tax revenues								
			Indirect taxes			Direct taxes				
	All	All	All	Goods and services taxes	Trade taxes	All	Income taxes	Personal income taxes	Corporate income taxes	Property taxes
Informal-sector share of GDP	3.91**	-1.62*	-1.33**	0.94	-0.47	-0.36	0.29	0.08	0.37	0.17
Control of corruption	-6.89	-3.13**	-2.92***	-3.01	-0.11**	-0.63	-0.99	-0.94	0.03	-0.45
Bureaucracy quality	-5.31	-4.84**	-2.32**	-2.16	0.19**	-2.12	-2.14	-0.18	-1.49*	-0.32
Absence of external conflict	-1.02*	-6***	-2.12***	-0.49	-1.25***	-2.57	-2.78*	-0.73	-1.62*	-0.19
Absence of internal conflict	-6.37**	-5.23***	-4.46***	-3.57**	-0.72**	-2.73**	-2.43**	-1.42**	-0.81	-0.28
Law and order	-7.94**	-0.33	-1.09*	-2.77	0.19*	0.6	0.1	-0.98	0.39	-0.12

Sources: International Country Risk Guide (ICRG); International Monetary Fund; Ohnsorge and Yu (2021); World Bank.
Note: Numbers show the difference between categories of revenues (in percentage points of GDP)—controlling for per capita GDP and commodity exporter status--between the worst and best quartiles among EMDEs by informal-sector share of GDP, control of corruption, bureaucracy quality, external and internal conflict and law and order. A negative number indicates that revenue ratios are lower in the worst quartile than in the best quartile. *** indicates a statistically significant difference at the 1 percent level, ** at the 5 percent level, and * at the 10 percent level. revenue-to-GDP ratios controlling for per capita GDP and commodity exporter status defined as the residual of a cross-sectional OLS regression of average revenue-to-GDP ratios (in percent of GDP) in 2019-21 on the logarithm of per capita GDP (at 2017 international U.S. dollar PPP) and a commodity exporter dummy.

TABLE 4.3 Difference in spending, with per capita GDP and commodity exporter status controlled for, between the means for the bottom and top quartiles among EMDEs, by indicator of institutional environment

	Infrastructure	Electricity infrastructure	Education	Health
Informal-sector share of GDP	0.10*	0.15	0.01	0.07
Control of corruption	-0.18**	-0.30**	-0.02	-0.10
Bureaucracy quality	-0.14	-0.21	-0.07*	-0.09
Absence of external conflict	-0.06	-0.09	-0.07*	-0.02
Absence of internal conflict	-0.09*	-0.12	-0.09***	-0.06
Law and order	-0.15***	-0.22**	-0.03*	-0.07*

Sources: International Country Risk Guide (ICRG); International Monetary Fund; Ohnsorge and Yu (2021); World Bank.

Note: Numbers show the difference between different spending efficiency indicators--controlling for per capita GDP and commodity exporter status--between the worst and best quartiles among EMDEs by informal-sector share of GDP, control of corruption, bureaucracy quality, external and internal conflict and law and order. A negative number indicates that revenue ratios are lower in the worst quartile than in the best quartile. *** indicates a statistically significant difference at the 1 percent level, ** at the 5 percent level, and * at the 10 percent level. Spending efficiency controlling for per capita GDP and commodity exporter status defined as the residual of a cross-sectional ordinary least squares (OLS) regression of average spending efficiency indicator in 2011-21 on the logarithm of per capita GDP (at 2010-19 average prices and market exchange rates) and a commodity exporter dummy.

References

ACLED (Armed Conflict Location & Event Data Project) database. Accessed on May 5, 2023. https://acleddata.com/data-export-tool/.

Akitoby, B., A. Baum, C. Hackney, O. Harrison, K. Primus, and V. Salins. 2018. "Tax Revenue Mobilization Episodes in Emerging Markets and Low-Income Countries: Lessons from a New Dataset." IMF Working Paper 18/234, International Monetary Fund, Washington, DC.

Akitoby, B., J. Honda, H. Miyamoto, K. Primus, and M. Sy. 2019. "Case Studies in Tax Revenue Mobilization in Low-Income Countries." IMF Working Paper 19/104, International Monetary Fund, Washington, DC.

Bergman, U. M, and M. Hutchison. 2015. "Economic Stabilization in The Post-Crisis World: Are Fiscal Rules The Answer?" *Journal of International Money and Finance* 52 (April): 82-101.

Cady, J., and A. Pellechio. 2006. "Sovereign Borrowing Cost and the IMF's Data Standards Initiatives." IMF Working Paper 06/78, International Monetary Fund, Washington, DC.

Cassidy, T. 2019. "The Long-Run Effects of Oil Wealth on Development: Evidence from Petroleum Geology." *The Economic Journal* 129 (623): 2745-78.

Chuku C., P. Samal, J. Saito, D. Hakura, M. Chamon, M. Cerisola, G. Chabert, and J. Zettelmeyer. 2023. "Are We Heading for Another Debt Crisis in Low-Income Countries? Debt Vulnerabilities: Today vs the Pre-HIPC Era." IMF Working Paper 23/79, International Monetary Fund, Washington, DC.

Clements, B. S., Gupta, and J.T. Jalles. 2022. "Fiscal Policy for Inclusive Growth in Asia." Working Paper 611, Center for Global Development, Washington, DC.

Coady, D., V. Flamini, and L. Sears. 2015. "The Unequal Benefits of Fuel Subsidies Revisited: Evidence for Developing Countries." IMF Working Paper 15/250, International Monetary Fund, Washington, DC.

Dabla-Norris, E., J. Brumby, A. Kyobe, Z. Mills, and C. Papageorgiou. 2012. "Investing in Public Investment: An Index of Public Investment Efficiency." *Journal of Economic Growth* 17 (September): 235-66.

Ebrill, L., M. Keen, and V. Perry. 2001. *The Modern VAT*. Washington, DC: International Monetary Fund.

Essl, S. M., S. Kilic Celik, P. Kirby, and A. Proite. 2019. "Debt in Low-Income Countries: Evolution, Implications, and Remedies." Policy Research Working Paper 8794, World Bank, Washington, DC.

Evenett, S., and B. Hoekman. 2004. "Government Procurement: Market Access, Transparency, and Multilateral Trade Rules." Policy Research Working Paper 3195, World Bank, Washington, DC.

Fardoust, S., S. G. Koeberle, M. Piatti-Fünfkirchen, L. Smets, and M. Sundberg. 2023. *Retooling Development Aid in the 21st Century: The Importance of Budget Support*. Oxford, U.K.: Oxford University Press.

Feeny, S., and M. McGillivray. 2009. "Aid Allocation to Fragile States: Absorptive Capacity Constraints." *Journal of International Development* 21(5): 618-32.

Foster, V., A. Rana, and N. Gorgulu. 2022. "Understanding Public Spending Trends for Infrastructure in Developing Countries." Policy Research Working Paper 9903, World Bank, Washington, DC.

García, S., and J. E. Saavedra. 2017. "Educational Impacts and Cost-Effectiveness of Conditional Cash Transfer Programs in Developing Countries: A Meta-Analysis." *Review of Educational Research* 87 (5): 921-65.

Goyal, A., and J. Nash. 2017. *Reaping Richer Returns: Public Spending Priorities for African Agriculture Productivity Growth.* Washington, DC: World Bank.

Gunter, S., D. Riera-Crichton, C. Vegh, and G. Vuletin. 2018. "Non-Linear Effects of Tax Changes on Output: The Role of the Initial Level of Taxation." Policy Research Working Paper 8668, World Bank, Washington, DC.

Gunter, S., D. Riera-Crichton, C. Vegh, and G. Vuletin. 2019. "Policy Implications of Non-Linear Distortion-Based Effects of Tax Changes on Output." Policy Research Working Paper 8720, World Bank, Washington, DC.

Gupta, S., A. Kangur, C. Papageorgiou, and A. Wane. 2014. "Efficiency-Adjusted Public Capital and Growth." *World Development* 57 (May): 164-78.

Hallegatte, S., J. Rentschler, and J. Rozenberg. 2019. *Lifelines—The Resilient Infrastructure Opportunity.* Washington, DC: World Bank.

Ho, G. and P. Mauro. 2016. "Growth—Now and Forever?" *IMF Economic Review* 64: 526-47.

Horn, S., C. Reinhart, and C. Trebesch, 2019. "China's Overseas Lending," NBER Working Paper 26050, National Bureau of Economic Research, Cambridge, MA.

Huidrom, R., M. A. Kose, and F. Ohnsorge. 2016. "Challenges of Fiscal Policy in Emerging and Developing Economies." Policy Research Working Paper 7725, World Bank, Washington, DC.

IMF (International Monetary Fund). 2015. *Making Public Investment More Efficient.* Washington, DC: International Monetary Fund.

IMF (International Monetary Fund). 2018a. *IMF Fiscal Monitor: Capitalizing on Good Times, April 2018.* Washington, DC: International Monetary Fund.

IMF (International Monetary Fund). 2018b. *Mozambique 2017 Article IV Consultation—Staff Report.* Washington, DC: International Monetary Fund.

IMF (International Monetary Fund). 2018c. *The Gambia 2017 Article IV Consultation—Staff Report.* Washington, DC: International Monetary Fund.

IMF (International Monetary Fund). 2020. "The Evolution of Public Debt Vulnerabilities In Lower Income Economies." Policy Paper 20/003, International Monetary Fund, Washington, DC.

IMF (International Monetary Fund). 2021. "Questions and Answers on Sovereign Debt Issues." International Monetary Fund, Washington, DC. https://imf.org/en/About/FAQ/sovereign-debt.

IMF (International Monetary Fund). 2023. "List of LIC DSAs for PRGT-Eligible Countries (As of April 30, 2023)." International Monetary Fund, Washington, DC.

Junquera-Varela, R.F., M. Verhoeven, G.P. Shukla, B. Haven, R. Awasthi, and B. Moreno-Dodson. 2017. *Domestic Resource Mobilization: Opportunities and Challenges.* Washington, DC: World Bank.

Kose, M. A., P. Nagle, F. Ohnsorge, and N. Sugawara. 2020. *Global Waves of Debt: Causes and Consequences.* Washington, DC: World Bank.

Kubota, M., and A. Zeufack. 2020. "Assessing the Returns on Investment in Data Openness and Transparency." Policy Research Working Paper 9139, World Bank, Washington, DC.

Lee, A., and F. Bachmair. 2019. "A Look Inside the Mind of Debt Managers. A Survey on Contingent Liabilities Risk Management." Treasury Public Debt Management, World Bank, Washington, DC.

Manghee, S., and C. Van den Berg. 2012. "Public Expenditure Review from the Perspective of the Water and Sanitation Sector: Guidance Note." Water Papers, World Bank, Washington D.C.

Mawejje, J., and R. K. Sebudde. 2019. "Tax Revenue Potential and Effort: Worldwide Estimates Using a New Dataset." *Economic Analysis and Policy* 63 (September): 119-29.

Montes, G., J. Bastos, and A. de Oliveira. 2019. "Fiscal Transparency, Government Effectiveness and Government Spending Efficiency: Some International Evidence Based on Panel Data Approach." *Economic Modelling* 79 (C): 211-25.

Mullins, P., S. Gupta, and J. Liu. 2020. "Domestic Revenue Mobilization in Low-Income Countries: Where To From Here?" Policy Paper 195, Center for Global Development, Washington, DC.

Muralidharan, K., J. Das, A. Holla, and A. Mohpal. 2016. "The Fiscal Cost of Weak Governance: Evidence from Teacher Absenteeism in India." Policy Research Working Paper 7579, World Bank, Washington, DC.

Newbery, D., and N. Stern, eds. 1987. *The Theory of Taxation for Developing Countries.* Oxford, U.K.: Oxford University Press.

Ohnsorge, F., and S. Yu, eds. 2021. *The Long Shadow of Informality: Challenges and Policies.* Washington, DC: World Bank.

Pessino, C., and R. Fenochietto. 2013. "Understanding Countries' Tax Effort." IMF Working Paper 13/244, International Monetary Fund, Washington, DC.

Rawlings, L. B., and G. M. Rubio. 2005. "Evaluating the Impact of Conditional Cash Transfer Programs." *World Bank Research Observer* 20 (1): 29-55.

Rivetti, D. 2022. "Achieving Comparability of Treatment under the G20's Common Framework." World Bank, Washington, DC

Sobjak, A. 2018. "Corruption Risks in Infrastructure Investments in Sub-Saharan Africa." 2018 OECD Global Anti-Corruption & Integrity Forum. Organisation for Economic Co-operation and Development, Paris.

Steinbach, R. 2019. "Growth in Low-Income Countries: Evolution, Prospects, and Policies." Policy Research Working Paper 8949, World Bank, Washington, D.C.

Stiglitz, J. E., and J. K. Rosengard. 2015. *Economics of the Public Sector (4th edition).* London: W.W. Norton and Company.

Strong, C., and C. Yayi. 2021. "Central Bank Independence, Fiscal Deficits and Currency Union: Lessons from Africa." *Journal of Macroeconomics* 68 (June): 103313.

Talvi, E., and C.A. Vegh. 2005. "Tax Base Variability and Procyclical Fiscal Policy in Developing Countries." *Journal of Development Economics* 78 (1): 156-90.

Thornton, J. 2014. "Does Foreign Aid Reduce Tax Revenue? Further Evidence." *Applied Economics* 46 (4): 359-73.

United Nations. 2021. *The Sustainable Development Goals Report 2021.* New York: United Nations.

Van Rijckeghem, C., and B. Weder. 2001. "Bureaucratic Corruption and the Rate of Temptation: Do Wages in the Civil Service Affect Corruption, and by How Much?" *Journal of Development Economics* 65 (2): 307-31.

World Bank. 2005. *World Bank Debt Servicing Handbook.* Washington, DC: World Bank.

World Bank. 2007. *Managing Public Debt: From Diagnostics to Reform Implementation.* Washington, DC: World Bank.

World Bank. 2015. *Global Economic Prospects: Having Fiscal Space and Using It.* Washington, DC: World Bank.

World Bank. 2017. *Education Public Expenditure Review Guidelines.* Washington, DC: World Bank.

World Bank. 2018a. "The Gambia—Joint Bank-Fund Debt Sustainability Analysis: 2018 Update." World Bank, Washington, DC.

World Bank. 2018b. "Republic of Guinea—Systematic Country Diagnostic: Overcoming Growth Stagnation to Reduce Poverty." World Bank, Washington, DC.

World Bank. 2018c. *World Development Report 2018: Learning to Realize Education's Promise.* Washington, DC: World Bank.

World Bank. 2019a. *Global Economic Prospects: Heightened Tensions, Subdued Investment.* Washington, DC: World Bank.

World Bank. 2019b. *Global Economic Prospects: Darkening Skies.* Washington, DC: World Bank.

World Bank. 2020. "Sustainable Development Finance Policy of the International Development Association: FY21 Board Update." World Bank, Washington, DC.

World Bank. 2021. "The International Development Association's Sustainable Development Finance Policy: An Early-Stage Evaluation." Independent Evaluation Group. Washington, DC: World Bank.

World Bank. 2022a. *Poverty and Shared Prosperity 2022: Correcting Course.* Washington, DC: World Bank.

World Bank. 2022b. *Public Expenditure and Revenue Review for Burkina Faso: Fiscal Reforms for Resilience.* Washington, DC: World Bank.

Real GDP growth

	Annual estimates and forecasts[1] (Percent change)						Quarterly estimates[2] (Percent change, year-on-year)					
	2020	2021	2022e	2023f	2024f	2025f	21Q4	22Q1	22Q2	22Q3	22Q4	23Q1e
World	-3.1	6.0	3.1	2.1	2.4	3.0	5.0	4.4	3.0	3.0	..	..
Advanced economies	-4.3	5.4	2.6	0.7	1.2	2.2	5.0	4.2	2.9	2.3	1.2	..
United States	-2.8	5.9	2.1	1.1	0.8	2.3	5.7	3.7	1.8	1.9	0.9	1.6
Euro area	-6.1	5.4	3.5	0.4	1.3	2.3	4.9	5.5	4.4	2.5	1.8	1.3
Japan	-4.3	2.2	1.0	0.8	0.7	0.6	1.0	0.7	1.5	1.6	0.4	1.3
Emerging market and developing economies	-1.5	6.9	3.7	4.0	3.9	4.0	5.0	4.7	3.1	4.0	..	..
East Asia and Pacific	1.2	7.5	3.5	5.5	4.6	4.5	4.3	4.8	1.3	4.5	3.2	4.6
Cambodia	-3.1	3.0	5.2	5.5	6.1	6.3	..	..	..	..	..	..
China	2.2	8.4	3.0	5.6	4.6	4.4	4.3	4.8	0.4	3.9	2.9	4.5
Fiji	-17.0	-5.1	16.1	5.0	4.1	3.5	..	..	..	..	..	..
Indonesia	-2.1	3.7	5.3	4.9	4.9	5.0	5.0	5.0	5.5	5.7	5.0	5.0
Kiribati	-1.4	7.9	1.2	2.5	2.4	2.3	..	..	..	..	..	..
Lao PDR	0.5	2.5	2.7	3.9	4.2	4.4	..	..	..	..	..	..
Malaysia	-5.5	3.1	8.7	4.3	4.2	4.2	3.6	4.8	8.8	14.1	7.1	5.6
Marshall Islands[3]	-2.2	1.1	1.5	1.9	2.1	2.3	..	..	..	..	..	..
Micronesia, Fed. Sts.[3]	-1.8	-3.2	-0.6	2.9	2.8	1.3	..	..	..	..	..	..
Mongolia	-4.4	1.6	4.7	5.2	6.3	6.8	-2.7	-3.8	6.9	6.9	7.3	7.8
Myanmar[3 6]	3.2	-18.0	3.0	3.0	..	..	..	..	..	..	..	..
Nauru[3]	0.7	1.5	3.0	1.0	2.0	2.5	..	..	..	..	..	..
Palau[3]	-8.9	-13.4	-2.8	12.3	9.1	4.7	..	..	..	..	..	..
Papua New Guinea	-3.2	0.1	4.5	3.7	4.4	3.1	..	..	..	..	..	..
Philippines	-9.5	5.7	7.6	6.0	5.9	5.9	7.9	8.0	7.5	7.7	7.1	6.4
Samoa[3]	-3.1	-7.1	-6.0	5.0	3.4	3.3	..	..	..	..	..	..
Solomon Islands	-3.4	-0.6	-4.1	2.5	2.4	3.0	..	..	..	..	..	..
Thailand	-6.1	1.5	2.6	3.9	3.6	3.4	1.9	2.2	2.5	4.6	1.4	2.7
Timor-Leste	-8.3	2.9	3.5	3.0	3.2	3.2	..	..	..	..	..	..
Tonga[3]	0.5	-2.7	-2.0	2.5	2.8	2.6	..	..	..	..	..	..
Tuvalu	-4.9	0.3	0.6	4.2	3.1	2.6	..	..	..	..	..	..
Vanuatu	-5.0	0.6	1.9	0.5	4.0	3.9	..	..	..	..	..	..
Vietnam	2.9	2.6	8.0	6.0	6.2	6.5	5.2	5.1	7.8	13.7	5.9	3.3
Europe and Central Asia	-1.7	7.1	1.2	1.4	2.7	2.7	7.0	4.9	0.6	-0.2	-0.3	..
Albania	-3.3	8.9	4.8	2.8	3.3	3.3	5.1	6.9	3.1	4.9	4.7	..
Armenia	-7.2	5.7	12.6	4.4	4.8	5.0	11.6	8.8	13.1	14.8	12.7	12.1
Azerbaijan	-4.2	5.6	4.6	2.2	2.5	2.6	..	..	..	..	..	..
Belarus	-0.7	2.4	-4.7	0.6	1.4	1.3	1.3	-0.5	-8.0	-5.4	-4.5	..
Bosnia and Herzegovina[5]	-3.0	7.4	3.9	2.5	3.0	3.5	7.8	5.9	5.8	2.6	1.7	..
Bulgaria	-4.0	7.6	3.4	1.5	2.8	3.0	7.7	5.1	4.5	3.1	2.1	2.0
Croatia	-8.6	13.1	6.3	1.9	3.1	3.3	12.3	7.8	8.7	5.3	3.5	2.8
Georgia	-6.8	10.5	10.1	4.4	5.0	5.0	8.6	15.0	7.2	9.8	9.7	..
Hungary	-4.7	7.2	4.6	0.6	2.6	2.6	7.6	8.2	6.5	4.0	0.4	-0.9
Kazakhstan	-2.6	4.1	3.3	3.5	4.0	3.6	5.4	4.6	2.7	1.9	4.0	..
Kosovo	-5.3	10.7	3.5	3.7	4.4	4.2	7.4	4.5	2.9	3.3	3.6	..
Kyrgyz Republic	-8.4	6.2	7.0	3.5	4.0	4.0	..	..	..	..	..	..
Moldova	-7.4	13.9	-5.9	1.8	4.2	4.1	18.3	1.1	-0.9	-10.3	-10.6	..
Montenegro[2]	-15.3	13.0	6.1	3.4	3.1	2.9	9.0	7.1	12.7	3.2	3.3	..
North Macedonia	-4.7	3.9	2.1	2.4	2.7	2.9	1.2	2.2	4.0	2.0	0.6	..
Poland	-2.0	6.9	5.1	0.7	2.6	3.2	8.6	8.8	6.1	3.9	2.3	-0.2
Romania	-3.7	5.8	4.7	2.6	3.9	4.1	2.4	6.3	5.0	3.7	4.5	2.3
Russian Federation	-2.7	5.6	-2.1	-0.2	1.2	0.8	5.8	3.0	-4.5	-3.5	-2.7	-1.9
Serbia[2]	-0.9	7.5	2.3	2.3	3.0	3.8	7.2	4.1	3.8	1.0	0.4	0.7
Tajikistan	4.4	9.4	8.0	6.5	5.0	4.5	..	..	..	..	..	..
Türkiye	1.9	11.4	5.6	3.2	4.3	4.1	9.6	7.6	7.8	4.0	3.5	..
Ukraine	-3.8	3.4	-29.1	2.0	..	..	6.3	-14.9	-36.9	-30.6	-31.4	..
Uzbekistan	2.0	7.4	5.7	5.1	5.4	5.8	..	..	..	..	..	..

Real GDP growth *(continued)*

	Annual estimates and forecasts [1] (Percent change)						Quarterly estimates [2] (Percent change, year-on-year)					
	2020	2021	2022e	2023f	2024f	2025f	21Q4	22Q1	22Q2	22Q3	22Q4	23Q1e
Latin America and the Caribbean	-6.2	6.9	3.7	1.5	2.0	2.6	4.3	3.8	4.5	4.0	..	..
Argentina	-9.9	10.4	5.2	-2.0	2.3	2.0	8.9	6.0	7.1	5.9	1.9	..
Bahamas, The	-23.8	13.7	11.0	4.3	2.0	1.9	..	..	..	..	..	..
Barbados	-13.7	0.7	10.0	4.9	3.9	3.1	..	..	..	..	..	..
Belize	-13.4	15.2	9.6	2.4	2.0	2.0	20.2	10.2	13.3	14.8	10.6	..
Bolivia	-8.7	6.1	3.1	2.5	2.0	2.0	0.2	4.1	4.5	4.3	1.4	..
Brazil	-3.3	5.0	2.9	1.2	1.4	2.4	2.1	2.4	3.7	3.6	1.9	..
Chile	-6.0	11.7	2.4	-0.4	1.8	2.2	12.7	7.5	5.2	0.2	-2.3	-0.6
Colombia	-7.3	11.0	7.5	1.7	2.0	3.2	11.1	8.2	12.2	7.3	2.1	3.0
Costa Rica	-4.3	7.8	4.3	2.9	3.0	3.2	9.7	6.6	4.4	2.5	3.8	4.0
Dominica	-16.6	6.9	5.8	4.7	4.6	4.2	..	..	..	..	..	..
Dominican Republic	-6.7	12.3	4.9	4.1	4.8	5.0	11.2	6.2	5.2	5.0	3.3	..
Ecuador	-7.8	4.2	2.9	2.6	2.8	2.7	4.9	3.4	1.4	2.7	4.3	..
El Salvador	-8.2	10.3	2.8	2.3	2.1	2.1	5.8	4.6	2.5	2.2	1.2	..
Grenada	-13.8	4.7	5.8	3.6	3.3	3.1	..	..	..	..	..	..
Guatemala	-1.8	8.0	4.0	3.2	3.5	3.5	4.9	4.8	4.5	3.8	3.5	..
Guyana	43.5	20.0	57.8	25.2	21.2	28.2	..	..	..	..	..	..
Haiti [3]	-3.3	-1.8	-1.7	-2.4	1.7	2.4	..	..	..	..	..	..
Honduras	-9.0	12.5	4.0	3.5	3.7	3.8	11.2	5.5	4.3	4.2	2.2	..
Jamaica [2]	-9.9	4.6	4.2	2.0	1.7	1.2	6.7	6.5	4.8	5.9	3.8	..
Mexico	-8.0	4.7	3.0	2.5	1.9	2.0	1.0	1.9	2.4	4.3	3.5	3.7
Nicaragua	-1.8	10.3	4.0	3.0	3.4	3.5	10.2	4.8	4.6	3.4	2.4	..
Panama	-17.9	15.3	10.5	5.7	5.8	5.9	16.3	13.6	9.8	9.5	..	..
Paraguay	-0.8	4.0	-0.3	4.8	4.3	4.3	0.3	-0.9	-3.3	2.9	1.7	..
Peru	-10.9	13.4	2.7	2.2	2.6	2.8	3.2	3.9	3.4	2.0	1.7	-0.4
St. Lucia	-24.4	12.2	15.4	3.6	3.4	2.5	..	..	..	..	..	..
St. Vincent and the Grenadines	-5.3	1.3	5.0	5.6	4.8	3.5	..	..	..	..	..	..
Suriname	-16.0	-2.7	1.9	2.4	3.2	3.1	..	..	..	..	..	..
Uruguay	-6.1	4.4	5.0	1.8	2.8	2.4	7.8	8.4	8.7	3.4	-0.1	..
Middle East and North Africa	-3.8	3.8	5.9	2.2	3.3	3.0	8.2	6.5	6.5	6.0	4.9	..
Algeria	-5.1	3.4	3.2	1.7	2.4	2.1	3.2	2.4	2.9	3.7	3.8	..
Bahrain	-4.6	2.7	4.9	2.7	3.2	3.1	6.2	5.3	6.8	3.3	4.1	..
Djibouti	1.2	4.8	3.0	4.4	5.4	5.9	..	..	..	..	..	..
Egypt, Arab Rep. [3]	3.6	3.3	6.6	4.0	4.0	4.7	8.3	5.4	3.3	4.4	3.9	..
Iran, Islamic Rep. [3]	1.9	4.7	2.9	2.2	2.0	1.9	6.7	5.0	2.5	3.4	4.7	..
Iraq	-12.0	1.6	7.0	-1.1	6.0	3.7	..	..	..	..	..	..
Jordan	-1.6	2.2	2.5	2.4	2.4	2.4	2.6	2.5	3.0	2.5	2.0	..
Kuwait	-8.9	1.3	7.9	1.3	2.6	2.4	..	..	..	..	..	..
Lebanon [6]	-21.4	-7.0	-2.6	-0.5	..	..	..	..	..	..	..	..
Libya [6]	-29.8	31.4	-1.2	..	..	..	..	..	..	..	..	..
Morocco	-7.2	7.9	1.1	2.5	3.3	3.5	7.6	0.3	2.0	1.6	0.5	3.0
Oman	-3.4	3.1	4.3	1.5	2.8	2.6	..	..	..	..	..	..
Qatar	-3.6	1.5	4.6	3.3	2.9	3.1	2.2	2.3	4.4	4.5	8.0	..
Saudi Arabia	-4.3	3.9	8.7	2.2	3.3	2.5	8.3	10.0	11.2	8.7	5.5	3.9
Syrian Arab Republic [6]	-0.2	1.3	-3.5	-5.5	..	..	..	..	..	..	..	..
Tunisia	-8.8	4.4	2.5	2.3	3.0	3.0	2.7	2.3	2.7	3.0	1.8	2.1
United Arab Emirates	-5.0	4.4	7.9	2.8	3.4	3.4	9.2	9.6	8.0	8.3	5.5	..
West Bank and Gaza	-11.3	7.0	3.9	3.0	3.0	3.0	11.1	5.7	3.4	4.6	2.2	..
Yemen, Rep. [6]	-8.5	-1.0	1.5	-0.5	2.0	..	..	..	..	..	..	..

Real GDP growth *(continued)*

	Annual estimates and forecasts [1] (Percent change)						Quarterly estimates [2] (Percent change, year-on-year)					
	2020	**2021**	**2022e**	**2023f**	**2024f**	**2025f**	**21Q4**	**22Q1**	**22Q2**	**22Q3**	**22Q4**	**23Q1e**
South Asia	**-4.1**	**8.3**	**6.0**	**5.9**	**5.1**	**6.4**	**5.1**	**3.9**	**12.6**	**5.8**	**3.9**	**..**
Afghanistan [6]	-2.4	-20.7	..	..	..	..	..	..	..	..	..	..
Bangladesh [3][4]	3.4	6.9	7.1	5.2	6.2	6.4	..	..	..	..	..	..
Bhutan [3][4]	-2.3	-3.3	4.3	4.5	3.1	4.3	..	..	..	..	..	..
India [3][4]	-5.8	9.1	7.2	6.3	6.4	6.5	5.2	4.0	13.1	6.2	4.5	6.1
Maldives	-33.5	41.7	13.9	6.6	5.3	5.9	55.5	20.5	29.4	8.1	1.8	..
Nepal [3][4]	-2.4	4.8	5.6	4.1	4.9	5.5	..	..	..	..	..	..
Pakistan [3][4]	-0.9	5.8	6.1	0.4	2.0	3.0	..	..	..	..	..	..
Sri Lanka	-4.6	3.5	-7.8	-4.3	1.2	2.0	1.4	-0.5	-7.4	-11.5	-12.4	..
Sub-Saharan Africa	**-2.0**	**4.4**	**3.7**	**3.2**	**3.9**	**4.0**	**4.1**	**3.6**	**2.8**	**3.7**	**2.9**	**..**
Angola	-5.6	1.1	3.5	2.6	3.3	3.1	..	..	..	..	..	..
Benin	3.8	7.2	6.0	6.0	5.9	6.1	..	..	..	..	..	..
Botswana	-8.7	11.8	6.5	4.0	4.0	4.0	6.0	6.8	5.2	5.3	5.9	..
Burkina Faso	1.9	6.9	2.5	4.3	4.8	5.1	..	..	..	..	..	..
Burundi	0.3	3.1	1.8	3.0	3.9	4.1	..	..	..	..	..	..
Cabo Verde	-14.8	7.0	15.0	4.8	5.4	5.3	..	..	..	..	..	..
Cameroon	0.5	3.6	3.4	3.9	4.2	4.5	..	..	..	..	..	..
Central African Republic	1.0	1.0	0.0	3.0	3.8	3.8	..	..	..	..	..	..
Chad	-1.6	-1.2	2.2	3.2	3.4	3.1	..	..	..	..	..	..
Comoros	-0.3	2.1	2.3	2.8	2.9	3.6	..	..	..	..	..	..
Congo, Dem. Rep.	1.7	6.2	8.6	7.7	7.6	7.5	..	..	..	..	..	..
Congo, Rep.	-6.2	-2.2	1.5	3.5	4.3	2.8	..	..	..	..	..	..
Côte d'Ivoire	1.7	7.0	6.7	6.2	6.5	6.5	..	..	..	..	..	..
Equatorial Guinea	-4.2	-2.8	2.9	-3.7	-6.0	-3.1	..	..	..	..	..	..
Eritrea	-0.5	2.9	2.5	2.7	2.9	2.8	..	..	..	..	..	..
Eswatini	-1.6	7.9	0.4	3.0	2.9	2.7	..	..	..	..	..	..
Ethiopia [3]	6.1	6.3	6.4	6.0	6.6	7.0	..	..	..	..	..	..
Gabon	-1.8	1.5	3.1	3.1	3.0	3.0	..	..	..	..	..	..
Gambia, The	0.6	4.3	4.3	5.0	5.5	5.8	..	..	..	..	..	..
Ghana	0.5	5.4	3.2	1.6	2.9	4.8	6.1	2.4	3.5	2.7	3.7	..
Guinea	4.9	4.3	4.7	5.6	5.8	5.6	..	..	..	..	..	..
Guinea-Bissau	1.5	6.4	3.5	4.5	4.5	4.5	..	..	..	..	..	..
Kenya	-0.3	7.5	5.2	5.0	5.2	5.3	8.6	6.3	5.2	4.3	3.8	..
Lesotho	-5.6	1.6	1.8	2.6	3.1	3.3	1.8	1.9	0.2	4.7	-4.0	..
Liberia	-3.0	5.0	4.8	4.3	5.5	5.6	..	..	..	..	..	..
Madagascar	-7.1	5.7	3.8	4.2	4.8	5.1	..	..	..	..	..	..
Malawi	0.8	2.8	0.9	1.4	2.4	3.0	..	..	..	..	..	..
Mali	-1.2	3.1	1.8	4.0	4.0	5.0	..	..	..	..	..	..
Mauritania	-0.9	2.4	5.2	4.5	5.6	6.8	..	..	..	..	..	..
Mauritius	-14.6	3.5	8.3	4.7	4.1	3.6	..	..	..	..	..	..
Mozambique	-1.2	2.3	4.1	5.0	8.3	5.3	3.6	4.2	4.7	3.6	4.2	4.2
Namibia	-8.0	2.7	3.5	2.4	1.7	2.1	5.0	7.3	5.4	3.9	1.9	..
Niger	3.6	1.4	11.5	6.9	12.5	9.1	..	..	..	..	..	..
Nigeria	-1.8	3.6	3.3	2.8	3.0	3.1	4.6	3.6	3.4	2.4	3.6	2.4
Rwanda	-3.4	10.9	8.1	6.2	7.5	7.5	10.3	7.9	7.5	10.0	7.2	..
São Tomé and Príncipe	3.1	1.9	0.9	2.1	3.4	3.7	..	..	..	..	..	..
Senegal	1.3	6.5	4.2	4.7	9.9	5.2	..	..	..	..	..	..
Seychelles	-8.6	5.4	8.8	3.8	3.0	3.1	0.0	13.8	4.0	13.9	..	..
Sierra Leone	-2.0	4.1	3.0	3.4	3.7	4.4	..	..	..	..	..	..

Real GDP growth *(continued)*

	Annual estimates and forecasts[1]						Quarterly estimates[2]					
	2020	2021	2022e	2023f	2024f	2025f	21Q4	22Q1	22Q2	22Q3	22Q4	23Q1e
Sub-Saharan Africa (*continued*)												
South Africa	-6.3	4.9	2.0	0.3	1.5	1.6	1.7	2.8	0.3	4.2	0.9	..
South Sudan[3]	9.5	-5.1	-2.3	-0.4	2.3	2.4	..	..	..	..	..	..
Sudan	-3.6	-1.9	-1.0	0.4	1.5	2.0	..	..	..	..	..	..
Tanzania	2.0	4.3	4.6	5.1	5.6	6.2	..	..	..	..	..	..
Togo	1.8	5.3	4.9	4.9	5.3	5.5	..	..	..	..	..	..
Uganda[3]	3.0	3.4	4.7	5.7	6.2	6.7	4.9	4.9	6.5	9.2	4.4	..
Zambia	-2.8	4.6	3.9	4.2	4.7	4.8	4.8	2.7	4.5	6.0	5.6	..
Zimbabwe	-7.8	8.5	3.4	2.9	3.4	3.4	..	..	..	..	..	..

Sources: World Bank; Haver Analytics.

Note: e = estimate; f = forecast. Since Croatia became a member of the euro area on January 1, 2023, it has been added to the euro area aggregate and removed from the EMDE and ECA aggregate in all tables to avoid double counting.

1. Aggregate growth rates calculated using GDP weights at average 2010-19 prices and market exchange rates.

2. Quarterly estimates are based on non-seasonally-adjusted real GDP, except for advanced economies, as well as Algeria, Ecuador, Morocco, and Tunisia. In some instances, quarterly growth paths may not align to annual growth estimates, owing to the timing of GDP releases. Quarterly data for Jamaica are gross value added. Quarterly data for Montenegro are preliminary. Data for Timor-Leste represent non-oil GDP. The 2023Q1 data for Serbia are a flash estimate.

Regional averages are calculated based on data from the following economies.

East Asia and Pacific: China, Indonesia, Malaysia, Mongolia, the Philippines, Thailand, and Vietnam.

Europe and Central Asia: Albania, Armenia, Belarus, Bosnia and Herzegovina, Bulgaria, Georgia, Hungary, Kazakhstan, Kosovo, Moldova, Montenegro, North Macedonia, Poland, Romania, the Russian Federation, Serbia, Türkiye, and Ukraine.

Latin America and the Caribbean: Argentina, Belize, Bolivia, Brazil, Chile, Colombia, Costa Rica, the Dominican Republic, Ecuador, El Salvador, Guatemala, Honduras, Jamaica, Mexico, Nicaragua, Panama, Paraguay, Peru, and Uruguay.

Middle East and North Africa: Bahrain, the Arab Republic of Egypt, the Islamic Republic of Iran, Jordan, Morocco, Qatar, Saudi Arabia, Tunisia, the United Arab Emirates, and West Bank and Gaza.

South Asia: India, Maldives, and Sri Lanka.

Sub-Saharan Africa: Botswana, Ghana, Kenya, Lesotho, Mozambique, Namibia, Nigeria, Rwanda, South Africa, Uganda, and Zambia.

3. Annual GDP is on fiscal year basis, as per reporting practice in the country.

4. GDP data for Pakistan are based on factor cost. For Bangladesh, Bhutan, Nepal, and Pakistan, the column labeled 2022 refers to FY2021/22. For India and the Islamic Republic of Iran, the column labeled 2022 refers to FY2022/23.

5. Data for Bosnia and Herzegovina are from the production approach.

6. Forecasts for Afghanistan (beyond 2021), Lebanon (beyond 2023), Libya (beyond 2022), Myanmar (beyond 2023), the Syrian Arab Republic (beyond 2023), Ukraine (beyond 2023), and the Republic of Yemen (beyond 2024) are excluded because of a high degree of uncertainty.

Data and Forecast Conventions

The macroeconomic forecasts presented in this report are prepared by staff of the Prospects Group of the Equitable Growth, Finance and Institutions Vice-Presidency, in coordination with staff from the Macroeconomics, Trade, and Investment Global Practice and from regional and country offices, and with input from regional Chief Economist offices. They are the result of an iterative process that incorporates data, macro-econometric models, and judgment.

Data. Data used to prepare country forecasts come from a variety of sources. National Income Accounts (NIA), Balance of Payments (BOP), and fiscal data are from Haver Analytics; the World Development Indicators by the World Bank; the World Economic Outlook, Balance of Payments Statistics, and International Financial Statistics by the International Monetary Fund. Population data and forecasts are from the United Nations World Population Prospects. Country- and lending-group classifications are from the World Bank. The Prospects Group's internal databases include high-frequency indicators such as industrial production, consumer price indexes, emerging markets bond index (EMBI), exchange rates, exports, imports, policy rates, and stock market indexes, based on data from Bloomberg, Haver Analytics, IMF Balance of Payments Statistics, IMF International Financial Statistics, and J. P. Morgan.

Aggregations. Aggregate growth for the world and all subgroups of countries (such as regions and income groups) is calculated using GDP weights at average 2010-19 prices and market exchange rates of country-specific growth rates. Income groups are defined as in the World Bank's classification of country groups.

Forecast process. The process starts with initial assumptions about advanced-economy growth and commodity price forecasts. These are used as conditioning assumptions for the first set of growth forecasts for EMDEs, which are produced using macroeconometric models, accounting frameworks to ensure national account identities and global consistency, estimates of spillovers from major economies, and high-frequency indicators. These forecasts are then evaluated to ensure consistency of treatment across similar EMDEs. This is followed by extensive discussions with World Bank country teams, who conduct continuous macroeconomic monitoring and dialogue with country authorities and finalize growth forecasts for EMDEs. The Prospects Group prepares advanced-economy and commodity price forecasts. Throughout the forecasting process, staff use macroeconometric models that allow the combination of judgement and consistency with model-based insights.

Global Economic Prospects: Selected Topics, 2015-23

Global Economic Prospects: Selected Topics, 2015-23

Growth and business cycles

Cross-border spillovers

Productivity

Investment

Forecast uncertainty

Fiscal space

Other topics

Global Economic Prospects: Selected Topics, 2015-23

Monetary and exchange rate policies

Financial spillovers of rising U.S. interest rates	January 2023, chapter 3
Asset purchases in emerging markets: Unconventional policies, unconventional times	January 2021, chapter 4
The fourth wave: Rapid debt buildup	January 2020, chapter 4
Price controls: Good intentions, bad outcomes	January 2020, Special Focus 1
Low for how much longer? Inflation in low-income countries	January 2020, Special Focus 2
Currency depreciation, inflation, and central bank independence	June 2019, Special Focus 1.2
The great disinflation	January 2019, box 1.1
Corporate debt: Financial stability and investment implications	June 2018, Special Focus 2
Recent credit surge in historical context	June 2016, Special Focus 1
Peg and control? The links between exchange rate regimes and capital account policies	January 2016, chapter 4
Negative interest rates in Europe: A glance at their causes and implications	June 2015, box 1.1
Hoping for the best, preparing for the worst: Risks around U.S. rate liftoff and policy options	June 2015, Special Focus 1
Countercyclical monetary policy in emerging markets: Review and evidence	January 2015, box 1.2

Fiscal policies

Fiscal policy challenges in low-income countries	January 2023, chapter 4
Resolving high debt after the pandemic: lessons from past episodes of debt relief	January 2022, Special Focus
How has the pandemic made the fourth wave of debt more dangerous?	January 2021, box 1.1
The fourth wave: Rapid debt buildup	January 2020, chapter 4
Debt: No free lunch	June 2019, box 1.1
Debt in low-income countries: Evolution, implications, and remedies	January 2019, chapter 4
Debt dynamics in emerging market and developing economies: Time to act?	June 2017, Special Focus 1
Having fiscal space and using it: FiscFal challenges in developing economies	January 2015, chapter 3
Revenue mobilization in South Asia: Policy challenges and recommendations	January 2015, box 2.3
Fiscal policy in low-income countries	January 2015, box 3.1
What affects the size of fiscal multipliers?	January 2015, box 3.2
Chile's fiscal rule—an example of success	January 2015, box 3.3
Narrow fiscal space and the risk of a debt crisis	January 2015, box 3.4

Commodity markets

Russia's invasion of Ukraine: Implications for energy markets and activity	June 2022, Special Focus 2
Commodity price cycles: Underlying drivers and policy options	January 2022, chapter 3
Reforms after the 2014-16 oil price plunge	June 2020, box 4.1
Adding fuel to the fire: Cheap oil in the pandemic	June 2020, chapter 4
The role of major emerging markets in global commodity demand	June 2018, Special Focus 1
The role of the EM7 in commodity production	June 2018, SF1, box SF1.1
Commodity consumption: Implications of government policies	June 2018, SF1, box SF1.2
With the benefit of hindsight: The impact of the 2014–16 oil price collapse	January 2018, Special Focus 1
From commodity discovery to production: Vulnerabilities and policies in LICs	January 2016, Special Focus
After the commodities boom: What next for low-income countries?	June 2015, Special Focus 2
Low oil prices in perspective	June 2015, box 1.2
Understanding the plunge in oil prices: Sources and implications	January 2015, chapter 4
What do we know about the impact of oil prices on output and inflation? A brief survey	January 2015, box 4.1

Globalization of trade and financial flows

High trade costs: causes and remedies	June 2021, chapter 3
The impact of COVID-19 on global value chains	June 2020, box SF1
Poverty impact of food price shocks and policies	January 2019, chapter 4
Arm's-length trade: A source of post-crisis trade weakness	June 2017, Special Focus 2
The U.S. economy and the world	January 2017, Special Focus
Potential macroeconomic implications of the Trans-Pacific Partnership Agreement	January 2016, chapter 4
Regulatory convergence in mega-regional trade agreements	January 2016, box 4.1.1
China's integration in global supply chains: Review and implications	January 2015, box 2.1
Can remittances help promote consumption stability?	January 2015, chapter 4
What lies behind the global trade slowdown?	January 2015, chapter 4

Prospects Group:
Selected Other Publications on the Global Economy, 2015-23

Commodity Markets Outlook	
Forecasting industrial commodity prices	April 2023
Pandemic, war, recession: Drivers of aluminum and copper prices	October 2022
The impact of the war in Ukraine on commodity markets	April 2022
Urbanization and commodity demand	October 2021
Causes and consequences of metal price shocks	April 2021
Persistence of commodity shocks	October 2020
Food price shocks: Channels and implications	April 2019
The implications of tariffs for commodity markets	October 2018, box
The changing of the guard: Shifts in industrial commodity demand	October 2018
Oil exporters: Policies and challenges	April 2018
Investment weakness in commodity exporters	January 2017
OPEC in historical context: Commodity agreements and market fundamentals	October 2016
From energy prices to food prices: Moving in tandem?	July 2016
Resource development in an era of cheap commodities	April 2016
Weak growth in emerging market economies: What does it imply for commodity markets?	January 2016
Understanding El Niño: What does it mean for commodity markets?	October 2015
How important are China and India in global commodity consumption?	July 2015
Anatomy of the last four oil price crashes	April 2015
Putting the recent plunge in oil prices in perspective	January 2015

Inflation in Emerging and Developing Economies: Evolution, Drivers, and Policies	
Inflation: Concepts, evolution, and correlates	Chapter 1
Understanding global inflation synchronization	Chapter 2
Sources of inflation: Global and domestic drivers	Chapter 3
Inflation expectations: Review and evidence	Chapter 4
Inflation and exchange rate pass-through	Chapter 5
Inflation in low-income countries	Chapter 6
Poverty impact of food price shocks and policies	Chapter 7

A Decade After the Global Recession: Lessons and Challenges for Emerging and Developing Economies	
A decade after the global recession: Lessons and challenges	Chapter 1
What happens during global recessions?	Chapter 2
Macroeconomic developments	Chapter 3
Financial market developments	Chapter 4
Macroeconomic and financial sector policies	Chapter 5
Prospects, risks, and vulnerabilities	Chapter 6
Policy challenges	Chapter 7
The role of the World Bank Group	Chapter 8

Global Waves of Debt: Causes and Consequences	
Debt: Evolution, causes, and consequences	Chapter 1
Benefits and costs of debt: The dose makes the poison	Chapter 2
Global waves of debt: What goes up must come down?	Chapter 3
The fourth wave: Ripple or tsunami?	Chapter 4
Debt and financial crises: From euphoria to distress	Chapter 5
Policies: Turning mistakes into experience	Chapter 6

Prospects Group:
Selected Other Publications on the Global Economy, 2015-23

Global Productivity: Trends, Drivers, and Policies	
Global productivity trends	Chapter 1
What explains productivity growth	Chapter 2
What happens to productivity during major adverse events?	Chapter 3
Productivity convergence: Is anyone catching up?	Chapter 4
Regional dimensions of productivity: Trends, explanations, and policies	Chapter 5
Productivity: Technology, demand, and employment trade-offs	Chapter 6
Sectoral sources of productivity growth	Chapter 7

The Long Shadow of Informality: Challenges and Policies	
Overview	Chapter 1
Understanding the informal economy: Concepts and trends	Chapter 2
Growing apart or moving together? Synchronization of informal- and formal-economy business cycles	Chapter 3
Lagging behind: informality and development	Chapter 4
Informality in emerging market and developing economies: Regional dimensions	Chapter 5
Tackling informality: Policy options	Chapter 6

Commodity Markets: Evolution, Challenges and Policies	
The evolution of commodity markets over the past century	Chapter 1
Commodity demand: Drivers, outlook, and implications	Chapter 2
The nature and drivers of commodity price cycles	Chapter 3
Causes and consequences of industrial commodity price shocks	Chapter 4

Falling Long-Term Growth Prospects	
Potential not realized: An international database of potential growth	Chapter 1
Regional dimensions of potential growth: Hopes and realities	Chapter 2
The global investment slowdown: Challenges and policies	Chapter 3
Regional dimensions of investment: Moving in the right direction?	Chapter 4
Potential growth prospects: Risks, rewards and policies	Chapter 5
Trade as an engine of growth: Sputtering but fixable	Chapter 6
Services-led growth: Better prospects after the pandemic?	Chapter 7

High-frequency monitoring	
Global Monthly newsletter	

ECO-AUDIT
Environmental Benefits Statement

The World Bank Group is committed to reducing its environmental footprint. In support of this commitment, we leverage electronic publishing options and print-on-demand technology, which is located in regional hubs worldwide. Together, these initiatives enable print runs to be lowered and shipping distances decreased, resulting in reduced paper consumption, chemical use, greenhouse gas emissions, and waste.

We follow the recommended standards for paper use set by the Green Press Initiative. The majority of our books are printed on Forest Stewardship Council (FSC)-certified paper, with nearly all containing 50-100 percent recycled content. The recycled fiber in our book paper is either unbleached or bleached using totally chlorine-free (TCF), processed chlorine-free (PCF), or enhanced elemental chlorine-free (EECF) processes.

More information about the Bank's environmental philosophy can be found at http://www.worldbank.org/corporateresponsibility.